DATE DUE

2 Jan '6

9 Jan '64 N

PERSONAL DEDUCTIONS
IN THE FEDERAL INCOME TAX

NATIONAL BUREAU OF ECONOMIC RESEARCH

FISCAL STUDIES

1. *Fiscal Planning for Total War*
   William Leonard Crum, John F. Fennelly, and Lawrence Howard Seltzer

2. *Taxable and Business Income*
   Dan Throop Smith and J. Keith Butters

3. *The Nature and Tax Treatment of Capital Gains and Losses*
   Lawrence H. Seltzer

4. *Federal Grants and the Business Cycle*
   James A. Maxwell

5. *The Income-Tax Burden on Stockholders*
   Daniel M. Holland

6. *Personal Deductions in the Federal Income Tax*
   C. Harry Kahn

PERSONAL DEDUCTIONS
IN THE FEDERAL
INCOME TAX

Charles

C. HARRY KAHN
RUTGERS UNIVERSITY

A STUDY BY THE
NATIONAL BUREAU OF ECONOMIC RESEARCH, NEW YORK

Fiscal studies, v. 6

PUBLISHED BY
PRINCETON UNIVERSITY PRESS, PRINCETON
1960

Printed in the United States of America
by Princeton University Press, Princeton, New Jersey

RELATION OF THE DIRECTORS TO THE WORK AND PUBLICATIONS OF THE NATIONAL BUREAU OF ECONOMIC RESEARCH

1. The object of the National Bureau of Economic Research is to ascertain and to present to the public important economic facts and their interpretation in a scientific and impartial manner. The Board of Directors is charged with the responsibility of ensuring that the work of the National Bureau is carried on in strict conformity with this object.

2. To this end the Board of Directors shall appoint one or more Directors of Research.

3. The Director or Directors of Research shall submit to the members of the Board, or to its Executive Committee, for their formal adoption, all specific proposals concerning researches to be instituted.

4. No report shall be published until the Director or Directors of Research shall have submitted to the Board a summary drawing attention to the character of the data and their utilization in the report, the nature and treatment of the problems involved, the main conclusions, and such other information as in their opinion would serve to determine the suitability of the report for publication in accordance with the principles of the National Bureau.

5. A copy of any manuscript proposed for publication shall also be submitted to each member of the Board. For each manuscript to be so submitted a special committee shall be appointed by the President, or at his designation by the Executive Director, consisting of three Directors selected as nearly as may be one from each general division of the Board. The names of the special manuscript committee shall be stated to each Director when the summary and report described in paragraph (4) are sent to him. It shall be the duty of each member of the committee to read the manuscript. If each member of the special committee signifies his approval within thirty days, the manuscript may be published. If each member of the special committee has not signified his approval within thirty days of the transmittal of the report and manuscript, the Director of Research shall then notify each member of the Board, requesting approval or disapproval of publication, and thirty additional days shall be granted for this purpose. The manuscript shall then not be published unless at least a majority of the entire Board and a two-thirds majority of those members of the Board who shall have voted on the proposal within the time fixed for the receipt of votes on the publication proposed shall have approved.

6. No manuscript may be published, though approved by each member of the special committee, until forty-five days have elapsed from the transmittal of the summary and report. The interval is allowed for the receipt of any memorandum of dissent or reservation, together with a brief statement of his reasons, that any member may wish to express; and such memorandum of dissent or reservation shall be published with the manuscript if he so desires. Publication does not, however, imply that each member of the Board has read the manuscript, or that either members of the Board in general, or of the special committee, have passed upon its validity in every detail.

7. A copy of this resolution shall, unless otherwise determined by the Board, be printed in each copy of every National Bureau book.

(Resolution adopted October 25, 1926 and revised February 6, 1933 and February 24, 1941)

FOREWORD

QUESTIONS of taxation, government expenditures, and public debt policies, always of lively public interest, have assumed a new importance in recent years because of the great increase in the magnitudes involved. Between 1929 and 1957, government purchases of goods and services increased from 8 to 15 per cent of the gross national product, and the sum of government transfer and net interest payments rose from 2.2 to 7.9 per cent of total personal income. While the gross national product in current dollars was rising to $4\frac{1}{3}$ times its 1940 level between that year and 1957, the aggregate annual tax revenues of the federal, state, and local governments of the United States—exclusive of social security taxes—rose to $6\frac{3}{4}$ times their 1940 level. The total of federal, state, and local government debt outstanding, exclusive of the amounts held by government agencies, accounted for 37 per cent of the aggregate volume of net public and private debt in 1957, as against 18 per cent in 1929 and 37.5 per cent in 1940.

In consequence of their new magnitudes, taxation, government expenditures, and public debt operations have become an important part of the economic climate in which individuals and business enterprises must make their decisions. This development has been so recent, and has been characterized by such frequent changes in important elements, that the accumulation of well-organized bodies of factual materials and analysis of them have lagged behind. To promote the growth of knowledge and understanding in the widening area of government fiscal operations, the National Bureau of Economic Research, with the aid of its Committee on Fiscal Research, has sponsored a number of studies in recent years. Among these are: *Fiscal-Planning for Total War*, by Crum, Fennelly, and Seltzer (1942); *Taxable and Business Income*, by Smith and Butters (1949); *The Nature and Tax Treatment of Capital Gains and Losses*, by Seltzer (1951); *Recent Developments in Dominion-Provincial Fiscal Relations in Canada*, by Maxwell (1948); *The Ownership of Tax-Exempt Securities, 1913-1953*, by Lent (1955); *Interest as a Source of Personal Income and Tax Revenue*, by Seltzer (1955); *The Income-Tax Burden on Stockholders*, by Holland (1958); and *City Expenditures in the United States*, by Brazer (1959).

Among the elements of the country's revenue structure none is more important than the federal individual income tax. It is by far the biggest single source of tax revenue in the United States. In 1957 it raised $36 billion or about 50 per cent of the net budget receipts of the national government.[1] All other tax sources of federal, state, and local governments ranked well behind: the federal corporation income tax yielded $21.5 billion, and the aggregate of state and local government taxes of all kinds about $28 billion.

The present-day importance of the personal income tax dates only from World War II. Before 1940, even under the high tax rates of World War I, the annual yield of the tax had never reached $1.5 billion. It averaged well under $1 billion in the prosperous decade of the 1920's, and fell to less than one-half that amount in several years of the 1930's. In most years before 1940, an income tax was paid by fewer than four persons in a hundred of all aged 15 or more, and by fewer than 6 per cent of all gainfully employed persons. An abrupt change accompanied American preparation for and participation in World War II. Sharp reductions in personal exemptions and steep increases in tax rates were applied to the rapidly expanding personal incomes resulting from rising output, employment, and prices. Annual collections from the tax rose from less than $1 billion in 1940 to $6.6 billion in 1943, to $18.3 in 1944, to $21 billion in 1948, to $32.5 in 1953, and, as noted, to $36 billion in 1957; and the number of taxable returns had risen to 47 million by 1957.

To raise sums of the magnitudes of those of recent years, the income tax must have wide coverage and must be levied at substantial rates. In truth, the tax now reaches the great bulk of personal incomes in at least some degree. In 1957, taxable returns accounted for about 86 per cent of the total amount of adjusted gross income estimated to have been received by all individuals in the United States. (Adjusted gross income is, roughly, net income before personal exemptions and personal deductions.) About 21 per cent of the total revenue yield was supplied by taxpayers with adjusted gross incomes under $5,000, and 60 per cent by those with adjusted gross incomes under $10,000. These revenues and the remaining 40 per cent were raised by income-bracket rates of tax on taxable income—after personal exemptions and personal deductions—ranging from a minimum of 20 per cent on the first dollar of taxable income to a maximum of 91 per cent.

The present monograph by C. Harry Kahn embodies the results of

[1] Total budget receipts less refunds and transfers to the highway and social security trust funds.

one segment of a broader study of the personal income tax being made by several scholars under the sponsorship of the National Bureau.

The point of departure of Kahn's monograph is the scope of taxable income. Although the coverage of the income tax is wide, in the sense that four-fifths of the country-wide total of adjusted gross income of individuals is reported on taxable returns, it is much narrower when judged by the proportion of total income included in what the statute now terms "taxable income"—that is, income actually subject to any of the bracket rates of tax. Taxable income in this sense, Kahn points out, embraced only $128 billion of the $273 billion of total adjusted gross income in 1955, about 47 per cent. The shrinkage of total adjusted gross income on its way to taxable income took place as follows: $43 billion did not appear on taxable returns, having been received by those whose incomes were less than the sum of their personal exemptions and their allowable personal deductions, and, assuming no estimating error, by those who failed to report or understated income; $71 billion of the amount appearing on taxable returns disappeared through personal exemptions; and $31 billion disappeared through personal deductions. In consequence, slightly more than 53 per cent of the total adjusted gross income of all individuals, and 44 per cent of the adjusted gross income of taxable individuals, was excluded from taxable income, that is, was not formally subject to any of the income-bracket rates of tax.

Since the tax rates now begin at 20 per cent of the very first bracket of taxable income, and are strongly graduated upward, elimination of any segments or types of income from the taxable category may confer substantial benefits upon some taxpayers at the expense of others. The basis for all such eliminations is properly subject to close scrutiny. Moreover, when taxable income is reduced roughly equally for all by such eliminations, Kahn asks whether the resulting higher nominal tax rates for the smaller amount of taxable income, to raise a given amount of revenue, do not have adverse effects upon incentives to work and invest, compared with a lower nominal rate structure for a larger base. For example, the disallowance of personal expense deductions would permit all bracket rates to be reduced by approximately one-fifth (the 50 per cent bracket rate could be cut to 40 per cent, and so on); or, alternatively, each bracket rate could be cut by 5 percentage points, Kahn estimates.

As Kahn recognizes, reductions in nominal tax rates brought about in this way would not have changed the aggregate tax liability of individuals nor, on the average, the effective marginal rates of tax at different income levels. Their principal effect would have been to shift a larger portion of the aggregate tax burden to those whose personal expense deductions exceeded their standard deductions. Apart from the possible advantage of reducing nominal rates without changing the actual aggregate tax burden or, on the average, the effective marginal tax rates, the desirability of reducing or eliminating the personal deductions turns on the rationale of the deductions themselves.

The personal deductions, the personal exemptions, the system of graduated tax rates, and various other provisions of the income tax law originate in the desire of Congress to take account of variations in the personal situations of the taxpayers. The formal rate structure, outside the starting rate, plays only a negligible role in determining the effective tax rates of the vast majority of taxpayers. More than three-fourths of all taxpayers are subject only to the starting rate. For them, a brisk graduation of effective rates is provided by the combination of the single starting rate, personal deductions, and personal exemptions. For significant numbers of taxpayers, the effective tax rates are also influenced importantly by other provisions of the law: exclusion from taxable income of certain kinds of retirement income, death benefits, and limited amounts of dividend income; credits against the tax otherwise payable for limited amounts of retirement income and dividends; and the special treatment of capital gains and losses. In short, the actual tax structure comprises a considerable variety of provisions besides the schedule of formal tax rates, and the nonbusiness expense deductions constitute but one type of such provisions.

Nevertheless, there is a useful sense in which the amounts of taxpayers' incomes may be considered the fundamental or presumptive basis for levying different effective tax rates; and all departures from this standard may be said, in this sense, to invite special scrutiny. It is from this point of view, implicitly, that Kahn reviews critically the conceptual basis and legislative history of each of the major personal expense deductions. He measures their quantitative importance for different income groups and in the aggregate. He devotes separate chapters, with much new material and analysis, to deductions for philanthropic contributions, nonbusiness tax payments, personal interest payments, medical expenses, and the standard deduction. His discussion and some of his findings raise the question whether a less liberal provision for personal deductions should not be considered.

However, the positive value of personal deductions and the possible advantage of expanding some of them, even if others are reduced, should not be overlooked. The "miscellaneous deductions," which Kahn does not discuss in detail, and which accounted for $2.9 billion or 14 per cent of the itemized deductions in 1956, include many negative-income or true expense items similar to the business expenses that are deductible *before* arriving at adjusted gross income. These so-called nonbusiness deductions—not allowed in arriving at adjusted gross income, and disallowed entirely if not deductible from adjusted gross income—include fees paid to accountants, investment advisers, attorneys, and custodians; professional and union dues; outlays for uniforms and tools; and other expenses incurred in the production of income. Some similar kinds of expenses are not now deductible from either gross or adjusted gross income, such as commutation fares and other transportation costs of employees in going to and from work, a considerable item for many. For the physically handicapped, they also include special expenses, as for taxicabs, incurred in order to earn a livelihood. The law now treats these as consumption outlays. While the per capita personal exemptions are regarded by some as a general allowance for all such expenses, they obviously offer no more allowance to those who actually incur them than to those who do not.

The personal deductions also allow Congress greater flexibility in determining the schedule of effective tax rates. In 1944, for example, and again in 1948, by enlarging the optional standard deduction, Congress reduced the effective tax rates on most moderate incomes without cutting the formal rates, or raising the level, or formally altering the uniformity of the per capita personal exemptions. In 1941-1943, a standard deduction, in the form of a 10 per cent reduction in tax, was available only to taxpayers with gross income from specified sources up to $3,000. In 1944 the optional standard deduction was made 10 per cent of adjusted gross income, with an upper limit of $500. In 1948 the upper limit was extended to $1,000 for married couples filing joint returns and for single persons (for married persons filing separate returns, the ceiling was kept at $500). Whereas in 1943 only 45 per cent of taxpayers chose the standard deduction, the proportion rose to 82 per cent in 1945, and approximated 80 per cent in 1948. It is not inconceivable that Congress might at some time prefer, for example, a modest tax cut in the form of an additional $100 to the standard deduction, or a transportation deduction of $100 for all employed persons rather than reducing the formal tax rates or raising the per capita exemptions.

Nevertheless, despite important grounds, equitable and other, for some of the nonbusiness deductions, all such allowances properly invite the closest scrutiny. The sums that they remove from the category of taxable income—$31 billion in the aggregate in 1955—are taken from each taxpayer's highest rate bracket. To the extent that some taxpayers are permitted the benefit of excessive allowances, the burden upon others must be increased. In this volume, Harry Kahn performs the valuable service of subjecting the whole category of the personal expense deductions, and each of its major components, to close quantitative and conceptual analysis.

LAWRENCE H. SELTZER

PREFACE

THIS monograph is intended to shed light on one aspect of our experience with personal income taxation. Personal deductions—such as those for philanthropic contributions, medical and dental expenses, personal interest payments, and nonbusiness taxes—have long been an important, though rather undefined, element of the individual income tax in the United States. They have a significant influence on the amount and the distribution of income that is ultimately subject to tax. They thus affect the distribution of tax liability among taxpayers and, by reducing the proportion of total personal income included in the tax base, they tend to raise the general level of nominal tax rates or lower the amount of income tax collected. While this is not a study of tax base definition, per se, it does constitute an attempt to throw light on one aspect of the derivation of the tax base as it has developed over past decades, and particularly as we know it today. We are indeed concerned with one facet of the relation between the income tax and its base.

The fact that without personal deductions the distribution of tax liability would be different—and either the nominal rates lower or the income tax yield higher—leads us to inquire into the nature of these deductions and the reasons for them, their place in the income tax, their size, and their relation to income and to the expense totals from which they are derived. This phase of the income tax has received little more than piecemeal attention until now. The personal allowances have never been studied as a whole, although important contributions have been made on each of the major deductions separately, both in the form of comment on their rationale and justification in principle, and in statistical information here and there.

In attempting a comprehensive picture of the personal expense allowances, we have concentrated on two approaches: (1) to assay the quantitative importance of personal deductions, both in the aggregate and for each major deduction; and (2) to explore, where possible, the reasons for enactment and the basis for continuation of the laws providing for personal expense deductions. Total personal deductions have been compared with, or studied in conjunction with, the magnitudes of such relevant figures as income, personal exemptions, the tax base, and tax liabilities. Several of the specific deductions were related to income, to the underlying expenditure aggregate, and where relevant

xv

to the specific purpose they are presumed to accomplish. In addition to annual totals for all income groups, we also present the amount of deductions claimed broken down by size of income as reported on tax returns. The tax return distribution of income and personal deductions was selected because, aside from the great difficulties involved in any attempt to transform that distribution into one of family units, it is also more relevant to problems in the income tax area. But still only a rough idea of the incidence of personal deductions by size of income can be obtained. The search for reasons leading to the introduction and continuance of personal expense deductions is important, because there is little or no recorded explanation for several of the deductions now allowed. For each of the major deductions we have briefly inquired into its relation to the concepts underlying an income tax, its relation to the other deductions, and the form it was given.

The two objectives were, of course, not treated apart from each other, and they are discussed separately only in the first three chapters. Chapter 1 deals solely with the nature and origin of the personal deductions, and sets the stage for Chapter 2, where the reader is given a picture of the quantitative development of personal deductions in the aggregate, and of the significance of the aggregates vis-à-vis other income tax magnitudes. Chapter 3 presents a brief survey of changes in the composition of the aggregate by types of deductions, and a breakdown by size of income reported. Each of the major types of deductions—philanthropic contributions, taxes paid, interest paid, medical expenses, and casualty losses of personal property—and the standard deduction, are dealt with separately in Chapters 4 to 8.

By far the major source of the data presented below, unless otherwise noted, is *Statistics of Income*, Part I, containing the annual tabulations by the Internal Revenue Service. As used in this study the figures are characterized by three limitations: 1) Although based on very large samples in most instances, they are nevertheless liable to some sampling error; this should be borne in mind when comparisons are made between *Statistics of Income* totals and other estimates, such as those of the Department of Commerce. 2) All figures, within the above qualification, constitute summations of those reported on tax returns, that is, they are pre-audit figures and therefore subject to such revisions as the reporting units or the revenue authorities later decide to make. 3) Because the *Statistics of Income* figures are transcribed from samples of tax returns, some discontinuities in historical series have resulted from changes in the tax law. Whenever feasible, we attempted to correct such discontinuities through estimates of our own.

I am indebted to many for advice, useful criticism, and aid in preparing the data. My gratitude is especially great to Lawrence H. Seltzer who first proposed this study to me, and from whose incisive comments and suggestions both this document and its author have benefited.

A number of persons reviewed the manuscript. Gerhard Bry and Thor Hultgren, members of the staff reading committee, made trenchant comments, most of which were in one form or another gratefully incorporated. Many helpful suggestions were received from V. W. Bladen, Martin Bronfenbrenner, Melvin G. de Chazeau, James S. Earley, Laszlo L. Ecker-Racz, Solomon Fabricant, Harold M. Groves, Daniel M. Holland, M. Slade Kendrick, Harry W. Laidler, Joseph A. Pechman, and Melvin I. White.

At all times I benefited from the prompt and courteous cooperation of government agencies, especially the Statistics Division of the Internal Revenue Service, whose annual compilations of data, as already pointed out above, constitute the major statistical source used in the study; the Treasury Department's Tax Advisory Staff of the Secretary (later Tax Division of the Analysis Staff); and the Commerce Department's National Income Division.

I received valuable material aid on particular aspects of the study from F. Emerson Andrews, then with the Russell Sage Foundation; Herbert E. Klarman, of the Hospital Council of Greater New York; Robert Lampman, of the University of Wisconsin; Morris Mendelson, of the National Bureau; Joseph A. Pechman, of the Committee for Economic Development; and Carl S. Shoup, of Columbia University. To Margaret T. Edgar, who expertly edited this final version and made valuable suggestions, I owe a particular debt of gratitude. A substantial part of the computations were performed by Sarah F. Cutter, Arnold Oliphant, Kathryn S. Marin, and Lola Stark. The charts are the skillful work of H. Irving Forman. Hannah W. Kahn read the manuscript and made many comments in the dual capacity of a student of public finance and a patient wife.

While I have hoped to thank all those who have aided me, it goes almost without saying that they do not necessarily approve of the contents of the book or share any responsibility for errors that remain.

CONTENTS

CONTENTS

CONTENTS

xxi

TABLES

APPENDIX TABLES

CHARTS

xxix

CHAPTER 1

Place of Personal Expense Deductions in the Income Tax

Relation of Deductions to Net Income

DIRECTLY related to that most vexing question of what constitutes personal income, in the context of an income tax, is the question of what expenditures should be allowed as deductions in the computation of a tax base. Under the federal personal income tax law—as indeed under many foreign and most state income tax laws—provision has been made for two kinds of deductions. There are, first, those intended to refine gross income to economic net income by subtraction from gross receipts of the expenses and losses incurred in the pursuit of income. Second, there are the deductions that, at the discretion of Congress, are intended to attain a particular goal of social or economic policy, or to help establish a measure of a person's capacity to pay taxes, which transcends the limits of a strictly economic concept of income. Thus the deduction allowable for philanthropic contributions is commonly regarded as a means of stimulating socially desirable expenditures; the allowance to deduct medical expenses above a certain percentage of income is usually considered a refinement of net income to take account of what are considered differences between the relative capacities of taxpayers to pay taxes.

The question of what deductions are appropriate and desirable in arriving at taxable income has thus depended in part on the concept of income upon which the tax is based, and in part on what particular policy objectives and equity considerations commend themselves to Congress as suitable to be dealt with through tax law adaptations. Consequently, the tax laws need not draw, and indeed have not always drawn, an explicit distinction between deductions stemming from the particular income concept adopted and deductions that serve some independent purpose. Yet such a distinction is valuable as a guide to policy, which is aided by more exact knowledge of identity and size of the deductions presently allowed on grounds other than the derivations of economic personal income.

While neither the Constitution nor successive income tax acts contain definitions that could be said to establish a concept of income for tax purposes,[1] the statutes, regulations, and judicial rulings have nevertheless resulted in a general, though not very precise, concept of taxable income. Briefly, the tax is based on realized net money income "from whatever source derived," including gains derived from dealings in property and, in some instances, nonmoney receipts that can be readily determined and evaluated.[2] The refinement of gross income

[1] The first federal income tax act did not even stipulate whether gross or net income was to be taxed, although it appears that the taxation of net income was desired. Senator James F. Simmons, author of the bill, remarked that he had thought of putting the word "net" in, "But I could see so many ways of evading it that I thought it better to let the Secretary of the Treasury prescribe his rules, and let the bill cover all incomes" (*Congressional Globe*, July 29, 1861, 37th Cong., 1st Sess., p. 315). The 16th amendment to the Constitution, from which the federal government has since 1913 derived its power to collect income taxes as we know them today, states simply that "Congress shall have power to lay and collect taxes on incomes from whatever sources derived. . . ." Subsequently, income tax laws have used the term "net income" and have enumerated at length some of the sources of "gains, profits and income" to be included, without, however, defining the term "net income" as such. This situation is by no means peculiar to the federal income tax. Great Britain's tax code also contains to this day no general definition of income. Moreover, the majority of the Royal Commission on the Taxation of Profits and Income, in its recent final report (Cmd. 9474, London, 1955), accepted the celebrated principle on which British courts have long based their interpretations, that "income tax is a tax on income." In the Commission's words, "We have not looked to refine upon this principle by producing a more precise definition" (p. 8). Henry C. Simons' characterization is possibly the most trenchant: "Tax laws do not really define income but merely set up rules as to what must be included and what may be deducted; and such rules by no means define income because they are neither exhaustive nor logically coherent." *Personal Income Taxation*, Chicago, 1938, p. 105.

[2] With small exceptions, such as monetary value of food and living quarters received as part of wages or salary, no attempts have been made at the federal level to go beyond money income and to impute income receipts in kind, although the latter clearly have some influence on the individual's relative capacity to pay. Since, at least in the Northern part of the United States, collection of the tax in anything but money form was never contemplated, it can be argued that the tax should also restrict itself to money income as a base. Otherwise, particularly at the time of the Civil War tax, some taxpayers might have been required to give up a very large part of their money income owing to the relative size of their income in kind. It is widely recognized that computation of income taxes has been based predominantly on money income: "Since an estimate of value has an extremely subjective character . . . it is clear . . . that courts and legislatures will tend to avoid such estimates so far as possible. This tendency leads to the limitation of the recognition of income for tax purposes to receipts either in money or susceptible of easy valuation therein." "Since the tax must be paid in money there is a tendency to include in taxable income only those receipts which can readily be measured in money" (Roswell Magill, *Taxable Income*, New York, 1936, pp. 21, 195). Speaking of income taxes, Pigou observed that "in general . . . the tax gatherer has to content himself, for his object of assessment, with money income" (A. C. Pigou, *A Study in Public Finance*, 3rd ed., revised, London, 1952, p. 78). Haig noted that "the net income which our 1918 Act attempts to reach is in the main money income." After offering his classic definition of taxable income from the point of view of "fundamental economics and equity" (see note 7 below) , he concludes that "the concept [of taxable income] as it stands in our own law is probably the closest approach to true economic income

to net income has been construed, broadly speaking, as deduction from the taxpayer's receipts of "ordinary and necessary" expenses connected with the creation of his income, and of losses that might be incurred in the course of activity directed toward the acquisition of income or gain. Conceivably, if size of net income were to be the only differentiation between taxpayers, this concept of net income could have constituted the base for the schedule of tax rates.

From the beginning, no such rigorous definition of the tax base was implicit in our tax laws. In fact, they went well beyond that definition in the direction of a narrower base, by two provisions. One, the allowable personal deductions, remained for a long time undefined and concealed; the other, the personal exemption, was at all times explicit in freeing from tax a part of what the statutes defined as income for a given year.[3] The personal exemption has, as a rule, varied in amount with the taxpayer's family status and the number of his dependents. The recent additional exemptions for taxpayers over 65 years of age, and for those wholly or partially blind, introduce some supplementary variation by age and by state of health. The reasons for such personal exemptions of given amounts of net income has been variously presented as the need for keeping untouched by the tax a subsistence amount of income, or a reasonable standard of living, and also the desire to eliminate as taxpayers those whose liability would be too small to warrant the expense of processing such returns.[4] In all the income tax laws from 1913 to 1954, personal exemptions were granted in the form of subtractions from whatever constituted statutory net

yet achieved by any country" (R. M. Haig, "The Concept of Income—Economic and Legal Aspects," in *The Federal Income Tax*, R. M. Haig, ed., 1921, pp. 23, 27).

[3] This view of the personal exemptions was most clearly stated as early as 1896 by Georg Schanz (the generally recognized "father" of the Haig-Simons concept of income, see note 7 below) in "Der Einkommensbegriff und die Einkommensteuergesetze" (The Income Concept and the Income Tax Laws), *Finanz Archiv*, XIII (1896), p. 33: "When the lawmaker leaves a subsistence minimum taxfree, or when he takes into consideration the number of persons in the family dependent on the income by allowing, for example, a deduction for minor children, then this has no connection with the income concept. It is simply that capacity to pay is not determined by size of income alone." (Translation ours.)

[4] The question of the rationale underlying the personal exemptions will be dealt with in more detail by Lawrence H. Seltzer in a later part of our study of the personal income tax. It is enough to note here merely two of many divergent views. "No clear guiding principle can be discerned for the determination of the amount of these allowances other than the revenue need" (Committee on Postwar Tax Policy, *A Tax Program for a Solvent America*, New York, 1945, p. 110). In contrast: "It is almost unanimously agreed that some exemption keyed to at least a minimum subsistence standard of living is desirable" (Walter J. Blum and Harry Kalven, Jr., *The Uneasy Case for Progressive Taxation*, University of Chicago, 1953, p. 4).

income at the time. Congress thereby made more or less explicit that net income was not considered enough of a refinement of gross income for determining the tax base; alternately, the revenue needs were not large enough to require using all of the tax base available under the net income concept adopted. In 1954, "statutory net income" disappeared from the vocabulary of both the tax return forms and the Revenue code. Personal exemptions are referred to in the new code as deductions, and on the tax return forms they are treated as deductions from adjusted gross income in computing taxable income.

Expense deductions, from the beginning of the modern income tax, have not been restricted to expenses and losses related to the production of taxable income. The income tax law of 1913 allowed deduction of all interest paid, taxes paid, and casualty losses (and bad debts, discussed below) without specific reference to their relation to taxable income. In practice, at that time and later, the personal deductions allowed in computing statutory income were nonbusiness interest, as paid on home mortgages and personal debts; nonbusiness tax payments, as personal income taxes and residential property taxes; and losses of personal property due to fire and storm (later also flood, theft, and accident) not compensated for by insurance.

The 1913 law, as well as later acts, allowed specifically for the deduction of worthless debts charged off during the taxable year. Several writers have included this item among the personal deductions.[5] Its retention (a legacy from the Civil War income tax) among deductions gave rise to some doubt in the Senate about its nature. Senator Albert B. Cummins, discussing the item described in the 1913 bill as "debts due to the taxpayer actually ascertained to be worthless and charged off within the year," spoke of a $100,000 note in his possession, presumably worthless: "I am permitted by this bill to deduct $100,000 from my income . . . although I had just as much income as though the man had remained solvent. I have simply lost a part of my capital or property, and it is proposed here to repair that loss by deducting

---

[5] "Usually, personal expenses are not deductible, but the federal income tax departs from this general rule by allowing deduction of . . . bad debts not contracted in business transactions. . . ." (Twentieth Century Fund, *Facing the Tax Problem*, New York, 1937, p. 562.) Magill speaks of "a debt ascertained to be worthless and charged off, even though the loan was unconnected with the taxpayer's business or professional activities" as among the deductions that "may be allowable, although they are entirely unconnected with the earning of the income which is the subject of the tax" (*op.cit.*, pp. 319-20). William J. Shultz and C. Lowell Harriss list "uncollectible debts . . . in some cases" among personal expense deductions (*American Public Finance*, 6th ed., New York, 1954, p. 281).

4

its amount from my income." It was the Senator's contention that the borrower had nothing to do with his income, had not contributed toward it, and was not interested in the source of his income.[6]

Yet it might be argued that this is at best a borderline case. The production of income (in the form of interest), which is usually taxable, may motivate the lender, even if a loan is not made in the ordinary course of business. A loss, in case of default, might have no more validity as a personal expense than losses incurred in the course of other activities directed toward earning income. More doubtful is the status of an interest-free loan to a friend or relative, who declares himself unable to repay—a loan probably more a personal gift than a financial asset. Even in terms of the Haig-Simons concept of taxable income such an unrepaid debt may not be deductible.[7]

Casualty losses on personal property, mentioned above, may also be considered a negative income item within the meaning of the Haig-Simons concept of income, since they may be said to constitute a diminution in the value of a person's "store of property rights." Indeed, the federal income tax law recognizes realized increases in the value of personal possessions and treats them as capital gains, but at the same time it does not allow deductions for realized losses sustained on assets not acquired for a "gainful" purpose.[8] Thus while losses realized through sale of personal possessions are not deductible, although realized gains from sale of such assets are taxable as capital gains, losses from theft, storm, or fire are fully deductible from ordinary income. For this reason the tax law may be said to establish a presumption, widely reflected in the literature, that the allowance for casualty losses on personal possessions is a personal expense deduction.[9] As in the case of bad debts, even the Haig-Simons concept of income does not tell when personal

---

[6] *Congressional Record*, 63rd Cong., 1st Sess., 1913, p. 3847.

[7] In accordance with what is widely known among students of public finance as the Haig-Simons concept of income, any loan made by a taxpayer—if initially considered as part of the taxpayer's assets—would become an allowable deduction if the debt has become uncollectible. Haig defined taxable income as "the money value of the net accretion to one's economic power between two points of time" (*op.cit.*, p. 7). Simons, similarly, defined personal income as the "algebraic sum of (1) the market value of rights exercised in consumption and (2) the change in the value of the store of property rights between the beginning and end of the period in question" (*op.cit.*, p. 50). This concept, too, leaves open the deductibility of worthless debts whenever the taxpayer's intent in making the loan comes into question.

[8] See Lawrence H. Seltzer, *The Nature and Tax Treatment of Capital Gains and Losses*, National Bureau of Economic Research, New York, 1951, p. 4.

[9] Twentieth Century Fund, *op.cit.*, p. 562; Magill, *op.cit.*, p. 320; William Vickrey, *Agenda for Progressive Taxation*, New York, 1947, p. 61; Joseph A. Pechman, "Erosion of the Individual Income Tax," *National Tax Journal*, March, 1957, p. 6.

property losses are essentially capital losses, and when a type of personal consumption. It may be argued that many of the losses allowed are generally anticipated and reckoned with as in the normal course of owning consumer durables.[10] We shall further explore this conceptual problem, as well as the quantitative importance of the casualty loss deduction, in chapter 7.

Brief Legislative History

The roots of the deductions mentioned reach back further than 1913, the beginning of the modern federal individual income tax.[11] Its forerunner, the Civil War income tax of 1861-1872, was in fact somewhat more liberal in this respect. In addition to permitting the deduction of all federal, state, and local taxes, interest, and various non-business losses, beginning with the act of 1863, it also allowed tenants to deduct the annual rent payments on their residences.[12] The rent deduction allowance was an attempt to place renters and homeowners on the same tax basis. It appears that the early law displayed more concern with the renter-debtor-owner problem than our modern income tax laws, although then, in contrast with current practice, the renter was treated more liberally than the owner.[13] The income tax law of 1894, declared unconstitutional before it could go into operation, also permitted deduction of all taxes, interest, and casualty losses, but did not include home rent among the deductions.

In 1917, prompted by the pressures exerted by high wartime revenue requirements, Congress eliminated federal income and profits taxes from the list of allowable deductions but added contributions made

[10] Cf. Vickrey, op.cit., pp. 61-62; Pechman, op.cit., p. 11.

[11] See Roy G. and Gladys C. Blakey, The Federal Income Tax, New York, 1940, p. 5.

[12] F. C. Howe goes so far as to state that "the householder was permitted to deduct the annual rental value of his homestead, whether occupied as tenant from another, or held in his own right" (see Charles J. Bullock, Selected Readings in Public Finance, Boston, 1906, p. 282). Actually, for the owner occupant, this was true only in the sense that the 1864 act stated specifically that homeowners were not required to include in their income the rental value of any residences occupied for their own use. The act of 1867, specific about another exclusion of income in kind, said that the taxable income of a person should include "the amount of sales of livestock, sugar, wool, butter, cheese, pork, beef, mutton, or other meats, hay and grain, or other vegetable or other productions, being the growth or produce of the estate of such person, not including any part thereof consumed directly by the family."

[13] Under current (1954) tax law, the homeowner's net imputed return on his investment in a home is not included in his income for tax purposes, and he is allowed to deduct property tax and any mortgage interest. But the sum of these falls short of the items covered by gross rent, which equals the explicit rent payments of the tenant.

6

within the taxable year to religious, charitable, scientific, and educational nonprofit organizations. The unlimited deduction of philanthropic contributions had been proposed, and rejected, in 1913. By 1917 there was much concern that high tax rates might shut off the flow of philanthropy and thus convert privately financed undertakings into public responsibilities. An amendment,[14] passed that year, permitted deduction of philanthropic contributions up to 15 per cent of net income. With some recent liberalizations, it has become a permanent feature of the income tax. The same wartime pressures led shortly afterwards to the disallowance of the deduction from income of federal income taxes paid in the preceding year.

Although in the course of a long Senate debate[15] the question of the relation of previously paid taxes to net income was brought up several times, the matter was apparently disposed of primarily on grounds of expediency.[16] Otherwise, it was argued, the tax rates would have to be commensurately higher to compensate for the revenue loss resulting from the deduction of the federal income tax on the previous year's income. Though one senator persistently raised the issue of the federal, state, and local taxes that remained deductible after 1917,[17] there appeared to be little interest in its solution. In part, this is explained by the fact that the remaining taxes had then relatively little effect on the size of the tax base (evidently the chief concern of Congress at that time). It is also partially explained by the apparent lack of distinction between taxes as a personal and as a business expense.[18] Federal excises and most state and local taxes continued to be deductible.

[14] Senator Henry F. Hollis, sponsor of the amendment, introduced it with the explanation that people usually "contribute to charities and educational objects out of their surplus. . . . Now, when war comes and we impose these very heavy taxes on incomes, that will be the first place where the wealthy men will be tempted to economize. . . . They will say, 'Charity begins at home!'" *Congressional Record*, 65th Cong., 1st Sess., 1917, p. 6728.

[15] *Ibid.*, pp. 6317-6327.

[16] "It seems to me purely a question of expediency as to whether or not we want to raise this amount of taxes by excepting the payments that are made to the government" (Senator John F. Shaffroth, *ibid.*, p. 6323). "Previously to this it has not made very much difference whether they did or not [deduct the federal tax], because the income tax was not very large; but I can not see any matter of morals or justice or principle in it. It is a pure matter of expediency. If you so arrange the income tax this year that you allow those who pay it to take back a third of it next year, you have simply got to put on a bigger tax. . . ." (Senator Hollis, *ibid.*, p. 6324.)

[17] See the remarks of Senator Porter S. McCumber: ". . . there is no more sense in excluding [from net income] taxes paid to a State than excluding those paid to the government. A tax is a tax" (*ibid.*, p. 6320).

[18] Several times during the 1917 debate the question arose whether taxes constitute an "expense." Examples were cited in which taxes were incurred in the

It was not until the beginning of the Second World War that personal deductions were further expanded and modified. In 1942 medical and dental outlays became, to a limited extent, deductible expenses. In the past such expenses had been considered adequately covered by the personal exemptions and dependency credits, but as these were lowered by successive revenue acts, the need for safeguarding unusual expenditures for medical care by special allowances was widely expounded. The medical expense allowance would undoubtedly have constituted a large separate subtraction from taxable net income, had it not been for the almost simultaneous introduction of the simplified tax return,[19] which incorporated a standard deduction.

To make the simplified return applicable to a large number of income recipients, many of whom had become newly liable to the income tax as a result of wartime increases in income and lowered personal exemptions, a new statutory income concept was required. It was this new income concept that at last drew a line between business deductions and personal deductions. In order to include allowance for personal deductions in the simplified tax return without causing extreme inequalities of treatment, it was necessary to place all taxpayers as nearly as possible on an equal before-deductions basis. So long as the standard deduction was granted on the basis of gross income—as it was from 1941 to 1943 for gross incomes not exceeding $3,000—its application on a grand scale was not possible without considerable inequity. A salaried worker and a storekeeper may have equal net incomes before personal deductions, but the gross income of the storekeeper would in most cases significantly exceed that of the employee. Therefore, the new statutory income concept that evolved to fill the need for simplification came close to being gross income less business deductions. It was closer than any previous definition used in tax legislation to what many economists would consider net income. It placed all taxpayers on a fairly comparable income basis before computation

ordinary course of business, and also in which taxes appeared as a personal expense. Senator Hollis, referring to property taxes deductible by homeowners but not by renters, concluded that the best solution would be to disallow deduction of all taxes, business and nonbusiness (*ibid.*, p. 6325). Senator McCumber cited the tax on a pleasure automobile to arrive at a similar conclusion (p. 6327). But there is no record of a proposal for separate treatment of taxes incurred as business expense and those incurred as a nonbusiness expense.

[19] This device gave taxpayers the option of determining their tax liability by use of a schedule stating the tax due, by size of income and number of exemptions, computed after a blanket allowance covering all personal deductions. The blanket allowance was to be sufficiently high to induce the majority of taxpayers to choose the simplified return rather than itemizing personal deductions.

of personal deductions. But its designation as "adjusted gross income," as if it were an intermediate income concept, was somewhat awkward.[20]

While beginning with 1944 an explicit distinction was attempted between expenses incurred in the creation of income and expenses incurred in its disposition (spending), the distinction is not yet complete. The catch-all category of deductions, miscellaneous, continues to include a substantial amount of business costs, that is, expenses incurred in the course of professional or occupational activity of wage and salary earners and some incurred for the management of property.[21] Apparently for administrative reasons these expenses were not allowed as deductions in arriving at adjusted gross income, but only as deductions from adjusted gross income by taxpayers not self-employed. Therefore, such taxpayers who elect to use the standard deduction cannot also separately deduct these miscellaneous items connected with the production of taxable income.[22]

Some Recent Developments

With the enactment of the 1954 Revenue code, personal deductions have been liberalized and some new ones added.[23] The most recent additions are likely to be important, both quantitatively and with regard to policy. They include expanded deductions for medical expenses, for interest paid on installment plan purchases, and for philanthropic contributions, and an entirely new type of deduction under the heading, "expenses for care of certain dependents."

[20] The meaning of the new income concept might have been better conveyed had it been named statutory net income, and the old net income changed to adjusted net income. Instead, from 1944 until 1954, when the term was abolished, statutory net income was used as in previous years for gross income less all deductions, business and personal. There was considerable confusion about the new term, adjusted gross income, when introduced as part of the tax simplification bill. In the House debate it was referred to as "gross income," "adjusted net income," and even "gross net income" (ibid., p. 4011).

[21] Examples are dues to labor unions and professional societies, tools and supplies, fees to employment agencies and investment counsel, rentals on safe deposit boxes, and amortizable bond premiums.

[22] Some arbitrariness is unavoidable in this type of arrangement. Taxpayers in a position to classify at their discretion part, or all, of their receipts may choose to designate them as business income in order to obtain both the miscellaneous business-type deductions and the standard deduction. Frequently, for example, salaried professional persons who have occasional receipts from professional activities outside their main employment, can, if they wish, declare them in the business schedule of the tax return.

[23] For a fuller discussion of the changes brought on by the 1954 code, see Joseph A. Pechman, "Individual Income Tax Provisions of the 1954 Code," National Tax Journal, March, 1955.

Of the expansions, that in the medical and dental allowance is quantitatively the most significant. The previous exclusion of 5 per cent of adjusted gross income, for which no deduction was allowed, was reduced to 3 per cent.[24] There is no evidence that new statistical findings on the pattern of private medical expenditures as such underlay this move. Rather, public concern with medical care and health in the postwar decade, at times as far reaching as the demand of part of the public for some kind of governmental health insurance plan, seems to account for Congress's revision of the original idea of extraordinary medical expenses.[25] In addition, the upper limit on the deductible amount was doubled to allow a married couple filing a joint return to deduct as much as $10,000 for medical expenses, and a single taxpayer (without dependents) as much as $2,500. But, as shown in Chapter 7, the increase in the ceiling has had no immediate significance for the majority of taxpayers.

Until 1954, interest charges on installment purchases were deductible only if the installment contract stated the interest separately from other carrying charges. Under the new law interest is deductible even if not clearly identified as such, but the deduction is limited to 6 per cent of the average unpaid balance due under the installment contract during the taxable year. The respective House and Senate committees parted company on this measure, but the House version as summarized above was eventually enacted. The House Committee was concerned with the inequity resulting from denying a deduction to those whose contracts did not identify interest specifically. The Senate Finance Committee deleted the provision for fear it might "encourage the practice of hiding the interest charge imposed under some other name"; because it might create a presumption that the proper interest charge is 6 per cent; and because most taxpayers who might have such unnamed interest charges are likely to choose the standard deduction, so

[24] For medicines and drugs a new and separate exclusion of 1 per cent of income was established with the intention of eliminating from the deduction most of the routine and ordinary household remedies, such as iodine, aspirins, and so forth. In effect, medical and dental expenses must thus exceed 3 to 4 percent of the taxpayer's income before a deduction can be made. To the extent that taxpayers succeed in having some of their expenses for pharmaceuticals transferred to doctors' and dentists' bills, the floor may be nearer to 3 than to 4 per cent.

[25] Both the House Ways and Means Committee and the Senate Finance Committee reported, in identical sentences: "There is general agreement that limiting the deduction only to expenses in excess of 5 per cent of adjusted gross income does not allow the deduction of all 'extraordinary' medical expenses" (*Internal Revenue Code of 1954*, H. Dept. 1337 to accompany House Report 8300, 83rd Cong., 2nd Sess., March 9, 1954, p. 20).

they would obtain no benefit from the provision.[26] In 1954, for the second time since 1952, Congress raised the ceiling on the amount of philanthropic contributions deductible, but the increase was restricted to gifts to churches, educational institutions, and hospitals. The new law raised the limit from 20 to 30 per cent of the taxpayer's adjusted gross income, provided the extra 10 per cent fell within any of the three categories mentioned. This innovation was "designed to aid these institutions in obtaining the additional funds they need, in view of their rising costs and the relatively low rate of return they are receiving on endowment funds."[27] The additional subsidy thus channelled to those institutions has probably been a modest one, as we shall see in Chapter 4, and the device adopted for it probably quite ineffectual in some cases. The taxpayer who already contributes 10 per cent of his income to his church, university, and a hospital can contribute the additional 20 per cent of his income for any recognized philanthropic purpose. In other words, even if a taxpayer expands his philanthropic contributions from 20 per cent of his income to 30 because of the increased deduction allowance, part or all of his increased gifts may go to other types of philanthropic organizations. The Finance Committee's Report estimated the resulting revenue cost at $25 million for the first year. For 1954 the amount of contributions reported in excess of 20 per cent of income on tax returns came to $67 million, of which $13 million was reported on nontaxable returns. This was a small increase in relation to the $3.9 billion itemized contributions reported on all tax returns for that year.

Beginning with 1954, working mothers were for the first time given an allowance for child-care expenses. The new allowance is carefully drawn to exclude all but those taxpayers whose child-care expenses are genuinely connected with earning a livelihood. A deduction of up to $600 is granted to working widows, widowers, and divorced persons for actual expenses incurred in the care of a child under 12 years of age, or of any dependent, including a working wife's husband, mentally or physically incapable of self care. The deduction may be claimed also by all other working wives provided they file joint returns with their husbands and their combined income does not exceed $4,500 after the deduction.

This new allowance represents a refinement of taxable income to-

---

[26] *Internal Revenue Code of 1954*, S. Dept. 1622 to accompany House Report 8300, 83rd Cong., 2nd Sess., June 18, 1954, p. 22.
[27] House Report 8300, p. 25.

ward increased interpersonal equity. Child-care expenses are commonly considered part of personal consumption outlays, though the House Ways and Means Committee explained that it had approved the deduction "because it recognizes that a widow or widower with young children must incur these expenses in order to earn a livelihood and that they, therefore, are comparable to an employee's business expenses."[28] If strictly adhered to, the comparison with an employee's business expenses could lead to a multiplicity of deductions covering outlays all of which are necessary in order to earn a livelihood. An alternative explanation is that offered by Pechman,[29] that the child-care deduction "is concerned with the fact that the value of services contributed by the housewife in the home is not included in taxable income." Thus when a housewife accepts employment outside the home and spends part of her earnings for child care, she is now taxed on a part of her income the equivalent of which was formerly untaxed. The situation is similar to that of residential housing, where imputed income from owner-occupied houses is untaxed. The issue can be resolved either by including an imputed amount of income in the taxable income of the housewife, or by allowing a compensating deduction to those who have substituted money income for income in kind. The new child-care allowance constitutes a compensating deduction, though only a very small one, from the substituted money income.

The child care allowance, like all other personal deductions, is available only to those itemizing their deductions. Since the standard deduction was not increased to allow for the additional deduction and the liberalizations of older ones noted above, the trend away from the standard deduction, which we shall observe in Chapters 3 and 8, became intensified from 1954 on.

Three Reasons for Deductions

Even though the tax laws have made it explicit that some personal and consumption expenses are deductible in computing taxable income, the haphazard enactment of these allowances over nearly forty years is more than evident. There has been no systematic legal review of the selection of personal expenses, if any, to be allowed as deductions from taxable income, or of the consistency of such choices with any underlying concepts of income or of social policy.

As we have seen in the foregoing historical sketch of personal deductions, there are three main explanations for their enactment. The first

28 *Ibid.*, p. 30.   29 *Ibid.*, p. 120.

is simply the lack of distinction between personal expenses on the one hand and business expenses and losses on the other, which appears to have been of significance in drawing up the first income tax laws. It is probably the primary reason that interest payments, various taxes, and casualty losses of property have always been allowable deductions, whether they occur as business or as personal consumption expenses.

The second reason is the desire to encourage certain expenditures, that is, to provide an incentive to expand or maintain private outlays of a specified type. The deduction for philanthropic contributions is usually explained on that ground.[30] From the point of view of the individual taxpayer, the federal government pays part of the cost of his donations. An alternative interpretation sometimes advanced, but not widely accepted, is that the deduction is granted in recognition that the taxpayer has parted with some of his income without any benefit to himself in return, so that gifts require treatment on a par with losses.

The third explanation for personal deductions lies in the desire for greater interpersonal equity than might be obtained with economic net income, however defined, alone. The equity consideration is served by shifting part of the tax load from those who are burdened with "unavoidable" and emergency type expenditures to others who have no such expenses or can "afford" to bear them. In this instance, the redistributive character of the allowance is the primary motive behind its enactment. The medical expense and child-care allowances are cases in point.

Of course the earliest group of deductions, enacted without any explicit considerations of incentive-subsidy or equity, nevertheless exert either or both of these influences. These are the considerations usually emphasized in present-day discussions of their merits. Like the medical expense allowance, those for casualty losses, alimony payments, state and local income, and sales taxes, may be said to serve some interpersonal equity purposes. As with the philanthropic contributions, the

---

[30] When the question of the deductibility of philanthropic contributions was first raised in 1913, the amendment's author pleaded that "if a man wants to make a gift of charity, he ought to be encouraged so to do and not discouraged" (*Congressional Record*, 63rd Cong., 1st Sess., 1913, p. 1259). And the liberalization of the allowance under the 1954 act in favor of schools, churches, and hospitals was expressly intended "to aid these institutions" (see note 23 above). See also C. Lowell Harriss, "Philanthropy and Federal Tax Exemption," *Journal of Political Economy*, August, 1939, p. 527; Vickrey, *op.cit.*, pp. 130-131; Melvin I. White, "Deductions for Nonbusiness Expenses and an Economic Concept of Net Income," *Federal Tax Policy for Economic Growth and Stability*, Papers submitted by panelists appearing before the Subcommittee on Tax Policy of the Joint Committee on the Economic Report, 84th Cong., 1st Sess., November 9, 1955, pp. 364-65; and Pechman, *op.cit.*, p. 7.

incentive-subsidy element, rather than equity, appears the paramount factor in the allowance of interest paid on personal loans, installment debts,[31] and home mortgages and taxes on owner-occupied residential property.

All the personal deductions have in varying degrees such a privileged expenditure character. They encourage the expansion of the deductible type of expenditures to the extent that the latter has some price elasticity. The deduction allowances for medical expenses, installment interest, and alimony payments[32] thus have some small incentive effect in addition to their equity function. The deductibility on the federal return of state and local income and sales taxes may make them more acceptable to the electorate, but it is difficult to say whether this feature has had any appreciable effect on the extent to which they are imposed.[33]

All the personal deductions also affect the distribution of income after tax. This is implied in the deductions that are intended for more equitable distribution of the tax burden. As they redistribute tax liability they redistribute a portion of after-tax income from the well

[31] Most writers tend to think of the personal interest deduction as lowering the cost of borrowing, viewing it as a subsidy to the borrower. In contrast, Melvin I. White, in examining the interest deductions for their consistency with "a systematically defined economic concept of personal income," assigns to interest on personal and installment loans primarily the characteristics of an equity device (see White, *op.cit.*, pp. 353ff). The deductibility of interest, he reasons, tends to right the balance between those who purchase a durable consumer good outright and those who purchase it with the help of credit. White thinks that the ideal solution would be to impute a return to the user-owner of durable goods, permitting interest payments as a deduction for the borrower-owner, but he acknowledges the difficulty of making such imputations for most durable goods. While imputation would remove inequities to those who purchase or rent their services, White holds that this group is comparatively small in durable goods other than houses. He concludes that a larger measure of equity results if installment and interest payments on consumer durables are allowed as deductions than if disallowed. In the case of housing, however, where renters are a very significant part of the consumer population, he concludes that an interest deduction increases the inequity to the renter, although it puts the debtor-owner on a more equitable footing with the clear owner. (For a more extended treatment of the nature of the interest deduction, see Chapter 6.)

[32] While deductibility is not likely to have affected the divorce rate any more than income-splitting has affected the number of marriages, it may nevertheless have permitted some alimony settlements to be more generous than they would otherwise have been.

[33] State income taxes, next to property taxes the most prominent instance of tax deductibility, have not risen significantly either in number or in rates since the 1930's. Yet since then the value of deductibility has risen steeply. It is particularly noteworthy that rate graduation in state income taxes stops, as a rule, at relatively low income levels. In 1953 over one-half of state income taxes reached their maximum rate at or below $10,000 of taxable income. See U.S. Treasury Department, Tax Analysis Staff, *Overlapping Taxes in the United States*, 1954, Table 12.

to the sick, from the young to the old, and from persons living in low-tax states to those in high-tax states. But redistribution also occurs through those deductions chiefly aimed at encouraging expenditures considered socially desirable. There is redistribution from tenants to homeowner occupants, and from "non-philanthropic" contributors to those who contribute money and property to philanthropies.[34]

If a deduction is primarily designed to stimulate private expenditures in areas of strong public interest, it may, in effect, become an indirect government expenditure. But more than an overlapping of private and public interest in certain expenditures, such as philanthropy and medical care, is necessary to genuinely equate a deduction allowance with indirect public expenditures. For the desired effect, taxpayers claiming the deductions must also expand their deductible expenditures as a result of the tax rebate. In other words, if a deduction is to serve as a tax incentive, the underlying expenditures must have a certain degree of price-elasticity. If taxpayers, despite the deduction, merely spend about the same they would have in any case, then the deduction allowance would in effect, although not by design, become solely a question of equity among taxpayers.

The distinction here between equity motivated deductions and deductions that serve as incentive devices is of more than merely formal significance. If an allowance, by way of refining a person's net income, is considered as part of the attempt to define capacity to pay tax, then a deduction from net income of that expense may be held appropriate. If, on the other hand, the allowance is part of a public policy to advance a given social or economic goal, it may be argued that a tax credit is called for. Reduction in tax resulting from a deduction depends on the size of the taxable income reported. A tax credit, provided it is granted at the same rate (20 or 30 per cent, for example) to everyone, brings, for a given deductible expenditure, a tax reduction that is the same for almost all taxpayers,[35] regardless of income size.

The question of the form allowed for the deduction has been frequently raised concerning the allowance for philanthropic contributions. Recently this has become particularly acute regarding a frequently proposed allowance for educational expenses.[36] Many have

34 See Robert J. Lampman, "The American Tax System and Equalization of Income," *Proceedings of the 49th Annual Conference on Taxation*, National Tax Association, 1956, p. 277.

35 An exception occurs when the tax credit to which a taxpayer is entitled exceeds his tax liability before credit.

36 See, for instance, The President's Committee on Education Beyond the High

favored a tax credit for educational expenses rather than a deduction from taxable income, on the ground that the latter "constitutes an upside down subsidy to education: the larger the income, the greater the subsidy in the form of tax savings. . . ."[37] This reasoning proceeds from the premise that the allowance would be intended to encourage greater private expenditures for education in place of greater budgetary appropriations. Others have favored simple deductions from income of all or selected educational expenses. Indeed, two such deductions connected with education are currently allowed on a limited scale. The 1954 Revenue code eliminates the $600 gross income test for determining the dependency status of children over 19 years of age still attending school, and it provides that scholarship aid need not be reckoned in determining whether a taxpayer provides over half the support of a child. Since 1958, outlays made by a teacher to further his education may be deducted even if such expenses are incurred voluntarily to improve professional status. Previously the latter expenses were deductible only if required to maintain existing salary and status.

Evidently, the kind of broad deduction that might be allowed in the future for educational expenses will depend, in some measure, on the distinctions we have attempted to bring out above. If educational expenses are an appropriate consideration in determining relative capacity to pay, equity among taxpayers being the governing principle, a deduction from income may be called for. In that case the personal investment aspect of education may be cited as the determining factor, and the deduction might take the form of a depreciation allowance. Needless to say, many do not view education as an investment, and many students do not pay their own expenses but receive them as gifts from parents or relatives. On the other hand, if education is to be made increasingly the object of communal investment, and the income tax is to be utilized for that purpose, a tax credit may be held most appropriate.

School, *Second Report to the President*, Washington, D.C., July, 1957, p. 56; National Science Foundation, *Basic Research—A National Resource* (a report to President Eisenhower), Washington, November, 1957, p. 50; and testimony by John F. Meck, on behalf of the American Council on Education, American Alumni Council, Association of American Colleges, and State Universities Association, at hearings before the House Ways and Means Committee on *Federal Revenue Revision*, 85th Cong., 2nd Sess., Part 1, January, 1958, pp. 1061-66.

[37] Walter W. Heller, "U.S. Tax Policy for 1958," *Canadian Tax Journal*, March-April, 1958, p. 95. (But Heller, while giving the edge to a tax credit over an income deduction, appears to favor neither for the purpose under consideration.)

CHAPTER 2

Quantitative Significance: Effect of Deductions on Tax Base and Liabilities

BEFORE dealing with each of the major personal deductions separately, an over-all quantitative view of them may be useful. To begin, we have placed the deductions within the context of other income tax magnitudes: adjusted gross income (the income concept in use since 1944), personal exemptions, and the tax base.[1] As pointed out in the preceding chapter, personal deductions and personal exemptions are the principal items that have stood, since 1913, between adjusted gross income and the tax base. Without these two allowances, adjusted gross income would in effect have constituted the tax base.

Tables 1 to 3 show the dollar amounts corresponding to the above concepts, in both absolute and relative forms. Table 1 traces for selected years, 1918 to 1955, the gap between estimated total adjusted gross income[2] and the tax base. Unfortunately, we possess fairly reliable estimates for only that part of the gap beginning with adjusted gross income on taxable returns (line 8). To cover the difference between total adjusted gross income and adjusted gross income on taxable returns (theoretically also explained by deductions and exemptions), we have only the information on nontaxable returns to guide us in making some crude estimates. Cast into the proverbial Scylla-and-Charybdis situation, with a set of very crude but mostly relevant data and a set of fairly accurate but less relevant data, we chose to present both.

---

[1] Tax base here means the amount of income to which any of the rates constituting the individual income tax schedule are applied in computing tax liability. Our tax base concept, a broad and synthetic one, corresponds approximately to the statutory concept, in the 1954 Internal Revenue code, of taxable income, which is income subject to normal and surtax plus income subject to capital gains tax. For more detail, see Appendix A.

[2] Total adjusted gross income is our estimate of the amount of income that would be reported on tax returns if there were no minimum filing requirements, and the public were scrupulously exact and correct in reporting income in accordance with the adjusted gross income concept. Total adjusted gross income differs from the Commerce Department's personal income concept mainly through its inclusion of net capital gains and losses, and employee contributions for social insurance, and because it excludes income in kind (such as imputed house rent, and goods produced and consumed on farms), state and local bond interest, accrued and imputed interest, a large part of military pay and family allowances, social security benefits, public assistance payments, and veterans' payments.

TABLE 1

Gap between Total Adjusted Gross Income and Tax Base, Distribution by Personal Deductions and Exemptions, Selected Years, 1918-1955

(millions of dollars)

	1918	1926	1933	1939	1946	1951	1953	1955
1. Estimated total adjusted gross income	50,301	69,431	36,445	64,674	156,065	226,603	254,450	272,723
2. Minus: adjusted gross income of nontaxable individuals and amount unexplained	35,367	50,076	28,155	47,207	37,344	42,668	43,966	43,128
3. Adjusted gross income of nontaxable individuals	32,805	46,385	26,210	43,379	18,238	21,481	20,763	21,083
4. Personal deductions	1,624	5,028	3,997	2,816	1,556	1,910	2,105	2,296
5. Personal exemptions	31,181	41,357	22,213	38,188	16,682	19,571	18,658	18,787
6. Earned income credit	—	—	—	2,375	—	—	—	—
7. Amount unexplained[a]	2,562	3,691	1,945	3,828	19,106	21,187	22,203	22,045
8. Equals: adjusted gross income on taxable returns	14,934	19,355	8,290	17,467	118,721	183,935	210,484	229,595
Minus:								
9. Personal deductions on taxable returns	1,041	1,982	917	1,663	13,245	22,504	26,961	30,524
10. Personal exemptions on taxable returns	5,772	6,244	3,094	6,564	39,653	61,428	67,896	71,182
11. Earned income credit on taxable returns	—	—	—	946	—	—	—	—
12. Equals: tax base[b]	8,121	11,179	4,279	8,294	65,823	100,003	115,627	127,889

[a] The amount of estimated total adjusted gross income (AGI) unexplained reflects possible estimating errors in the personal income figure from which total AGI was derived, in our adjustments to obtain AGI, and in the reported income tabulations in Statistics of Income; it also reflects underreporting due to taxpayers' errors or evasion. For years beginning with 1946, this is the residual amount of AGI after subtracting from total AGI all AGI reported on tax returns and an estimated amount not reported by persons whose AGI falls below the filing requirement. For the four years 1918-1939 shown above, the unexplained amount was assumed to be 15 per cent of all reported AGI. For details, see Appendix A.
[b] The tax base includes all income to which tax rates were actually applied.

Source: See Appendix A.

Relative Effect of Deductions and Exemptions in Computing Tax Base, Taxable Returns

Beginning with income reported on taxable returns, we find that the amount of personal deductions shows an almost uninterrupted rise from an estimated 7 per cent of such income in 1918, to 13.3 per cent in 1955 when it amounted to $30.5 billion (Table 2).[3] Personal exemptions have been considerably larger but have exhibited little, if any, long-run change in relation to income on taxable returns (Chart 1). They accounted, somewhat surprisingly, for roughly one-third of the income reported in each of the seven years shown in Table 2: 39 per cent in 1918, 32 in 1926, 38 in 1939, about 33 in 1946, 1951, and 1953, and 31 per cent in 1955.[4] In view of what we know about the movement of exemptions and incomes during the period, we might have expected a steeply declining ratio of exemptions to income. This is true of the ratio of exemptions to total adjusted gross income, as we shall see below. For accuracy in stating the quantitative importance of exemptions, we must consider also nontaxable incomes, for these are excluded from the tax base primarily by virtue of the exemptions. If the ratio is computed with taxable returns only, there is no a priori reason why the ratio of exemptions to income should move in one direction rather than another as incomes and the size of exemptions change. When the amount of allowed exemptions is lowered or national income rises, or both, the exemption-income ratio for taxpayers already on the rolls tends to fall, while the ratio for new taxpayers who are only now entering the taxable group tends, on average, to be very high. The two groups therefore have an offsetting effect on the over-all ratio of exemptions to income. When the exemptions are raised or incomes fall, or both, the opposite occurs: the taxpayers with the highest exemption-income ratios drop out of the tax-paying group, but the exemption-income ratios of those who remain rise. In a period of 38

[3] There is some overstatement in these figures because of the inclusion of occupational and professional expenses in the miscellaneous deductions category, as explained in Chapter 1, the end of section 2. On the assumption that since 1944 about one-half of miscellaneous deductions were really expenses incurred in the production of taxable income, the overstatement of personal deductions shown in Table 1 would amount to about one-tenth of the postwar total; or, only about nine-tenths of the amount included was truly personal. While the overstatement does not affect the trends discussed in this chapter, it must be borne in mind that the deduction figures cited (except those in Table 6) suffer from an undetermined amount of overstatement.

[4] For other years, see Appendix Table D-3.

TABLE 2

Deductions and Exemptions on Taxable Returns, Selected Years, 1918-1955

(dollars in millions)

	1918	1926	1933	1939	1946	1951	1953	1955
1. Adjusted gross income[a]	14,934	19,355	8,290	17,467	118,721	183,935	210,484	229,595
2. Minus: a) Deductions	1,041	1,932	917	1,663	13,245	22,504	26,961	30,524
b) Exemptions	5,772	6,244	3,094	6,564	39,653	61,428	67,896	71,182
3. Equals: tax base	8,121	11,179	4,279	9,240[b]	65,823	100,003	115,627	127,889
				PER CENT				
4. Adjusted gross income	100.0	100.0	100.0	100.0	100.0	100.0	100.0	100.0
5. Minus: a) Deductions	7.0	10.0	11.1	9.5	11.2	12.2	12.8	13.3
b) Exemptions	38.6	32.3	37.3	37.6	33.4	33.4	32.3	31.0
6. Equals: tax base	54.4	57.8	51.6	52.9[b]	55.4	54.4	54.9	55.7

[a] For years beginning with 1946, the adjusted gross income figure is that given in *Statistics of Income*. For earlier years the figures are our estimates based on *Statistics of Income* data, since the concept was actually not introduced until 1944.

[b] This figure differs from that in Tables 1 and 3 by the amount of earned income credit shown in line 11 of Table 1. It was included here to make the 1939 tax base figure more comparable to those of other years. Actually, without the earned income credit, all the 1939 magnitudes would have been slightly larger than shown since some incomes that were not taxable would presumably have been taxable. However, the effect of adjusting for this on the percentages shown would be negligible.

Source: Table 1.

CHART 1

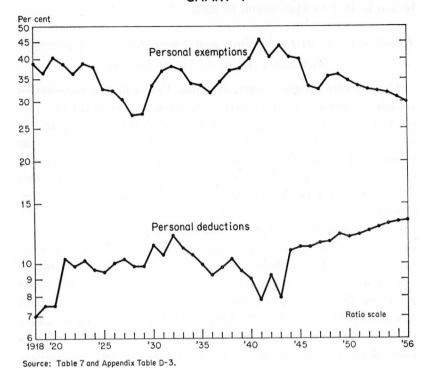

Source: Table 7 and Appendix Table D-3.

Total Personal Deductions and Personal Exemptions Reported on Taxable Returns as Per Cent of Adjusted Gross Income Reported, 1918-1956

years, 1918-1955, the exemptions-income ratio has stayed within the range of 0.32 to 0.38 almost two-thirds of the time.[5]

While the exemptions moved from about 39 per cent of adjusted gross income on taxable returns in 1918 to 31 per cent in 1955, personal deductions increased from 7 to 13 per cent over the same period. In both years the tax base was nearly the same proportion of income

[5] The above observations are substantially similar to Vickrey's findings in his investigation of the income elasticity of various components of the tax base. Letting X = total income of the persons taxed (from the context it appears that Vickrey used statutory net income), and B = tax base, Vickrey equated the income elasticity of a simple flat-rate tax on income above a given exemption to X/B. A progressive income tax schedule may be broken down into components—as many as its bracket rates—each step-up in bracket rate constituting a flat tax on all income above the step-up level. For years before 1943, Vickrey obtained X/B values varying between 1.4 and 1.9, and he concluded that "as a first approximation the elasticity of the tax yield may be considered to fall within this range" (William Vickrey, "Some Limits to the Income Elasticity of Income Tax Yields," *Review of Economics and Statistics*, May, 1949, pp. 141-42). X/B values may be obtained for the aggregate

reported by taxpayers, although in absolute amount it rose from $8 billion in 1918 to $128 billion in 1955.

Relative Effect of Deductions and Exemptions in Arriving at Tax Base, Adjusted Gross Income

The gap between the amount of adjusted gross income reported on taxable returns and total adjusted gross income amounted to over 70 per cent of the total during most of the period 1918-1939. By 1955 it had declined to about 16 per cent. If we include the nontaxed income in our calculations, thus moving on to total adjusted gross income, our percentages for deductions and exemptions become somewhat more meaningful to the interpretation of these items, but also less reliable.

It is a truism that, except for underreporting and statistical errors in estimating, the adjusted gross income not reported on taxable returns is answered for by deductions and exemptions. Part of this income was reported on nontaxable returns; part was not reported because it was below the figure set as a filing requirement, or because some with incomes too low to be taxable ignored the filing requirement; and a third part was not reported due to error and evasion.[6] The first two parts of the gap are accounted for by deductions and exemptions.

---

tax base in the same manner from Table 2 by dividing lines 1-2a by line 3 as shown below:

	1918	1926	1933	1939	1946	1951	1953	1955
X (billions)	13.9	17.4	7.4	15.8	105.5	161.4	183.5	199.1
B (billions)	8.1	11.2	4.3	9.2a	65.8	100.0	115.6	127.9
X/B	1.7	1.6	1.7	1.7	1.6	1.6	1.6	1.6

a Includes earned-income credit.

Vickrey's findings for the various components of the tax base appear to hold also for the total tax base. This is significant as a first approximation to the income elasticity of the tax, in light of what we know about the behavior of the average rate of tax with respect to the total tax base in the short run. Pechman showed that the income tax has behaved almost like a flat-rate tax with respect to the total tax base over the period 1948-1953 (Joseph A. Pechman, "Yield of the Individual Income Tax during a Recession," *National Tax Journal*, March, 1954. See also note 9 in Chapter 3). To the extent that this is so, the income elasticity of the tax base is also the income elasticity of the tax.

6 The approximate size of the third part—statistical error and underreporting— was estimated as a residual for the four most recent years in Table 3. To the amounts reported on all returns was added an estimated amount of adjusted gross income received by those whose incomes fell below the filing requirement in those years, and the sum was subtracted from total adjusted gross income. The relationship between "amount unexplained" and the income reported on all tax returns was assumed to hold also for the four selected pre-World War II years. For details on the method of computation, see Appendix A.

Some rough estimates of how each subtraction helps make the two parts of the gap nontaxable are possible by use of the information supplied on nontaxable returns.

As expected, personal exemptions cover over nine-tenths of the adjusted gross income of nontaxable individuals. Inclusion of this segment of income in our computations raises the ratio of exemptions to adjusted gross income to a much higher level for the early years (1918-1939) than was the case with income reported on taxable returns only (see Table 2). In 1918 almost three-fourths of total adjusted gross income was not part of the tax base because of personal exemptions (Table 3). This figure declined to 36 per cent in 1946 and 33 per cent in 1955. The personal deductions moved in the opposite direction: from only 5 per cent of total adjusted gross income in 1918 to 12 per cent in 1955. Thus while in 1918 the amount of personal exemptions was nearly 14 times as large as that for personal expense allowances, by 1955 it was less than three times as large.

These figures reveal two important features in the development of the modern income tax. First, they show a decline in the relative amount of income eliminated by statute from the aggregate conceptually designated as the tax base (as opposed to income types that lie conceptually outside the tax base, that is, are not included in adjusted gross income). The amount eliminated is, nevertheless, still large. The amount not directly subject to tax because of deductions and exemptions has dropped from an estimated 76 per cent of total adjusted gross income in 1939 to 45 per cent in 1955. Yet after allowing for some leakage, due to underreporting and possible estimating error, the figures also show that only 47 per cent of income conceptually constituting the tax base was actually part of it. The reader is reminded that a sizable portion of income not in the actual tax base for the reasons stated is, nevertheless, part of the income of taxpayers; some (a smaller amount in recent years) is part of the income of persons not subject to tax. Thus the income not in the tax base includes not only all the adjusted gross income of nontaxpayers, but also some of the adjusted gross income of all taxpayers. Income not in the tax base, therefore, refers not to nontaxable income, but rather to the adjusted gross income not subject to the formal tax rates.[7] Second, the figures

[7] The size of the amount of income removed from the actual tax base does not constitute an argument against the allowances responsible for the removals. But its size may pertain to consideration of policy decisions, which take into account the cost of particular objectives of allowances granted on grounds other than that of consistency with the underlying income concept.

TABLE 3

Relative Importance of Personal Deductions and Exemptions in Accounting for Gap between Total Adjusted Gross Income and Tax Base, Selected Years, 1918-1955

(dollars in millions)

	1918	1926	1933	1939	1946	1951	1953	1955
1. Total adjusted gross income	50,301	69,431	36,445	64,674	156,065	226,603	254,450	272,723
2. Minus: Estimated deductions[a]	2,665	6,960	4,914	4,479	14,801	24,414	29,066	32,820
Estimated exemptions[b]	36,953	47,601	25,307	44,752	56,335	80,999	86,554	89,969
Amount unexplained	2,562	3,691	1,945	3,828	19,106	21,187	23,203	22,045
3. Equals: Tax base	8,121	11,179	4,279	11,615[c]	65,823	100,003	115,627	127,889
				PER CENT				
4. Total adjusted gross income	100.0	100.0	100.0	100.0	100.0	100.0	100.0	100.0
5. Minus: Estimated deductions	5.3	10.0	13.5	6.9	9.5	10.8	11.4	12.0
Estimated exemptions	73.5	68.6	69.4	69.2	36.1	35.7	34.0	33.0
Amount unexplained	5.1	5.3	5.3	5.9	12.2	9.3	9.1	8.1
6. Equals: Tax base	16.1	16.1	11.7	18.0	42.2	44.1	45.4	46.9

a Line 4 + line 9 of Table 1.
b Line 5 + line 10 of Table 1.
c As shown in Table 1, the earned income credit reduced the tax base by an estimated $3,321 million, which was omitted here for the sake of simplicity.
Source: Table 1.

for exemptions and deductions indicate a change in composition of the amount of income eliminated from the tax base. The amount is less related to family size or population than previously, more to some types of personal expenses and, because of the standard deduction, to size of income.

Influence of Deductions and Exemptions on Distribution of Effective Rates among Income Groups

We may carry a step further our analysis of personal deductions within the context of other income tax magnitudes, by comparing the influence of personal deductions and exemptions on the pattern of effective rates. Aside from the difference in the total amounts of the two allowances, there is a significant difference in their distribution among income groups, which are in turn subject to varying marginal rates of tax. Table 4 shows the 1953 distribution of deductions and exemptions reported on taxable returns, by adjusted gross income

TABLE 4

Personal Deductions and Exemptions Claimed on
Taxable Returns, by Adjusted Gross Income Groups, 1953

(dollars in millions)

ADJUSTED GROSS INCOME GROUPS ($000's)	Adjusted Gross Income		Personal Exemptions		Personal Deductions	
	Amount	Per Cent of Total	Amount	Per Cent of Total	Amount	Per Cent of Total
Under 2	9,311	4.4	4,844	7.1	1,097	4.1
2-3	17,650	8.4	7,901	11.6	2,186	8.1
3-5	63,117	30.0	26,363	38.8	8,140	30.2
5-10	81,753	38.8	24,775	36.5	10,812	40.1
10-20	19,702	9.3	3,005	4.4	2,430	9.0
20-50	12,037	5.7	857	1.3	1,337	5.0
50-100	3,994	1.9	120	0.2	486	1.8
100-500	2,392	1.1	29	a	376	1.4
500 and over	528	0.3	1	a	97	0.4
Total	210,484	100.0	67,896	100.0	26,961	100.0

a Less than 0.05 per cent.
Source: *Statistics of Income.* The data were adjusted to exclude returns with self-employment tax only. For method, see Appendix B.

groups. Almost three-fifths of the exemptions were claimed on returns with less than $5,000 of adjusted gross income, but only somewhat over two-fifths of the deductions fell into that income range. From the $20,-000 income level up, deductions exceeded exemptions, in absolute amount, even though they were only a little over one-third the size of exemptions for all returns. This is because exemptions can vary only from $600 to a few multiples of it and therefore tend to decline in relation to adjusted gross income (except for a small range at the bottom of the income scale). Deductions varied on average from about $70 per return at the bottom to over $1 million at the top. Their distribution, as shown in Table 4, closely paralleled that of income.

The influence of deductions and exemptions on effective tax rates (tax liabilities divided by adjusted gross income) is shown in Table 5 and Chart 2 by means of four tax base variants constructed with figures reported on 1953 taxable returns. The first variant corresponds to the actual 1953 tax base, with both deductions and exemptions al-

TABLE 5

Effective Tax Rates Estimated from 1953 Distribution of Income
Reported on Taxable Returns, with Varying Tax Base
Assumptions, by Adjusted Gross Income Groups

(dollars in millions)

ADJUSTED GROSS INCOME GROUPS ($000's)	Adjusted Gross Income (1)	1953 Tax Liability[a] Computed with:			
		Deductions and Exemptions (2)	Exemptions Only (3)	Deductions Only (4)	No Deduction or Exemptions (5)
Under 2	9,311	748	992	1,823	2,068
2-3	17,650	1,679	2,170	3,454	3,971
3-5	63,117	6,415	8,307	12,375	14,337
5-10	81,753	10,453	13,048	16,389	19,176
10-20	19,702	3,573	4,334	4,487	5,275
20-50	12,037	3,334	3,996	3,734	4,414
50-100	3,994	1,638	1,970	1,719	2,052
100-500	2,392	1,206	1,515	1,228	1,538
500 and over	528	320	409	321	410
Total	210,484	29,366	36,741	45,530	53,241
		EFFECTIVE RATES OF TAX (PER CENT)[b]			
Under 2		8.0	10.7	19.6	22.2
2-3		9.5	12.3	19.6	22.5
3-5		10.2	13.2	19.6	22.7
5-10		12.8	16.0	20.0	23.5
10-20		18.1	22.0	22.8	26.8
20-50		27.7	33.2	31.0	36.7
50-100		41.0	49.3	43.0	51.4
100-500		50.4	63.3	51.3	64.3
500 and over		60.6	77.5	60.8	77.7
Total		14.0	17.5	21.6	25.3

a 1953 rate schedule.
b Tax liabilities divided by adjusted gross income.
Source: See Appendix C.

lowed; the second allows personal exemptions only; the third allows
deductions only; and the fourth allows neither exemptions nor deductions, meaning that adjusted gross income was used as the tax base.
To isolate the influence of deductions and exemptions on effective rates
of tax, the same rate schedule was applied to all four variants of tax

CHART 2

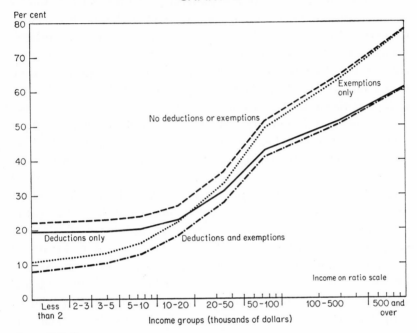

Source: Table 5.

Effective Tax Rates for Four Tax Base Variants, by Income Levels,
Taxable Returns, 1953

base. We chose for convenience the 1953 rate schedule, but any other
rate schedule of recent times would have produced substantially the
same results (and the reader can easily experiment with other rate
schedules by using the detailed tax base figures shown in Appendix C).
With the rate schedule held constant, and applied to one hypothetical
tax base to another, the results do not imply that Congress—in the
absence of provision for deductions and exemptions—would have set
a rate schedule like that of recent years. The figures in Table 5, therefore, are not intended to suggest the increase in tax liabilities that
would be realized if there were no allowance for personal deductions
and exemptions.

The effective rate patterns for the two variants that allow either exemptions or deductions, but not both, differ markedly (columns 3 and 4). For the variant that includes only exemptions, the rates in the lower part of the income scale are close to the current tax-base rates, and in the upper part they approach the rates that would result with the adjusted-gross-income base. If only deductions are included we obtain the opposite effective rate pattern: at the bottom it is similar to that of the adjusted-gross-income base, and at the top it resembles the current base pattern. The two effective rate curves cross slightly below the $20,000 level. A most striking contrast emerges in the differential effect of deductions and exemptions on the progression of effective rates. When deductions alone are eliminated, the ratio of tax to income rises from 11 per cent at the lowest income level to 78 per cent at the top. When exemptions are omitted it rises only from 20 per cent to 61 per cent. Thus the personal deductions, as a whole, have tended to dampen progression in effective rates whereas the exemptions have added considerably to effective rate progression. Without personal exemptions the ratio of tax to income shows hardly any increase for the income groups with up to $10,000 income, indicating the extent to which the exemptions have recently been responsible for effective rate progression among the great majority of taxpayers. A major reason why the exemptions explain so much progression up to the $10,000 income level is the provision of income splitting between husbands and wives, effective since the 1948 tax law. Married couples filing joint returns have virtually been permitted to double the size of their rate brackets; for example, the first $4,000 of their joint taxable income is subject to the same rate a single individual pays on the first $2,000.

Effect of Deductions on Level of Liabilities and Rates

Deductions from income in computing the tax base affect either the yield of the tax or, if a given yield requirement must be satisfied, the level of tax rates. The following quantitative analysis of the short-run[8] effects of deductions shows that the magnitudes involved are large, probably larger than commonly thought. But the quantification should not suggest a particular policy and its results. As such it would be considered unrealistic by many.[9] Without implying suggested

---

[8] It may be argued that, over longer periods of time, the flow of income itself is modified in one direction or another by some of the personal deductions, so that their net effect on tax yields, or rates, may be greater or less than shown below.

[9] For a treatment that does propose drastic reductions in personal deductions, and

changes in policy, we find merit in presenting some of the results of policy, as embodied in current tax law.

The significance of personal deductions in terms of total tax liability is estimated in Table 6 for 1953.[10] Enlarging the tax base by the

TABLE 6

Effect of Personal Deductions on Tax Liability, 1953

(millions of dollars)

| | | Tax Liability on Income | | |
	Tax Base (1)	Reported on Taxable Returns (2)	Not Reported on Taxable Returns (3)	Total (4)
x base after deductions	115,627	29,366	—	29,366
x base before deductions	142,027	36,017	421	36,438
crease, line (2)— (1)	26,400	6,651	421	7,072
r cent increase in total liability, e (3) ÷ (1) × 100				24.1
te reduction possible (equal proportinate change in all rates)				19.4

Source, by column

(1) Table 1. The personal deductions were reduced by one-half of estimated miscellaneous deductions (see text note 3).

(2) Table 5. Adjusted for omission of one-half of miscellaneous deductions.

(3) Figure in line 4 of Table 1, reduced as in column 1, multiplied by lowest bracket rate 1953.

(4) Rate reduction possible equals $(1 - \dfrac{29,366}{36,438}) \times 100$.

amount of personal deductions claimed in that year, we find the number of taxable returns increases somewhat and hence also the total amount of adjusted gross income reported on taxable returns.[11] We assume in our computations that all of the roughly $2 billion of adjusted gross income not reported on taxable returns because of deductions (see Table 1) would have been taxable at the lowest bracket rate

presents estimates of the effect of the reductions in terms of increased tax liabilities and possible rate reductions, see Joseph A. Pechman, "Erosion of the Individual Income Tax," *op.cit.*, pp. 1ff.

10 The figures in Table 6, unlike those in the preceding tables, are presumed to exclude the part of miscellaneous deductions which consists of professional and occupational expenses incurred in the production of taxable income. The adjustment made is as indicated in note 3 above, and is therefore only approximate.

11 This was not taken into account in Table 5, since our data for income not reported on taxable returns are too sketchy to be distributed by income groups. Table 5 thus shows only the redistribution of tax liability within the adjusted gross income aggregate reported on taxable returns in 1953.

in the absence of these allowances. This is undoubtedly correct for all but a small amount. At 1953 rates, tax liabilities were reduced from an estimated $36.4 to $29.4 billion, that is, by $7.1 billion. In that year the revenue cost of the deductions was somewhat less than one-fourth of the actual yield of the personal income tax.

Another way to see the significance of personal deductions is to determine how much individual income tax rates could be reduced, rather than how much more revenue could be obtained at existing rates, if the tax base were not lowered by the amount of the personal deductions.[12] This view has merit in the eyes of those who think that tax rates would not have risen to their current level without the type of tax base in existence. To hold the total tax liability approximately constant, the increase in the tax base from $116 billion to $142 billion, resulting from removing the deductions, might have permitted an equal proportionate reduction of all bracket rates by almost one-fifth in 1953. Alternatively, a reduction of all rates by close to 5 percentage points would have offset roughly the increase in the tax base. The overall average rate of tax (total tax liability divided by tax base) would then have been 20.7 instead of 25.4 per cent. But with an approximately constant tax liability, a lowering of rates commensurate with the widening of the base would not, of course, produce any change in the average tax burden (tax liability divided by income). Nominal rates would be lower, but the real rate of taxation would, on average, remain the same. It follows also that increments to income, though taxed at lower nominal rates, would still be generally subject to the same effective marginal rates as before. The possible merits of broadening the tax base are that (1) a higher tax yield is possible at given nominal rates, or (2) a given tax yield can result from nominal rates that are closer to actual effective rates. The lower level of rates will, of course, benefit those who had only relatively small deductions. Conversely, only the same taxpayers suffer from the higher nominal rates necessary with a smaller tax base.

The rather impressive size of the personal deductions and their

[12] This is the general approach taken by, among others, William F. Hellmuth, Jr., "Erosion of the Federal Corporation Income Tax Base," *Proceedings of the Annual Conference on Taxation, 1955*, National Tax Association, 1956, pp. 315-350; Pechman, "Erosion of the Individual Income Tax," *op.cit.*; Vickrey, *Agenda for Progressive Taxation*. In discussing the possible elimination of the mortgage interest deduction, Vickrey reasons that it "will increase the tax base and thus permit the rates to be decreased to a corresponding degree. This may be a distinct advantage in so far as it decreases the intensity of such other inequities as cannot be eliminated and reduces the effect of the tax on incentives to production" (pp. 23-24).

effect on the income tax are offset, for some students, by the stringent allowance for personal expenses necessary to earn a livelihood. To these critics, the new allowance under the 1954 Revenue code for child-care expenses—not reflected in the above tax liability estimates—is only a faint beginning in the right direction. They point to the nondeductible quasi-business expenses of the physically handicapped, as, for example, the necessary taxicab fares to and from work; they cite the moving expenses to new places of employment, in some cases seasonal; and the educational costs incurred by those whose professional and business plans require higher education, such as accountants, physicians, and teachers. Some go further and suggest the capitalization and charging off against future income of all expenditures for higher education.[13] Though the arguments for deduction of such quasi-business expenses are persuasive, it is difficult to determine the fine line of distinction between business and personal expenditures in each of these expense categories.[14] Many of these demands for more liberal allowances imply overstatement of income not only on tax returns, but also in the current national income accounts of the Department of Commerce.

[13] These suggestions, and many more, can be found in the records of hearings held by Congressional Committees. For a recent example, see Hearings before the Committee on Ways and Means, *General Revenue Revision*, 83rd Cong., 1st Sess., 1953, Part 1. For an earlier, and more disinterested treatment, see Paul J. Strayer, *The Taxation of Small Incomes*, New York, 1939, particularly pp. 71 and 116-18. The most recent report advocating deduction from taxable income of higher education expenses is the *Second Report to the President*, President's Committee on Education Beyond the High School, Washington, D.C., July, 1957, p. 56.

[14] This difficulty has been widely acknowledged throughout the literature on personal income taxation. For instance: "The problem of distinguishing sharply between business expense and personal expense is one which is the occasion of much practical difficulty and upon which wide differences of opinon exist." R. M. Haig, "The Concept of Income—Economic and Legal Aspects," *op.cit.*, p. 13.

CHAPTER 3

Quantitative Significance: Changes in Composition, Cyclical Sensitivity, and Distribution, 1918-1956

IN THE preceding chapter, the quantitative significance of personal deductions was analyzed, by comparing them over time with income and exemptions, and by examining their effects upon the tax base and upon the yield of the individual income tax. This broad, rather sweeping view of deductions in the context of the income tax structure will now be supplemented by a detailed view of three of their quantitative aspects: changes over time in composition of deductions; their effects on the built-in flexibility of the income tax; and the distribution of deductions among income classes.

As we have seen, there has been a slow, but steady, upward trend in personal expense deductions in relation to income reported on taxable returns.[1] Table 7 shows that in the four years 1918-1921 deductions absorbed, on average, about 8 per cent of adjusted gross income. During the latest years of our period, 1952-1956, the ratio rose to 13 per cent. In the 1920's deductions averaged close to 10 per cent of adjusted gross income; in the first half of the 1930's slightly over 11 per cent; and in the 1940's, after an initial sharp dip, they moved steadily toward their 1956 level of 13.4 per cent of income. It is also apparent from Table 7 that in the interwar years they were somewhat less sensitive than taxpayers' incomes to cyclical fluctuations in economic activity. They rose abruptly to 10 per cent of adjusted gross income in 1921; to a three-decade peak of 12 per cent in 1932; and—after a decline to 9.2 per cent in 1936—to 10.3 per cent in 1938. The relative stability of the deductions, with consequent changes in the ratio to income, made the tax base slightly more sensitive to business cycles than it would have been had the ratio of deductions to income remained the same during business cycles.

Changes Over Time in Composition

The upward trend of total personal deductions in relation to income,

[1] Unless otherwise noted, our data in this and the following chapters are for taxable returns. The tabulated information for nontaxable returns is less complete and detailed than that for taxable returns, and filing nontaxable returns appears to have been highly subject to the vagaries of administrative practice and change in tax laws.

TABLE 7

Total Personal Deductions Reported on Taxable Returns as
Per Cent of Adjusted Gross Income Reported, 1918-1956

YEAR	AGI *(billions of dollars)* (1)	Deductions *(billions of dollars)* (2)	Deductions as Per Cent of AGI (3)
1918	14.9	1.0	7.0
1919	19.1	1.4	7.5
1920	21.9	1.7	7.5
1921	15.0	1.5	10.3
1922	16.7	1.6	9.8
1923	19.4	2.0	10.2
1924	21.5	2.1	9.6
1925	19.3	1.8	9.4
1926	19.4	1.9	10.0
1927	20.2	2.1	10.3
1928	23.3	2.3	9.8
1929	22.7	2.2	9.8
1930	15.4	1.7	11.3
1931	10.4	1.1	10.6
1932	9.0	1.1	12.1
1933	8.3	0.9	11.1
1934	9.3	1.0	10.6
1935	11.1	1.1	9.9
1936	15.7	1.4	9.2
1937	16.9	1.6	9.7
1938	14.1	1.5	10.3
1939	17.5	1.7	9.5
1940	25.9	2.3	9.0
1941	49.3	3.8	7.8
1942	72.7	6.7	9.2
1943	104.6	8.2	7.9
1944	115.2	12.5	10.9
1945	118.1	13.2	11.2
1946	118.7	13.2	11.2
1947	135.9	15.7	11.5
1948	142.7	16.6	11.6
1949	139.1	16.9	12.1
1950	159.3	19.2	12.0
1951	183.9	22.5	12.2
1952	197.3	24.7	12.5
1953	210.5	27.0	12.8
1954	209.7	27.5	13.1
1955	229.6	30.5	13.3
1956	249.6	33.5	13.4

Source: Appendix Table D.

33

shown in Table 7, does not characterize all components. The number of deductions included in the total, as well as the relation of each to income, has changed over time (Tables 8 and 9). Before the 1930's, 40 per cent of the total was interest paid on nonbusiness loans, about 25 per cent nonbusiness taxes, and close to 20 per cent philanthropic contributions. In the course of the 1930's, with the decline of interest rates and private indebtedness on the one hand, and the rise of most deductible taxes on the other, the quantitative relationships changed significantly. By 1940—the last year before the introduction of the optional standard deduction device—nonbusiness taxes amounted to almost 40 per cent of total deductions, contributions to almost 25 per cent, and personal interest payments to only 20 per cent.

In 1941 an optional standard deduction and in 1942 an allowance for medical expenses were added to the list of deductible items. The medical expense deduction has not played as important a quantitative role as is suggested by the size of personal medical expenditures in the United States—$12.1 billion in 1956, for instance. In that year the medical expense deduction on all tax returns was less than $3.5 billion, and on taxable returns it was less than $3 billion. During 1942-1956, the medical allowance accounted each year for substantially less than one-tenth of personal deductions. One reason for this is that the medical expense allowance is the only one designed to benefit principally taxpayers with large expenses relative to income. In effect, the lower income groups thereby tend to be the main beneficiaries (see Chapter 7). The other reason is the standard deduction, in force a year before the medical deduction. The same groups who tend to benefit from the medical deduction are also the major users of the standard deduction.

The standard deduction was first introduced on a moderate scale and only for those at the bottom of the income distribution. It gave taxpayers the opportunity of filing a short, simplified return, including in the rate structure an automatic allowance for personal deductions, without regard to the individual taxpayer's actual deductions.[2] From 1941 to 1943 the standard deduction accounted for one-tenth to one-fifth of total deductions. Beginning with 1944, when the new adjusted gross income concept was introduced, the standard deduction was made more generous and applicable to all taxpayers: 10 per cent

[2] For a detailed description and discussion of the development of the standard deduction, see Chapter 8.

TABLE 8

Major Personal Expense Deductions, Taxable Returns, Selected Years, 1920-1956

(millions of dollars)

YEAR	Contributions	Taxes Paid	Interest Paid	Losses (fire, theft, storm, etc.)	Medical Expenses	Child-Care	Miscellaneous[a]	Optional Standard Deduction	Total Deductions	Adjusted Gross Income
1920	349b	372b	700b	17b	—	—	214	—	1,651	21,880
1927	423	537	827b	11b	—	—	268	—	2,067	20,157
1929	441	560	922	19b	—	—	289	—	2,232	22,725
1932	231	353b	352b	10b	—	—	141	—	1,086	9,006
1936	312	532	397	17b	—	—	187	—	1,445	15,664
1940	570	901	467	22	—	—	356	—	2,317	25,875
1942	1,320	1,893	1,010	91	534	—	762	1,112	6,721	72,670
1944	1,235	1,152	696	149	722	—	695	7,883	12,532	115,173
1945	1,424	1,225	683	128	836	—	1,027	7,873	13,195	118,104
1946	1,559	1,269	694	137	906	—	1,225	7,455	13,245	118,721
1947	1,875	1,547	855	193	1,156	—	1,517	8,541	15,682	135,891
1948	1,756	1,500	903	179	1,040	—	1,648	9,545	16,571	142,667
1949	1,897	1,812	1,106	171	1,170	—	1,656	9,082	16,895	139,108
1950	2,129	2,068	1,372	248	1,260	—	1,940	10,135	19,152	159,256
1951	n.a.	n.a.	n.a.	n.a.	n.a.	—	n.a.	11,566	22,504	183,935
1952	2,968	3,034	2,095	293	1,843	—	2,440	12,069	24,742	197,331
1953c	3,383	3,453	2,585	326	2,043	—	2,638	12,533	26,961	210,484
1954c	3,671	3,826	2,985	359	2,482	73	2,479	11,600	27,476	209,669
1955c	n.a.	n.a.	n.a.	n.a.	n.a.	n.a.	n.a.	12,027	30,524	229,595
1956c	4,650	5,543	4,544	295	2,993	95	2,916	12,471	33,508	249,551

In this and all other tables, n.a. = not available.

a Until 1944 the miscellaneous deductions were computed as a residual by "estimating out" certain other items for which independent estimates were possible.

b Estimated.

c Excludes fiduciary returns.

TABLE 9

Major Personal Expense Deductions as Per Cent of Adjusted Gross Income and as Per C of Total Deductions, Taxable Returns, Selected Years, 1920-1956

YEAR	Contri-butions	Taxes Paid	Interest Paid	Losses (fire, theft, storm, etc.)	Medical Expenses	Child-Care	Miscel-laneous	Optional Standard Deduction	T
			PER CENT OF ADJUSTED GROSS INCOME						
1920	1.6	1.7	3.2	0.1	—	—	1.0	—	
1927	2.1	2.7	4.1	0.1	—	—	1.3	—	]
1929	1.9	2.5	4.1	0.1	—	—	1.3	—	
1932	2.6	3.9	3.9	0.1	—	—	1.2	—	]
1936	2.0	3.4	2.5	0.1	—	—	1.2	—	
1940	2.2	3.5	1.8	0.1	—	—	1.4	—	
1942	1.8	2.6	1.4	0.1	0.7	—	1.0	1.5	
1944	1.1	1.0	0.6	0.1	0.6	—	0.6	6.8	]
1945	1.2	1.0	0.6	0.1	0.7	—	0.9	6.7	]
1946	1.3	1.1	0.6	0.1	0.8	—	1.0	6.3	]
1947	1.4	1.1	0.6	0.1	0.9	—	1.1	6.3	]
1948	1.2	1.1	0.6	0.1	0.7	—	1.2	6.7	]
1949	1.4	1.3	0.8	0.1	0.8	—	1.2	6.5	]
1950	1.3	1.3	0.9	0.2	0.8	—	1.2	6.4	]
1951	n.a.	n.a.	n.a.	n.a.	n.a.	—	n.a.	6.3	]
1952	1.5	1.5	1.1	0.1	0.9	—	1.2	6.1	]
1953	1.6	1.6	1.2	0.2	1.0	—	1.3	6.0	]
1954	1.8	1.8	1.4	0.2	1.2	a	1.2	5.5	]
1955	n.a.	n.a.	n.a.	n.a.	n.a.	n.a.	n.a.	5.2	]
1956	1.9	2.2	1.8	0.1	1.2	a	1.2	5.0	]
			PER CENT OF TOTAL DEDUCTIONS						
1920	21.1	22.5	42.4	1.0	—	—	12.9	—	1C
1927	20.4	26.0	40.0	0.5	—	—	13.0	—	1C
1929	19.8	25.1	41.3	0.9	—	—	13.0	—	1C
1932	21.3	32.5	32.4	0.9	—	—	13.0	—	1C
1936	21.6	36.8	27.5	1.2	—	—	12.9	—	1C
1940	24.6	38.9	20.2	0.9	—	—	15.4	—	1C
1942	19.6	28.2	15.0	1.4	7.9	—	11.3	16.5	1C
1944	9.9	9.2	5.6	1.2	5.8	—	5.5	62.9	1C
1945	10.8	9.3	5.2	1.0	6.3	—	7.8	59.7	1C
1946	11.8	9.6	5.2	1.0	6.8	—	9.2	56.3	1C
1947	12.0	9.9	5.5	1.2	7.4	—	9.7	54.5	1C
1948	10.6	9.1	5.4	1.1	6.3	—	9.9	57.6	1C
1949	11.2	10.7	6.5	1.0	6.9	—	9.8	53.8	1C
1950	11.1	10.8	7.2	1.3	6.6	—	10.1	52.9	1C
1951	n.a.	n.a.	n.a.	n.a.	n.a.	—	n.a.	51.4	1C
1952	12.0	12.3	8.5	1.2	7.4	—	9.9	48.8	1C
1953	12.5	12.8	9.6	1.2	7.6	—	9.8	46.5	1C
1954	13.4	13.9	10.9	1.3	9.0	0.3	9.0	42.2	1C
1955	n.a.	n.a.	n.a.	n.a.	n.a.	n.a.	n.a.	39.4	1C
1956	13.9	16.5	13.6	0.9	8.9	0.3	8.7	37.2	1C

Source: Table 8.
a Less than 0.05 per cent.

of income up to $500 per taxpayer. In that year almost two-thirds of the amount of the deductions was taken in the package form, and the number of taxpayers using it exceeded 80 per cent of the total. The amount of standard deduction thus rose from $1.8 billion in 1943 to $7.9 billion in 1944, or by over $6 billion. Probably about $2.5 billion, or 40 per cent, of the rise was caused by the inclusion in the enlarged standard deductions of a portion of income that would have been in the tax base in the absence of the 10 per cent standard deduction. Most of the rest of the increase was caused by the shift of taxpayers from itemized to standard deductions.[3] However, the shift did not continue after 1944. Despite some further liberalization in 1948 of the standard deduction, it accounted for less than 40 per cent of the total in 1956, in contrast to 63 per cent in 1944.

From the available evidence, it appears that the relative decline in use of the standard deduction is attributable to rises in both incomes and deductible expenditures since 1944. Despite the dramatic increase in incomes over the decade, most taxpayers have stayed within the income range to which the standard deduction of 10 per cent of income applies, particularly since its ceiling was raised to $1,000 in 1948. But within this income range the preference for the standard deduction declines with rising income, and incomes have shifted upwards considerably within the $0-10,000 income group during 1944-1956. In addition the relative rise in deductible expenditures has brought about a fall of the proportion of standard deduction returns at any given income level in the years since 1944.[4] Reported philanthropic contributions seem to have continued their mild upward trend in relation to income. Nonbusiness interest payments have reversed their previously noted relative decline throughout the 1930's and the war years, with the postwar firming of interest rates and growth of consumer and mortgage debt. State and local tax payments have risen steeply in relation to income in the postwar period, a rise reinforced for deductible purposes by the increase of homeownership since World War II. The medical expense deductions, rather stable until 1950, have also risen sharply since then, largely because of the removal of the exclu-

---

[3] This estimate is based on the assumption that without the more generous standard allowance, the 1944 relationship between deductions and income would not have differed appreciably from that of 1942-1943. This resulted in a hypothetical deductions estimate of $10.0 billion for 1944 compared to the actual of $12.5 billion. (The 1943 figures are shown in Appendix D, Table D-1.)

[4] These observations will be dealt with in more detail in Chapter 8. See particularly Table 52.

sion of 5 per cent of income from the medical expenses of taxpayers 65 and older, and because of the reduction of the exclusion for all taxpayers in 1954.

Thus of $33.5 billion deductions on taxable returns in 1956, we find $12.5 billion in the optional standard form and $21 billion in the itemized form. Of the latter, $5.5 billion are for state and local taxes, another $4.6 billion for philanthropic contributions, $4.5 billion for personal interest payments, and $3 billion for medical expenses. As we shall see later, the relative size of these deductions is not indicative of the relative size of the underlying aggregate expenditures. Personal interest payments are probably larger than philanthropic donations, and medical expenditures exceed both of them, even though on tax returns medical deductions are smaller than either of the other two. The large proportion of the total coming from the standard deduction may have some effect on the cyclical sensitivity of the personal deduction aggregate, referred to earlier. Conversion of a large amount of the deductions into a flat 10 per cent of income has made the cyclical variability of the deductions more akin to that of income, and hence seems to make the tax base somewhat less cycle-sensitive than formerly.[5] We shall explore the effect on built-in flexibility in the next section.

The amount of deductions classified as miscellaneous has fluctuated, on average, between one-tenth and one-fifth of the total. Serving as a catch-all for items we could not estimate separately, its composition has been neither constant over time, nor made up solely of personal expense items. In recent years it has included, among other items, deductions for alimony payments, gambling losses, the taxpayers' share of interest and taxes on cooperative apartment houses, and such business-type expenses as amortizable bond premiums, and outlays in connection with employment (for example, union dues, tools and supplies, and employment agency fees).

Effect on Built-in Flexibility of the Income Tax

In what direction have personal deductions affected the built-in

---

[5] The evidence on this is as yet rather inconclusive. In the 1948-1949 and 1953-1954 recessions, the total of deductions did not decline as the total of reported income did. The standard deductions declined sharply, but the itemized deductions more than offset the drop. For 1954 the revisions in the tax code may account for it in part. A possible generalization on these two experiences would be that the effect of the standard deduction on built-in flexibility was not as great as suggested above, although in the same direction.

flexibility of the income tax? If we define built-in flexibility[6] as the change in tax accompanying a given change in income, or $\dfrac{\Delta T}{\Delta Y}$, where $T =$ tax liability and $Y =$ income, it is likely that with a given rate structure changes in tax liability, in response to changes in income, will be larger without than with personal deductions. This would be true as long as personal deductions varied in the same direction as income—not always the case as we shall see below. It was probably with a constant rate structure assumption in mind that Brown concluded: "Greater output stabilization can be achieved . . . through elimination of deductions that vary with output or income such as those for charitable contributions and for other taxes."[7]

The effect of personal deductions on built-in flexibility is not so obvious if we start with the supposition that tax rates would be different (that is, lower) in the absence of deductions. Suppose Congress wants to raise a given amount of revenue from the income tax, in some initial year, regardless of whether any deductions are allowed. For simplicity's sake, let us assume a flat rate of tax on all taxable income. Will the tax with deductions show cyclical responses similar to those of the tax without deductions? If the ratio of deductions to tax base moves inversely to the business cycle—falling as the tax base rises, and rising when the tax base declines—then the tax with deductions has the greater built-in flexibility than that without. If the ratio of deductions to tax base rises as the tax base rises, and falls as the tax base falls, then deductions lessen built-in flexibility. If deductions change by the same relative amounts as the tax base, built-in flexibility is unaffected by personal deductions.

Table 10 compares personal deductions to the tax base for the pre-

6 Built-in flexibility, as used here, is not synonymous with, but merely ancillary to, automatic stabilization. The latter concept is concerned with the effect of induced changes in tax liabilities (or some other stabilizer) on output and income. The definition adopted here is that presented by Pechman, "Yield of the Individual Income Tax During a Recession," op.cit.

7 E. Cary Brown, "The Statistic Theory of Automatic Fiscal Stabilization," *Journal of Political Economy*, October, 1955, p. 433. In a similar but more general vein, Norman Ture stated: ". . . We should be concerned with the impact of narrowing the tax base on the potential of the federal revenue system in automatically counteracting changes in the level of economic activity. . . . It appears evident to me that adopting a tax provision which narrows the tax base in relation to income increases the possibility that changes in income will not involve effective compensating changes in tax liabilities." See round table on "Federal Tax Problems," *Proceedings of the Annual Conference on Taxation, 1955*, National Tax Association, 1956, p. 362.

war period 1932-1939, and the ten postwar years 1946-1955. The two periods were chosen because both permitted year-to-year comparisons undisturbed by legal changes in exemptions, which would of course exert a strong influence on the size of the tax base.[8] Deductions on tax

TABLE 10

Relation of Personal Deductions to Tax Base, 1932-1939 and 1946-1955

(dollars in millions)

| | Personal Deductions | | | Tax Base before Deductions | | Deductions as Per Cent of Tax Base before Deductions | |
| | on Taxable Returns | Estimated Total Effective Deductions | Tax Base | | | | |
YEAR	(1)	(2)	(3)	(1)+ (3) (4)	(2)+ (3) (5)	(1)÷ (4) (6)	(2)÷ (5) (7)
1932	1,086	5,649	4,489	5,575	10,138	19.5	55.7
1933	917	4,914	4,279	5,196	9,193	17.6	53.5
1934	987	4,565	4,740	5,727	9,305	17.2	49.1
1935	1,106	4,447	5,773	6,879	10,220	16.1	43.5
1936	1,445	4,427	8,544	9,999	12,971	14.5	34.1
1937	1,633	4,599	8,669	10,302	13,268	15.9	34.7
1938	1,453	4,370	6,702	8,155	11,072	17.8	39.5
1939	1,663	4,479	8,294	9,957	12,773	16.7	35.1
1946a	12,571	14,801	56,656	69,227	71,457	18.2	20.7
1947a	15,089	17,273	65,688	80,777	82,961	18.7	20.8
1948	16,571	18,716	75,208	91,779	93,924	18.1	19.9
1949	16,895	19,095	71,980	88,875	91,075	19.0	21.0
1950	19,152	21,232	84,861	104,013	106,093	18.4	20.0
1951	22,504	24,414	100,003	122,507	124,417	18.4	19.6
1952	24,742	26,818	108,054	132,796	134,872	18.6	19.9
1953	26,961	29,066	115,627	142,588	144,693	18.9	20.1
1954	27,476	29,852	115,227	142,703	145,079	19.3	20.6
1955	30,524	32,820	127,889	158,413	160,709	19.3	20.4

a Figures for 1946 and 1947 in columns 1 and 3 were adjusted for comparability with later year figures by assuming a $600 per capita exemption instead of the actual $500 exemption in force in those years. The 1946 and 1947 figures are therefore somewhat smaller than corresponding figures in other tables.

Source: Column 1: Appendix Table D-1; columns 2 and 3: estimated as described in notes to Table 1 (Appendix A).

returns and total "effective" deductions indicate the same characteristic relative to the tax base: they rose relatively less than the tax base when the latter rose, and they declined by a relatively smaller amount

[8] Since the exemptions were changed in 1948 from $500 per capita to $600, we adjusted the 1946 and 1947 tax base figures to a $600 exemption basis, which was possible with a fair degree of accuracy. However, the estimates of effective deductions for 1946-1947 do not take this into account and are therefore very slightly on the high side.

when it fell—a relationship more marked in the 1930's[9] than in the postwar years. But for both periods the figures indicate that deductions slightly increased the built-in flexibility of the tax, if the tax rate is set to obtain a given yield. The figures for deductions on taxable returns are far more reliable than those for total effective deductions since, with some estimated adjustments, they are based on reported figures. The total effective deductions (a very crude series of estimates as noted in Chapter 2) are conceptually the most relevant, since not only the deductions reported on taxable returns, but also some not so reported would have become taxable in the absence of the corresponding allowances.

In the postwar years the relation between deductions and the tax base was apparently much more stable than in the '30's. Nevertheless, in the 1948-1949 and 1953-1954 recessions, the decline in the tax base was evidently reinforced by the presence of the deductions; indeed, in these instances the latter rose while the tax base dropped off. On the supposition that Congress raised the same amount of tax revenues in 1946 with or without deductions, we applied a constant flat rate of tax to each of the tax bases in columns 3 and 5 of Table 10, computed to give a tax liability of $16.3 billion for 1946 for each type of base.[10] The figures are shown in Table 11. For 1948-1949, the liabilities obtained with the base allowing deductions drop from $21.6 billion to $20.7 billion; those derived from the base allowing no deductions decline from $21.4 to $20.8 billion. The deductions thus make for slightly greater built-in flexibility than in their absence, given the assumption that the same yields would be sought regardless of whether or not deductions are allowed. Similar computations for the '30's give the

---

[9] See also Adolph J. Goldenthal, *Concentration and Composition of Individual Incomes, 1918-1937*, Temporary National Economic Committee, Monograph No. 4, Washington, D.C., 1940, pp. 99-100. Goldenthal observes, in a somewhat different context, that "deductions from economic income are a larger proportion of economic income in years of diminished incomes than in years of increased incomes," during the period 1918 to 1937.

[10] The figure of $16.3 billion corresponds to that actually reported in *Statistics of Income* for 1946. The application of a constant flat tax rate to the tax bases of the postwar years is not unreasonable in the light of Pechman's (*op.cit.*, p. 9) and our own findings. When we use a given rate schedule, the rates under the 1954 code, for instance, we find that the tax has behaved almost like a flat-rate tax with respect to the total tax base over the period 1946-1955:

1946	24.1	1951	23.9
1947	23.8	1952	23.3
1948	24.2	1953	22.9
1949	23.8	1954	23.3
1950	24.5	1955	23.4

same results for 1937-1938, a period when deductions did not continue to rise as they did in 1948-1949 (Table 10). Built-in flexibility is nevertheless greater with than without the deductions in this instance, too. If we hold rates constant while studying the effect of deductions on

TABLE 11

Tax Liabilities Obtained with Assumed Flat Rate on Tax Base before and after Personal Deductions, 1933-1939 and 1946-1955

(millions of dollars)

YEAR	With Current Tax Base (1)	With Tax Base Before Deductions (2)
	(rate: 0.074)	*(rate: 0.033)*
1932	330	330
1933	317	303
1934	351	307
1935	427	337
1936	632	428
1937	642	438
1938	496	365
1939	614	422
	(rate: 0.287)	*(rate: 0.228)*
1946	16,281	16,281
1947	18,852	18,915
1948	21,585	21,415
1949	20,658	20,765
1950	24,355	24,189
1951	28,701	28,367
1952	31,011	30,751
1953	33,185	32,990
1954	33,070	33,078
1955	36,704	36,642

$330 million for 1932 and $16,281 million for 1946 are the reported tax liabilities for these two years in *Statistics of Income*. Rates for each column were obtained by dividing these two liabilities by the respective tax base figures for those years, as given in Table 10.

Source: Column 1: rate times column 3, Table 10; column 2: rate times column 5, Table 10.

built-in flexibility, then built-in flexibility is likely to be lessened by the operation of deductions, as illustrated by the 1937-1938 experience. The absolute decline in tax base is smaller with deductions allowed. By the same token the 1948-1949 and 1953-1954 experiences do not confirm this: deductions rose in that period and the absolute decline in the tax base is therefore in this instance greatest when deductions are allowed.

42

In any case, it should be evident from the foregoing that the effect on built-in flexibility attributed to deductions depends heavily on what the relation between level of tax rates and deductions is assumed to be. In the short run, any change in tax law or practice regarding deductions is more likely to affect revenue than tax rates. When the rate structure remains thus unchanged, any change in deductions may well cause an opposite change in built-in flexibility, as Brown has pointed out. Over the long run, budgetary requirements may exert the dominant influence in determining the amount of revenue raised by the income tax. Within broad limits, statutory changes in the size of the tax base may affect the level of statutory rates rather than revenue. In the same way, the allowance of deductions may in the long run affect the level of statutory rates rather than the level of revenue and, as has been shown above; their existence may thus tend to increase built-in flexibility by some small amount.

Distribution by Size of Income on Tax Returns

The change over time in the composition of the personal deductions, described in the first section of this chapter, has been accompanied by changes in their distribution by income groups.[11] Until 1941 deductions exhibited a tendency to rise in relation to taxpayers' income; since then the curve describing this relationship has been U-shaped. This is shown by the percentages in Table 12.

The percentages are given both inclusive and exclusive of the miscellaneous deductions, because that category has always contained some negative income (that is, expense and loss) items. This was particularly true of the earlier years and has tapered off in time.[12] For instance, the 1918 and 1928 miscellaneous deductions include the net losses of sole proprietors and partners of unincorporated businesses, and before 1937 they also include amounts that were distributed to beneficiaries and hence deducted from income on fiduciary tax returns. But the

[11] All figures are deductions as per cent of adjusted gross income. But in distributing the returns by income size groups, statutory net income is used for years up to 1943 and adjusted gross income thereafter. This change in classification moves some taxpayers into a higher group than the one they were in before 1944. Therefore, the change results in a slightly lower ratio of deductions to income for a given income group when the ratio is a rising function of income. The opposite results when the deduction-income ratio is a declining function of income. When the curve describing the ratios is U-shaped, the change in classification raises the declining portion and lowers the rising portion of the curve slightly.

[12] For an enumeration of the various items included under miscellaneous in the different years, see the notes to this Table in Appendix E.

TABLE 12

Personal Deductions as Per Cent of Adjusted Gross Income on Taxable Returns,
by Size of Income, Selected Years, 1918-1956

INCOME GROUPSa ($000's)	1918	1928	1933	1937	1943	1945	1947	1949	1952	1954	1956
INCLUDING MISCELLANEOUS DEDUCTIONSb											
Under 2	4.5		8.2	8.2	9.0	11.3	11.4	11.4	11.6	11.6	11.8
2-3	6.3	8.9	10.7	9.7	8.3	11.6	11.4	11.7	12.1	12.4	12.7
3-5	7.5		13.0	11.0	7.7	11.9	12.5	12.5	12.7	13.3	13.6
5-10	15.3	12.0	15.0	11.9	7.9	11.0	11.6	13.0	13.0	13.6	14.0
10-25	14.1	12.9	15.7	12.0	7.4	8.5	9.2	11.3	12.0c	12.5c	12.6
25-50	13.6	12.4	17.8	12.0	7.3	8.2	8.9	9.9	10.5c	11.2c	11.3
50-100	14.8	12.1	21.3	12.7	7.6	9.3	10.0	10.4	11.3	12.0	12.3
100-500	15.1	11.1	24.0	14.7	8.7	11.8	12.0	12.8	14.4	15.9	17.1
500 and over	20.9	9.4	19.4	16.7	9.0	12.3	12.6	13.4	15.3	18.8	19.3
Averaged	10.6	11.3	14.2	11.3	8.2	11.1	11.5	12.1	12.5	13.1	13.4
EXCLUDING MISCELLANEOUS DEDUCTIONSb											
Under 2		4.3	5.8	5.8	8.2	11.0	11.1	11.0	11.3	11.3	11.5
2-3		4.4	7.6	6.7	7.5	11.1	10.9	11.3	11.7	12.0	12.2
3-5		7.4	9.4	7.9	6.8	11.0	11.6	11.6	12.0	12.6	12.8
5-10		8.8	11.0	8.8	6.7	9.7	10.0	11.6	11.8	12.5	12.9
10-25		9.7	11.2	9.0	6.1	7.1	7.5	9.5	10.3c	11.0c	11.2
25-50		9.6	12.8	9.2	6.0	6.8	7.1	8.0	8.6c	9.4c	9.7
50-100		9.5	15.3	10.2	6.2	7.6	7.8	8.3	9.0	9.8	10.4
100-500		8.8	16.8	12.1	7.1	9.6	9.4	9.9	11.4	13.1	14.5
500 and over		8.3	12.5	13.8	7.6	10.5	10.0	11.0	12.6	16.6	17.3
Average		8.5	10.2	8.4	7.3	10.4	10.5	11.1	11.4	12.1	12.4

a Statutory net income classes until 1943; adjusted gross income classes thereafter.

b In the tabulation that includes the miscellaneous deductions, the latter were also part of adjusted gross income. When the miscellaneous category was excluded, it was omitted from adjusted gross income as well as from the deductions total.

c For 1952 and 1954 the percentages given are for the income group $10-20 thousand and 20-50 thousand.

d The ratio of total deductions to income in this table does not correspond to that shown in Table 11. In the latter table an attempt was made to present both deductions and adjusted gross income free of most business deductions. It was not possible to do the same for each income group.

miscellaneous category also includes such personal expense items as losses due to fire, storm, and theft until 1937, and gambling losses in excess of gains until 1933. The figures excluding miscellaneous deductions are probably closer to the total of truly personal deductions.

It is evident from both tabulations in the table that before World War II the personal deductions as a whole removed a larger proportion of income from the tax-base of high-income taxpayers than of low-income ones. For 1928 the ratio of personal deductions (excluding miscellaneous) to income rises from 4 per cent for taxpayers with $3,000

44

and under, to almost 10 per cent for those in the $10 to $50 thousand range, and then declines to 8 per cent for incomes of $500 thousand and over. For 1933 the rise is from 6 per cent at the bottom to 17 per cent for incomes in the $100 to $500 thousand range, and 12.5 per cent in the highest income group. On 1937 tax returns, the percentage rises smoothly from 6 to 14 without any hump in the middle. The picture is not altered when we include the miscellaneous deductions in the distribution. The percentages are at a higher level, but the pattern remains the same.

Beginning with 1942, the ratio of personal deductions to income no longer rises throughout the income scale. It was lifted sharply at the bottom to a level about as high as that near the very top, mainly because of the introduction of the standard allowance optional for those with gross incomes of $3,000 or less, and the medical expense allowance with a fixed percentage exclusion. The percentages from that time on started at a high level at the lower income ranges, sagged at the middle income ranges, and rose to their initial level at high-income ranges. With surprising regularity, the ratio reached its low point at the $25 to $50 thousand income range in every year during the 1942-1953 period. It was not until 1952 that, for the first time since 1940, it went above 10 per cent at that income range. This was also the first time that personal deductions (including the miscellaneous category) exceeded one-tenth of the reported income of taxpayers in all income groups.

From 1944 on, when the 10 per cent standard deduction was inaugurated, there is a mild rise in the percentages at the lower end of the income distribution extending to the point where the upper limit of the standard deduction is reached.[13] The rise occurs because, as we move up in the income scale, relatively more taxpayers choose to itemize. Yet on returns with itemized deductions, the latter decline as a percentage of income until the $25 to $50 thousand income range is reached. The reasons for the behavior of the percentages will become clearer after we analyze in succeeding chapters the major items in the totals of deductions for each income group. Philanthropic contributions is the subject of that analysis in the next chapter.

[13] Until 1947 the upper limit of the 10 per cent deduction was $500 per return and it was reached at $5,000 of adjusted gross income. From 1948 on the limit became $1,000 for virtually all taxpayers and was reached at $10,000 income.

CHAPTER 4

Philanthropic Contributions

THE present status under the 1954 Revenue code of the allowance for deduction of philanthropic contributions in computing taxable income, the reader will recall, is deduction of such gifts up to 30 per cent of annual income, provided that 10 per cent of income is given to certain institutions. The brief legislative history of personal deductions given in Chapter 1 will now be supplemented by a sketch of the background of current legislation on contributions.

Legislative Background

Until recently, public debate of any consequence concerning the tax treatment of philanthropic gifts had occurred only twice. The first time, in 1917 when the United States entered World War I, there was widespread anxiety that established habits of giving and periodic appeals might no longer be sufficient to maintain the flow of private philanthropy. The general consensus, among those of the press and in Congress who were seriously concerned, tended toward the notion that persons in the habit of contributing to philanthropic causes would now seek to offset increases in tax liabilities with cuts in their philanthropic giving. From then on, until the limit was raised in 1952, gifts to philanthropic organizations were deductible up to 15 per cent of the taxpayer's income.

The question arose once more after the United States entered World War II. The 1944 proposal to extend the standard deduction to tens of millions of taxpayers was, for many, a threat to the continued existence of private non-profit activity. Obviously, the standard deduction made gifts to philanthropy no cheaper than any nondeductible expenditure. There was, therefore, a justifiable fear that the generous flow of funds to private, nonprofit institutions might shrink to a mere trickle. As in 1917, some of the more vociferous advocates of undiminished nongovernmental financing and control of such activities saw in it the first steps toward their nationalization.[1] But the predominant Congressional opinion in 1944, unlike that in 1917, appeared to be that most contributions are made independently of tax considerations. Representative Robert L. Doughton, then chairman of the House Ways

---

[1] Representative Carl T. Curtis of Nebraska expressed the fear that the standard deduction would cripple the institutions supported by private donations, and thus start us on "the road toward totalitarianism" (*Congressional Record*, 78th Cong., 2nd Sess., 1944, pp. 3972, 4029). Similar fears had been expressed in 1917: a *Wash-*

and Means Committee, argued that the mass of contributors do not give "for the purpose of securing a tax reduction, but because of the worthy causes such contributions advance."[2] And Senator Walter F. George, chairman of the Senate Finance Committee, stated that "the committee does not believe it can be proved that a tax incentive has been an important factor in the making of such gifts by individuals having less than $5,000 of adjusted gross income, and certainly the $500 standard deduction will not remove the tax incentive for persons in the higher brackets, upon whom the charities depend for contributions in substantial amounts."[3] It might be argued that this statement suggests no real departure from the thinking of 1917, since the committee believed only those with modest incomes to be insensitive to the influence of the tax upon giving. But the tax rate on the lowest bracket of taxable income in 1944 exceeded all but the marginal rates on the very highest brackets in 1917.

The change in Congressional thinking may be accounted for in part by the intense pressure on Congress in the early 1940's to simplify the tax return form. The "simplification" of the deductions seemed a key point in this task. But the change in thinking was also the result of the common belief that giving to philanthropic causes had become an ingrained habit with most Americans, irrespective of any tax concessions. As far back as 1933, a member of the President's Research Committee on Social Trends concluded, on the basis of the 1922 to 1929 income tax experience, that "the ratio between income and contributions is so consistent throughout the period as to suggest that giving is more definitely regulated by habit or tradition than by changes in income, tax rate, or any external circumstance."[4]

Whatever the reasons underlying the change in Congressional philosophy, the statistical record of the past three decades may throw light on some of the questions raised. Of course, the available data give little information about the donors' ultimate motives, which were not an object of the statistical study. In addition to personal values that ac-

---

ington Post editorial, inserted into the Congressional Record (65th Cong., 1st Sess., 1917, p. 6728), warned that unless a citizen's donations for the public good are allowed as a deduction the government itself will have to "support all those works of charity and mercy and all the educational and religious works which in this country have heretofore been supported by private benevolence. . . ."

[2] Congressional Record, 78th Cong., 2nd Sess., 1944, p. 3975.

[3] Ibid., p. 4702.

[4] Sydnor H. Walker, "Privately Supported Social Work" in Recent Social Trends in the United States (Report of the President's Research Committee on Social Trends), Vol. II, New York, 1933, p. 1219.

count for the volume of philanthropic giving (religious beliefs, interest in particular causes such as education or science, social emulation, and so on), the tax saving may reduce the cost to the donor—in some cases even match it.[5] The complex motives are frequently not clear cut even to the donor. Our figures do, however, indicate somewhat the trend in volume of individual philanthropic contributions in the course of changing incomes, tax rates, and allowances for deductions. The statistical data may shed light on some of the policy problems raised above. And their examination is valuable because tax return data have been the chief reliance in past studies of philanthropic giving.[6]

Trend in Amounts Deducted for Contributions, 1917-1956

The total amounts annually deducted as philanthropic contributions by individuals on their tax returns through nearly four decades are shown in Table 13. The totals for 1920 to 1939 stayed within the range of $250 to $550 million. Since 1942 the amounts have exceeded $1 billion in every year, despite the introduction of the standard deduction which has been taken by the majority of taxpayers. For 1956 a total of $4.9 billion was reported. Of this $4.7 billion, or 95 per cent, was reported on taxable returns and hence had a direct effect on the total tax revenue and its distribution among taxpayers. On the basis of estimated adjusted gross income for 1957, total itemized contributions may be close to $5.5 billion. The steep rise since the beginning of World War II is largely explained by many newcomers to the tax-return universe whose incomes had previously been below the filing requirements.[7] Thus to distill some meaning from the fig-

---

[5] A gift made in property rather than cash can be costless to the donor. In such a transfer of property any accrued capital gains are not considered realized, and hence not taxed; yet the gift is deductible at the full market value of the property. The tax saving from the deduction from income of the gift may, in a few cases, exceed what the donor could have realized had he sold the asset and paid the tax on the accrued capital gain.

[6] See, among others, Sydnor H. Walker, op.cit., pp. 1216-1220; Seymour E. Harris, How Shall We Pay for Education?, 1948, Chapters 8 and 9; F. Emerson Andrews, Philanthropic Giving, Chapter 1, and Philanthropic Foundations, Chapter 13 (both published by Russell Sage Foundation, New York, 1950 and 1956); John Price Jones, The American Giver, 1954; Thad L. Hungate, Financing the Future of Higher Education, Teachers College, Columbia University, New York, 1946, Chapter 5.

[7] It is occasionally overlooked that a time series based on tax returns is likely to have an upward growth bias. Thus Harris (op.cit., p. 133), compared changes in contributions between 1941 and 1943 as reported on tax returns with changes in national income: "In 1943 income was about 55 per cent above that of 1941; and

TABLE 13

Philanthropic Contributions and Adjusted Gross Income on Tax Returns with Itemized Deductions, 1917-1956

(dollars in millions)

YEAR	Taxable Returns			All Returns		
	Contributions (1)	Adjusted Gross Income (2)	Ratio of Contributions to AGI (per cent) (1) ÷ (2) (3)	Contributions (4)	Adjusted Gross Income (5)	Ratio of Contributions to AGI (per cent) (4) ÷ (5) (6)
1917a	235	11,004	2.14	245	11,664	2.10
1920b	348	21,880	1.59	387	25,571	1.51
1922	343	16,678	2.06	425	23,577	1.80
1923	422	19,396	2.18	535	27,481	1.95
1924	441	21,541	2.05	533	28,468	1.87
1925	371	19,280	1.92	442	24,356	1.81
1926	395	19,355	2.04	484	24,606	1.97
1927	423	20,157	2.10	508	25,368	2.00
1928	459	23,307	1.97	541	28,473	1.90
1929	441	22,725	1.94	540	28,225	1.91
1930	357	15,429	2.31	434	21,116	2.06
1931	242	10,405	2.32	354	16,067	2.20
1932	231	9,006	2.56	317	13,830	2.29
1933	185	8,290	2.23	282	12,964	2.18
1934	200	9,331	2.14	280	14,524	1.93
1935	227	11,140	2.04	310	16,683	1.86
1936	312	15,664	1.99	390	21,241	1.84
1937	352	16,897	2.08	445	23,478	1.90
1938	310	14,123	2.20	414	21,026	1.97
1939	387	17,467	2.22	499	25,518	1.96
1940	570	25,875	2.20	740	39,921	1.85
RETURNS WITH ITEMIZED DEDUCTIONS ONLY						
1941	876	38,780	2.26	1,002	45,501	2.20
1942	1,320	54,134	2.44	1,450	59,594	2.43
1943	1,813	74,315	2.44	1,836	75,062	2.45
1944	1,235	32,468	3.80	1,258	32,694	3.85
1945	1,424	34,779	4.09	1,450	34,955	4.15
1946	1,559	38,173	4.08	1,639	39,569	4.14
1947	1,875	44,499	4.21	1,974	45,862	4.30
1948	1,756	42,912	4.09	1,881	44,890	4.19
1949	1,897	44,795	4.23	2,032	46,825	4.34
1950	2,129	53,109	4.01	2,260	55,116	4.10
1951	n.a.	63,236	—	n.a.	65,261	—
1952	2,968	71,682	4.14	3,116	73,643	4.23
1953	3,383	80,817	4.19	3,556	82,871	4.29
1954	3,671	89,381	4.11	3,893	92,334	4.22
1955	n.a.	104,641	—	n.a.	108,528	—
1956	4,650	119,731	3.88	4,878	123,719	3.94

Figures include returns of fiduciaries up to 1944, and after that exclude fiduciary return figures.
a For net incomes above $2,000 only.
b For net incomes above $1,000 only.
Source: *Statistics of Income.*

ures shown, we must view them against the background of another series, such as income reported on tax returns and the countrywide aggregate of philanthropic contributions.

For the two decades up to 1940 it is possible to compare total contributions and total income reported on taxable returns for the years up to 1940. For those years we observe a fairly stable relationship, contributions remaining close to 2 per cent of total income reported (Chart 3). In the 1920's annual contributions on taxable returns varied typically between 1.9 and 2.2 per cent of reported income; in the four depression years 1930-1933 they rose to a level of 2.2 to 2.6 per cent; and thereafter (1934-1940) the relation of contributions to income dropped back to a level of 2.0 to 2.2 per cent.[8]

The gradual introduction, beginning with 1941, of the standard deduction makes it difficult to compare philanthropic gifts and income as reported on tax returns for recent years. For 1941-1943 the standard deduction applied only to taxpayers with less than $3,000 income. Assuming for this group a contributions-to-income ratio similar to that for 1940, we obtain the following figures for all returns comparable to the 1917-1940 series shown in Table 13:[9]

	Taxable Returns	All Returns
1941	2.13	1.98
1942	2.14	2.03
1943	2.18	2.12

contributions and gifts were about 100 per cent above the 1941 figure. *In other words, contributions and gifts seem to have a high income elasticity: with a given percentage rise (decline) of income, the increase (reduction) in the percentage of gifts and contributions is large.*" (Author's italics.) It is widely thought, and with good reason as we shall see below, that the opposite is the case: contributions tend to change relatively less than income.

[8] On nontaxable returns, contributions were relatively lower in the interwar period. Thus for all returns (taxable and nontaxable) the percentages were typically 1.8 to 2.0 per cent in the 1920's; 2.1 to 2.3 for 1930-1933; and 1.8 to 2.0 for 1934-1940.

[9] The figures underlying these percentages are:

	Reported	Estimated	Total	Adjusted Gross Income
		(taxable returns)		
1941	876	174	1,050	49,319
1942	1,320	233	1,553	72,670
1943	1,813	462	2,275	104,562
		(all returns)		
1941	1,002	252	1,254	63,032
1942	1,450	304	1,754	85,310
1943	1,836	466	2,302	106,149

The column group heading "Contributions" spans Reported, Estimated, and Total.

CHART 3

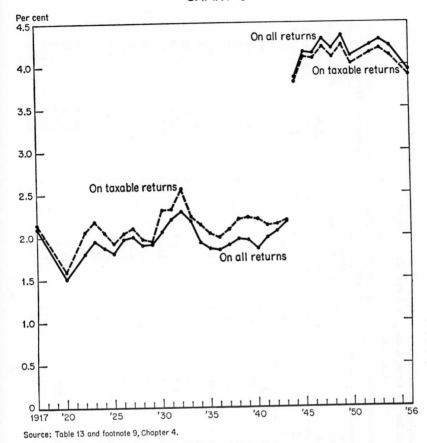

Source: Table 13 and footnote 9, Chapter 4.

Contributions as Per Cent of Adjusted Gross Income on Tax Returns with
Itemized Deductions, 1917-1956

This projection appears not unreasonable in the light of the reported figures for returns with incomes under $3,000 for 1922-1940,
and for returns with incomes over $3,000 for 1922-1943 (Table 14 and
Chart 4). On average, contributions on taxable returns with incomes
over $3,000 remained practically unchanged relative to incomes: they
averaged 2.10 per cent of adjusted gross income in 1922-1924 and 2.09
per cent in 1941-1943. For the group with incomes under $3,000 we
observe a similarly stable relation between reported gifts and income
from 1932 to 1939. But the stable ratio represents a sharp upward
shift from that of 1922 to 1932, the year when personal exemptions
were lowered with a consequent increase in the number of family-tax

51

TABLE 14

Reported Philanthropic Contributions and Estimated Adjusted Gross Income on Taxable Returns of Three Income Groups, for Three Periods, 1922-1956

(dollars in millions)

YEAR	Under $3,000			$3,000 and Over			$50,000 and Over		
	Contributions (1)	Adjusted Gross Income (2)	Ratio of Contributions to AGI (per cent) (1) ÷ (2) (3)	Contributions (4)	Adjusted Gross Income (5)	Ratio of Contributions to AGI (per cent) (4) ÷ (5) (6)	Contributions (7)	Adjusted Gross Income (8)	Ratio of Contributions to AGI (per cent) (7) ÷ (8) (9)
1922	67	4,015	1.66	276	13,334	2.07	63	2,063	3.08
1923	80	4,618	1.74	341	15,677	2.17	73	2,140	3.43
1924	82	4,739	1.72	360	17,469	2.06	91	2,649	3.45
1925	31	2,165	1.42	340	17,797	1.91	112	4,190	2.68
1926	34	2,258	1.50	361	17,532	2.06	125	4,257	2.92
1927	34	2,098	1.64	389	18,225	2.13	145	4,922	2.95
1928	34	2,102	1.59	425	21,599	1.97	176	7,041	2.49
1929	29	1,996	1.44	412	21,149	1.95	173	6,721	2.58
1930	33	2,025	1.66	324	13,986	2.32	104	2,790	3.74
1931	24	1,367	1.78	217	9,123	2.38	59	1,361	4.36
1932	50	2,132	2.37	180	6,584	2.74	40	586	6.76
1933	42	1,877	2.23	143	6,251	2.29	29	770	3.77
1934	37	1,718	2.13	163	7,878	2.07	34	981	3.47
1935	41	2,035	2.03	186	9,403	1.98	42	1,304	3.25
1936	57	2,779	2.06	255	13,244	1.92	70	2,194	3.21
1937	70	3,417	2.04	282	13,990	2.02	73	2,014	3.62
1938	69	3,208	2.16	241	11,340	2.12	43	1,273	3.41
1939	96	4,331	2.21	291	13,542	2.15	57	1,454	3.89
1940	220	10,108	2.18	350	16,107	2.17	65	1,694	3.84

(concluded on next page)

YEAR	Under $3,000			$3,000 and Over			$50,000 and Over[a]		
	Contributions (1)	Adjusted Gross Income (2)	Ratio of Contributions to AGI (per cent) (1) ÷ (2) (3)	Contributions (4)	Adjusted Gross Income (5)	Ratio of Contributions to AGI (per cent) (4) ÷ (5) (6)	Contributions (7)	Adjusted Gross Income (8)	Ratio of Contributions to AGI (per cent) (7) ÷ (8) (9)
1941				443	21,572	2.05	73	2,266	3.21
1942				611	29,593	2.06	76	2,799	2.71
1943				973	44,996	2.16	95	3,423	2.79
1944							130	3,285	3.96
1945							173	3,801	4.55
1946							198	4,466	4.43
1947							209	4,460	4.69
1948							249	6,084	4.09
1949							240	5,404	4.44
1950							298	7,676	3.88
1951							n.a.	7,888	n.a.
1952							363	7,246	5.01
1953							352	6,583	5.35
1954							438	7,826	5.60
1955							n.a.	9,116	n.a.
1956							574	9,892	5.80

a Returns for individuals with itemized deductions only, beginning 1944.
Source: *Statistics of Income*.

CHART 4

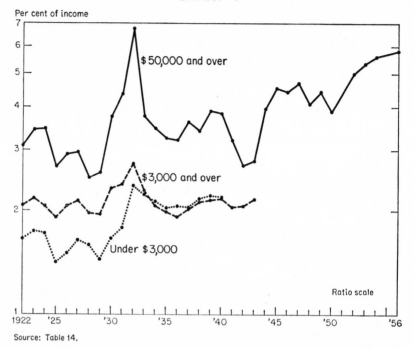

Philanthropic Contributions Reported on Taxable Returns as Per Cent of Income Reported, for Three Selected Income Groups, 1922-1956

returns filed in the low-income ranges. Further lowering of exemptions in 1940 might be expected to produce a similar effect in the years up to 1944, but available evidence does not suggest it (see Table 19 below). It appears that the relation between reported gifts and income on tax returns remained virtually unchanged from the early 1920's through 1943.

No simple conjectures are possible for years after 1943, which are marked by extension of the optional standard deductions to all taxpayers. The upper limit on its dollar amount, however, tended to make its choice relatively most frequent among taxpayers with low or modest incomes. For those continuing to itemize their deductions, contributions fluctuated around a fairly stable level of 4 per cent of income between 1944 and 1956 (Table 13). For 1956, the percentage was 3.9 per cent, and for the intervening 9 years for which there are figures, they were consistently somewhat over 4 per cent of income. But interpretation of this apparent stability is more difficult when it is viewed in conjunction with the steady rise since 1944 in the proportion of taxpayers choosing to file itemized returns. Between 1944 and 1956, the number of taxable returns with standard deduction declined from 82 to 63 per cent of the total; and the dollar amount of standard deductions declined from 63 to 37 per cent of total personal deductions.[10]

The pronounced shift from the standard to itemized deductions raises the possibility that the level trend of 1944-1956 in the ratio of contributions to income, as reported on returns with itemized deductions, does not genuinely indicate a stable relation for those years comparable to that for 1917-1943. Table 14 and Table 19 below show that for income groups of $50,000 and over, the ratio of contributions to income has risen considerably since 1943. Because of the $1,000 limit on the standard deduction, only a small number of taxpayers in those groups made use of it; consequently, the relation between gifts and incomes revealed on these returns does not suffer the same distortion as that on returns farther down the income distribution. The same upward trend in the ratio of reported contributions to income might have obtained for taxpayers in all income groups, had it not been for the sustained changeover, at lower levels of income, from the standard to itemized deductions.

The changeover appears to be strongly associated with the postwar rise in homeownership, that is, with itemized deduction of property taxes and mortgage interest, and the liberalization of the medical expense deduction allowance. As a result, returns with contributions somewhat below the previous average for those who itemize, may have been swept into several income groups, covering up an over-all rising trend of contributions to income reported. This reasoning is supported, when we observe the change in number, between 1944 and 1956, of tax returns reporting deductions for contributions and for the three other items. The frequencies for the $3,000 to $10,000 income range, from which about 60 per cent of the deducted contributions for 1956 were reported are shown in the tabulation below.

	Philanthropic Contributions	Taxes Paid	Interest Paid	Medical Deductions	Itemized Deductions
			NUMBER WITH		
			(in thousands)		
1944	2,764	2,691	1,786	1,038	2,923
1956	12,581	12,734	10,523	7,549	13,010
	PER CENT OF RETURNS WITH ITEMIZED DEDUCTIONS				
1944	94.6	92.1	61.1	35.5	100.0
1956	96.7	97.9	80.9	58.0	100.0

10 See Tables 54 and 55 in Chapter 8.

Returns with deductions for interest on personal indebtedness rose from three-fifths to four-fifths of the total number itemizing, and the number with medical expense deductions from 35 to 58 per cent in the $3,000 to $10,000 income group. The number with deductions for taxes paid, less than the number with deductions for contributions in 1944, exceeded that number in 1956. The same developments were even more pronounced for the $5,000 to $10,000 income group, which accounted for two-fifths of all itemized contributions in 1956. The decline of its ratio of contributions to income (from 4.1 in 1949 to 3.5 in 1956; see Table 19) supports the hypothesis that it was the rise in homeownership with its attendant deductions, and the liberalization of the medical deduction, rather than the size of contributions, that influenced the increasing choice of the long-form return. The observed movement in the ratio of contributions to income for returns with itemized deductions cannot be assumed to characterize standard deduction returns, for which the trend could well have been upwards for recent years.

Tax Equivalent of Deductions for Philanthropic Contributions

Figures for the annual flow of philanthropic contributions as deducted on personal income tax returns, the subject of our discussion so far, tell us little about the resulting tax reduction for contributors and the so-called revenue cost to the government. Estimates are presented in Table 15 for the period 1924-1956. Successive rises in tax rates chiefly account for the continuing rise of the government's participation in deductible gifts: from an average of over 10 per cent before 1932, to about 15 per cent in the years before World War II, and to about 30 per cent in the years since our entrance into World War II (Chart 5). We estimate that the tax cost of itemized contributions reached 38 per cent, or $539 million in 1945, when tax rates were at their wartime peak, and about 32 per cent or nearly $1.5 billion in 1956.

To round out the picture, there are other ways in which the federal government, through the tax system, offers rebates on funds donated for philanthropic purposes. The laws for the corporation income tax, estate tax, and gift tax (property transfers) all permit deductions for gifts to philanthropy. In addition, the income of nonprofit organizations is also tax free. Finally, there is the revenue foregone on some

56

TABLE 15

Contributions Reported on Taxable Returns, Cost of Deductions to
Government, and Net Cost of Contributions to Taxpayers, 1924-1956

(dollars in millions)

YEAR	Contributions Reported on Taxable Returns (1)	Cost to the Government[a] (2)	Net Cost to the Contributors (1) — (2) (3)	(2) ÷ (1) (per cent) (4)	Effective Rate of Tax Liability[b] (per cent) (5)
1924	441	54	388	12.2	3.3
1925	371	41	330	11.0	3.8
1926	395	45	350	11.3	3.8
1927	423	50	373	11.8	4.1
1928	459	58	401	12.6	5.0
1929	441	52	388	11.9	4.4
1930	357	38	319	10.7	3.1
1931	242	24	218	9.8	2.4
1932	231	35	196	15.0	3.7
1933	185	27	158	14.5	4.5
1934	200	33	167	16.3	5.5
1935	227	39	189	17.0	5.9
1936	312	64	248	20.4	7.8
1937	352	68	285	19.2	6.8
1938	310	47	262	15.3	5.4
1939	387	52	335	13.4	5.3
1940	570	85	485	15.0	5.8
1941	876	175	701	19.9	9.2
1942	1,320	358	961	27.2	14.2
1943	1,813	542	1,271	29.9	19.5
1944	1,235	445	791	36.0	20.7
1945	1,424	539	885	37.8	21.2
1946	1,559	531	1,028	34.1	19.5
1947	1,875	613	1,262	32.7	18.2
1948	1,756	487	976	27.7	14.9
1949	1,897	504	1,393	26.6	13.7
1950	2,129	603	1,526	28.3	15.3
1951	n.a.	n.a.	n.a.	n.a.	16.4
1952	2,968	1,030	1,939	34.7	16.6
1953	3,383	1,133	2,251	33.5	15.7
1954	3,671	1,144	2,527	31.2	14.1
1955	n.a.	n.a.	n.a.	n.a.	14.1
1956	4,650	1,465	3,185	31.5	14.2

a For method of calculation, see Appendix G.

b Tax liability as reported in *Statistics of Income* divided by adjusted gross income on taxable returns (as shown in Table 13).

CHART 5

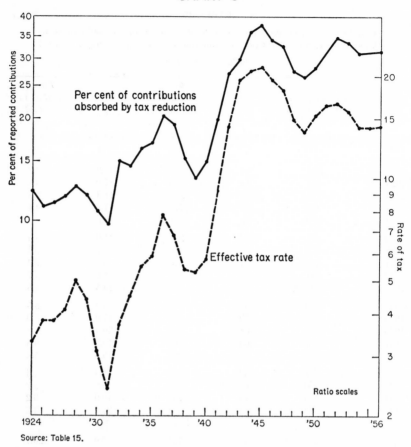

Per Cent of Taxpayers' Reported Contributions Absorbed by Tax Reduction, and Effective Rate of Tax Liability on Returns with Itemized Deductions, 1924-1956

fraction of the standard deduction. In round numbers, the 1956 tax cost of $1.5 billion on individual itemized returns would be raised to around $2.6 billion by addition of the tax cost of corporation gifts, property transfers, income of nonprofit organizations,[11] and the por-

[11] This estimate takes account only of tax concessions accorded philanthropy in particular. No attempt is made to estimate the tax equivalent of the income of philanthropic organizations received in the form of gifts. Since gifts are not taxable to the recipient in the federal income tax, philanthropy is in this instance accorded no tax concession that is not equally available to others. Only the deductibility for the donor of gifts made to philanthropic organizations is unique. Many hold that gifts should be taxable as income to the recipient in the same manner as any other receipts that add to his spending power (see, for instance, Henry C. Simons, *Personal Income Taxation*, Chapter 6). But we are not concerned with this larger problem here.

tion of the standard deduction allotted to philanthropic contributions.[12]

Comprehension of the figures showing the amount of tax reduction to contributors is not as simple as the frequent descriptions of a "tax loss" to the government and a subsidy to philanthropy suggest. The tax cost must be interpreted in the light of the effect on government expenditures if part of the deducted contributions were not made. Whether the tax reduction is actually an indirect subsidy to philanthropy depends upon the influence of the deduction allowance on private gifts. The significance of the tax cost of the deduction depends on both considerations.

To the extent that government expenditures might have to replace a part of private expenditures in the absence of allowable deductions, larger tax collections would be required. To avoid this, public action can be attempted, as it has been, in the form of tax relief measures.[13] To the extent that such measures are successful, the government's budget understates its share in the determination of output. In the case of tax relief for donors to philanthropy, no government subsidy is active unless private gifts increase with tax relief. If gifts show little or no sensitivity to the tax rebate conditional on them, then the cost of the deduction simply amounts in effect, though not by intent, to rewarding taxpayers for contributing to socially desirable activities.

Thus the tax cost of the deduction has differing significance depending on two considerations: (1) The degree of public interest in the activities financed by the contributions. The tax cost figures, as

[12] Estimated tax cost of the four categories outside itemized personal deductions was obtained as follows: for the corporation tax 43 per cent of the $413 million of gifts reported by net income corporations in *Statistics of Income*, 1956-1957, was included. For bequests and gifts of property, the amount reported in *Statistics of Income*, 1954, was multiplied by the ratio of reported gross tax to net estate after specific exemption. Hypothetical tax liability on income of nonprofit organizations was reached by assuming a 4 per cent rate of return on $15.8 billion of corporate securities and mortgages, and 3 per cent on $5.8 billion of government securities, owned in 1955 (see Morris Mendelson, *The Flow of Funds through the Financial Markets, 1953-1955*, unpublished mimeo, National Bureau of Economic Research, Table 24-1) . On $800 million of investment income thus computed, we estimated tax liabilities at $300 million. Finally, we computed the fraction for the standard deduction under the personal income tax by assigning about 17 per cent of the standard deduction to philanthropy. Tax liability on this amount was then computed in the manner set forth in the note to Table 15, given in Appendix G.

[13] For a recent discussion of this point, see Clarence D. Long and Selma Mushkin, "Welfare Programs and Economic Growth and Stability," in *Federal Expenditure Policy for Economic Growth and Stability*, Subcommittee on Fiscal Policy, Joint Economic Committee, 85th Cong., 1st Sess., 1957, pp. 1,028-30.

shown by Table 15, are relevant in a consideration of costs, but their meaning depends on whether the absence of some of the contributions would require increased government outlays, and hence increased tax collections, or not. (2) The first consideration is important only to the extent that contributions vary with the amount of tax rebate. It matters little whether or not private expenditures stand as substitutes for public expenditures (as they may in education, health, and welfare) if the flow of contributions is not significantly affected by the deduction. If the flow were maintained without the deductions, the government would not have to increase its expenditures in areas where private and public expenditures supplement each other.[14] In that case the deduction allowance would become only an equity question: should the allowance be given mainly in recognition of the consignment by taxpayers of part of their income to the public good without direct and immediate benefit to themselves?

Whether the subsidy or the equity motive underlay enactment of the deduction is a question to which Congress has so far not directly addressed itself. While the deduction is usually regarded as an encouragement of socially desirable expenditures, its form—a deduction from income rather than a tax credit—would lead one to infer that it was intended as an equity measure.

Tax Cost in Relation to Fields of Philanthropy

What factual evidence can we present on the question of the degree of public (governmental) interest in the purposes for which private contributions are made, and on the related question of the sensitivity of contributions to the amount of tax rebate?

To begin, we have the estimated distribution of contributions by broad areas of activity. In 1954, about two-thirds of the contributions made by living donors went to religious purposes; somewhat over one-fifth to health, education, and welfare; and the remainder to private foreign aid, foundations, and miscellaneous activities.[15] It is of course

---

[14] But even if the deduction were found unnecessary to maintain private gifts, the tax cost need not be viewed as a loss to the Treasury in the usual sense. To the extent that the loss in tax base caused by the deduction is compensated by higher rates, there is no actual revenue loss to the Treasury. Rather, there is a redistribution of the tax load, and possibly some loss to the community because of the economic effects of higher marginal rates.

[15] For the estimates on which this distribution is based, see Appendix F. F. Emerson Andrews has made similar estimates for gifts to philanthropy from all sources (living donors, bequests, and corporations). He estimates that one-half went to

difficult to measure the degree of public interest attached to those categories. Philanthropy now encompasses a wide variety of activities, some so recognized as in the public interest that for them a high degree of substitutability may be said to exist between private and governmental spending; in others the governmental interest is negligible. In some areas of health, education, and welfare, the government has tended, for some time, to supplement, if not at times to supplant,[16] private nonprofit institutions. In contrast, government's participation in the arts, literature, and religion has been slight—almost nonexistent in areas touching religion.

Substitutability, therefore, does not appear to be the only test that has been applied in determining what areas are appropriate for indirect government participation.[17] The 1954 Tax code, as noted previously, raised the deduction ceiling from 20 to 30 per cent for those taxpayers who contribute at least 10 per cent of their income to churches, hospitals, or educational institutions. While substitutability of public for private activity is high in health and education, both are areas into which the federal government has moved tardily and, especially in education, with great reluctance. That religious organizations were included among those for which the allowance was extended suggests that official public interest in a field is not Congress' sole criterion for selecting contributions to merit favorable treatment under the income tax.

---

organized religion, and 43 per cent to education, health, and welfare in 1954. See Andrews, *Philanthropic Giving*, p. 73. (The percentages cited are Andrews' unpublished revisions of his earlier estimates.)

16 Andrews estimates that "government expenditure (including federal, state, and local) is now about nine times voluntary giving for purposes which a generation or two ago would have been deemed to lie wholly within the field of private 'charity'." *Ibid.*, pp. 43ff.

17 However, see the opinion of Sylvester Gates and John R. Hicks quoted in note 36 below. Gates and Hicks argue that total exemption from tax should be reserved to philanthropies performing functions "which are a well recognized responsibility of the state. When this condition is satisfied, it may be argued that, since any tax which was levied would have to be offset by a grant or subvention, the one can be cancelled against the other." They hold that the bulk of philanthropic activity, though desirable, is not indispensable and hence "will not appreciably diminish the State's own responsibilities or, consequently, the amount of money required to be raised by taxation. If, the amount to be raised by taxation remaining constant, the sector of income on which tax can be levied is reduced, a correspondingly added burden is cast on the remaining sector."

Effect of Income Tax on Level of
Philanthropic Contributions

Next, we inquire, how sensitive have contributions by individuals been to changes in the amount of tax rebate offered to them? The data in Table 13 suggest that, despite significant changes in tax rates during the 1930's and 1940's, reported contributions showed little, if any, change in relation to income. Beginning with 1941, however, figures for reported contributions do not include amounts contributed by taxpayers choosing the standard deduction, and therefore give only a partial picture (see the section of this chapter dealing with the trend in contributions reported on tax returns). For a more reliable picture, annual figures of total contributions by living individuals would be preferable. Unfortunately we have only rough estimates in the area of private philanthropy, be it of income or of assets. To some extent the lack of information may be ascribed to the vagueness of the term philanthropy, making it often more difficult to compare figures from different sources, and to the fact that nonprofit and charitable organizations, because of their very nature, do not report systematically on their receipts and financial condition.

In Table 16, three estimates of total gifts by living donors are shown with the totals of itemized contributions reported on tax returns for the period 1929-1954. The series in columns 1 and 2 are based largely on various institutional reports. The third series, by F. Emerson Andrews, is based primarily on tax returns with some "correction allowance for the probably too-high rate for reported incomes."[18] Despite Andrews' correction, the annual figures in his series based on tax returns exceed those of the other two by large amounts from 1941 on. This is shown graphically in Chart 6. While the Andrews series shows a very steep rise in the early forties, the two other series show a much less pronounced rise during that period. For 1954, our estimate, extending the Commerce Department figures, is $4.15 billion and that by Andrews $4.79 billion. Either of these estimates may approximate the true figure. The Commerce estimates and our extrapolation of them may have omitted significant amounts, or Andrews' correction for overstatement may be too small.[19]

[18] Andrews, op.cit., p. 292.
[19] A recent estimate of $4.5 billion for 1954 by Surveys and Research Corporation came to our attention too late for use in this study. See *Stimulating Voluntary Giving to Higher Education and Other Programs*, American Association for the Advancement of Science, Washington, D.C., 1958, p. 40.

TABLE 16

Philanthropic Gifts by Individuals, Three Estimates, 1929-1954

(dollars in millions)

| | | | | Returns with Itemized Deductions | |
| | Extrapolated Commerce Series (1) | Jenkins (2) | Andrews (3) | Contributions Reported (4) | Income Reported as % of Total Income (5) |
YEAR					
1929	1,449	1,206	1,067	540	37.3
1930	1,378	1,190	981	434	33.9
1931	1,264	1,329	843	354	32.8
1932	990	1,188	702	317	37.4
1933	806	982	637	282	35.6
1934	832	862	662	280	32.9
1935	902	868	727	310	34.4
1936	952	919	830	390	36.8
1937	1,099	1,000	943	445	38.1
1938	990	1,006	884	414	37.8
1939	970	1,068	967	499	39.5
1940	1,053	1,044	1,064	740	56.9
1941	1,060	1,089	1,556	1,002	53.5
1942	1,259	1,277	2,108	1,450	55.6
1943	1,568	1,456	2,535	1,836	58.2
1944	1,824	1,852	2,691	1,258	23.8
1945	2,045	2,103	2,772	1,450	24.9
1946	2,151	2,242	2,929	1,639	25.4
1947	2,191	2,219	3,240	1,974	26.7
1948	2,446	2,366	3,319	1,881	24.3
1949	2,549	—	3,447	2,032	25.4
1950	2,729	—	3,688	2,260	27.4
1951	2,931	—	4,286	n.a.	28.8
1952	3,350	—	4,545	3,116	30.6
1953	—	—	4,779	3,556	32.6
1954	4,141	—	4,789	3,893	36.5

Source, by column

(1) For 1929-1942, from *Survey of Current Business*, Department of Commerce, June 1944, Table 3. Figures for 1943-1951 are projections based on data for only a small number of components. The figures for 1952 and 1954 are our rough estimates based on a variety of sources as explained in Appendix F.

(2) Edward C. Jenkins, *Philanthropy in America*, pp. 172-173.

(3) F. Emerson Andrews, *Philanthropic Giving*, p. 72. The figures in this column are a revised series supplied by Andrews.

(4) *Statistics of Income.*

(5) Adjusted gross income reported on tax returns as a per cent of total adjusted gross income (countrywide) as derived from Commerce Department statistics on personal income.

The correct figure for 1954 may well be within the range of those two estimates, $4.2 to $4.8 billion. If the lower one based on a variety of institutional reports were more nearly correct, it would suggest the

CHART 6

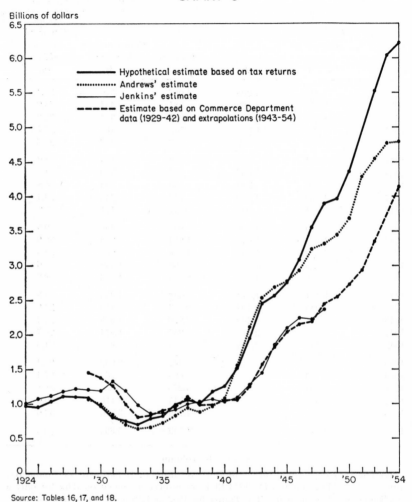

Billions of dollars

Hypothetical estimate based on tax returns
Andrews' estimate
Jenkins' estimate
Estimate based on Commerce Department data (1929-42) and extrapolations (1943-54)

Source: Tables 16, 17, and 18.

Total Philanthropic Contributions by Individuals, Four Estimates, 1924-1954

possibility of extensive overreporting of contributions on itemized returns, which amounted to $3.9 billion for 1954. This would leave contributions of only $0.26 billion for returns with the standard deduction on which the reported income was $137 billion. The implied ratio of contributions to income would be less than 0.2 per cent in contrast to 4.2 per cent for returns with itemized deductions. But even the higher estimate of $4.8 billion would leave contributions of only $0.90 billion for taxpayers electing the standard deduction, implicitly less than 0.7 per cent of income.

The Commerce Department estimates for 1929-1942, our extension of them up to 1954, and the other two estimates all suggest a sizable overstatement in the reported contributions on tax returns after 1940. We might hazard a guess at the size of the overstatement by attributing to standard deduction returns for all the years 1944-1954 the same ratio of contributions to income as may reasonably be assumed would have been reported on these returns for 1944.[20] When this amount is added to the reported figures in column 4 of Table 16, the tax return figures become conceptually comparable to the estimates for all individuals shown in the first three columns of the table. It amounts to attributing to returns with standard deductions contributions of somewhat over 1.5 per cent of income reported on these returns and assuming that the ratio would have been stable during 1944-1954. In view of the findings for itemized returns (Tables 13 and 14), it is unlikely that the ratio would have shown a decline, hence the assumption that it remained stable is more likely to give the hypothetical estimate a downward bias than an upward one.

The figures are shown in Table 17, plotted along with the other three series in Chart 6. The hypothetical estimates, like Andrews', exceed the other two from 1941 on by large absolute amounts. From 1945 on, the hypothetical estimates based on tax returns consistently exceed those by Andrews, whose corrections for overreporting appear to have been larger from after that date.[21] For 1952 and 1954 the three estimates are given below.

[20] The ratio of contributions to income for all returns in 1943 was used to obtain an estimate of the amount of contributions that would have been reported in 1944 in the absence of the 10 per cent standard deduction. This does not seem unreasonable in view of the percentages shown in Table 14 and Chart 3. An estimate of contributions that would have been reported on returns with standard deduction in 1944 was derived residually, by subtracting from the estimated total the amount actually reported.

[21] Andrews gives no explanation of the kind of correction allowance he used. For 1944 he imputes to those who reported no contributions a ratio of 0.4 of the reported ratio for that year, and lowers this rate to 0.35 for 1945, 0.3 for 1946 and 0.25 thereafter (op.cit., p. 292).

TABLE 17

Contributions Itemized on Tax Returns and Hypothetical Estimates for All
Individuals, Assuming Tax Return Ratios of Contributions to Income, 1924-1954

(millions of dollars)

YEAR	Itemized Contributions (1)	Hypothetical Estimate of Total Contributions (2)	Total Adjusted Gross Income (3)
1924	533	973	62,049
1925	442	954	67,137
1926	484	1,031	69,431
1927	508	1,114	70,130
1928	541	1,100	73,545
1929	540	1,084	75,597
1930	434	969	62,233
1931	354	805	48,969
1932	317	751	36,978
1933	282	700	36,445
1934	280	790	44,127
1935	310	828	48,447
1936	390	985	57,676
1937	445	1,057	61,559
1938	414	1,001	55,561
1939	499	1,177	64,674
1940	740	1,254	70,152
1941	1,002	1,520	85,101
1942	1,450	1,944	107,172
1943	1,836	2,449	129,035
1944	1,258	2,567	137,495
1945	1,450	2,762	140,185
1946	1,639	3,088	156,065
1947	1,974	3,559	171,563
1948	1,881	3,898	184,795
1949	2,032	3,966	184,292
1950	2,260	4,359	201,446
1951	n.a.	—	226,603
1952	3,116	5,521	240,645
1953	3,556	6,036	254,450
1954	3,893	6,216	252,987

Source: Column 1: *Statistics of Income*; column 2: see Appendix F; column 3:
see Appendix A, Notes to Table 1, line 1.

66

	1952	1954
	(billions of dollars)	
(1) Based on tax returns (Andrews)	4.5	4.8
(2) Based on reports of organizations	3.35	4.1
(3) Hypothetical, based on tax returns (assuming 1944 ratio of contributions to income for returns with standard deduction)	5.5	6.2
(3) ÷ (1)	1.2	1.3
(3) ÷ (2)	1.6	1.5

A number of explanations are possible for the large gap between the hypothetical tax return figure and the estimate based on institutional sources. First, there may be definitional differences. Taxpayers may have included a wider area under philanthropy than is covered by the estimates which start at the other end of the transactions. The concept of philanthropy is vague and fuzzy. Second, gifts of property may be evaluated at higher figures by donors than by recipients. Third, the roughness of some components of the estimates based on reports of organizations are subject to error: for example, the component estimate of gifts to foundations, particularly family foundations, may be on the low side. Fourth, we have made no allowance for gifts to so-called "rackets" (from which no reports could be available), but such gifts reported as deductions would also constitute a form of over-reporting. Finally, the previously noted possibility that taxpayers may have considerably overstated their contributions under the impact of high tax rates in the 1940's and 1950's, suggests an explanation for the discrepancy between the estimates.[22] The explanations for discrepancies between estimates may in varying degrees be related to changes in the level of tax rates. Differences in values reported for property transfers are likely to have increased with the rising importance of the income tax. The unknown, but certainly rising, number of family foundations are a product of the tax structure.

[22] Overstatement of contributions on tax returns is difficult to check because of the present form of the deduction allowance. A revamping of the provisions for the deduction along the lines of the current British method would remove practically all possibility of tax evasion due to faulty reporting. The British tax law allows what amounts to a flat-rate tax credit for charitable contributions. The rebate goes to the eligible institution directly, upon its submission of a claim. The taxpayer merely remits his "net gift" to the philanthropy in question. For a more detailed discussion of the method, see pp. 87ff. of this chapter.

A casual inspection of Chart 6 may tempt one to attribute the large gap between the two tax-return series and the two series obtained from recipients' reports to the sharp rise in tax rates during World War II. But the evidence is not clear cut. In Chart 7 we compare the movements of the two types of series by expressing the hypothetical estimates based on tax returns as a per cent of estimates based on

CHART 7

Per cent

As per cent of estimate based on Dept. of Commerce data

As per cent of Jenkins' estimate

Source: 1924-32: column (2), Table 17 ÷ Jenkins' estimates shown in Tables 16 and 18;
1929-54: column (2), Table 17 ÷ column (1), Table 16.

Estimates of Contributions Based on Tax Data as Percentage of Estimates Based on Recipients' Reports, 1924-1954

recipients' reports. While there is no clear indication of a trend until after 1935, it is nevertheless clear that the tax-return figures began to rise relative to the Commerce Department estimates, and to exceed them before 1940. Is it likely that the turning point in the taxpayers' zeal to report gifts to philanthropy came well before the 1940's?

The fraction of contributions reported on taxable returns that represented a cost to the government was shown in Table 15 and Chart 5 above. There was a significant jump in this fraction in the early '30's. Some tax increases occurred in 1932 and 1936.[23] They may have had sufficient influence on subsequent taxpayer behavior to produce the results observed, although the early rises were mild compared to those that took place in the '40's. The amount of reported contributions that was paid for by the Treasury rose from a level of 10 per cent of the total in 1929-1931 to 15 per cent in 1932, and reached a high of 20 per cent in 1936. During World War II there were further increases in this percentage to a level well above 20 per cent. In 1945, the peak year, 38 per cent of the amount reported acted as a reduction in tax rather than in income. A similar pattern is produced when we plot the average effective rate of tax liability on income reported on tax returns (Chart 5). It rose from 2.4 in 1931 to 7.8 per cent in 1936; and again from 5.3 in 1939 to 21.2 per cent in 1945. This evidence is consistent with the hypothesis that the rise in deducted contributions, relative to the estimates developed independently of reports by donors, may have occurred in response to taxation developments of the 1930's as well as the 1940's.

In addition to some indication of how taxation developments have affected the reporting of contributions, we want to know whether, and how, taxation may have influenced the actual volume of contributions. Even with excellent estimates of the actual volume of contributions—currently not available—the answer would require some knowledge of what the volume of contributions would have been in the absence of rising tax rates. We possess no such knowledge. Nevertheless, rather than retreat from the question entirely, we can reach a partial and qualified answer.

In Table 18 and Chart 8 the estimates by Andrews and those from reports of recipient institutions are expressed as percentages of estimated total adjusted gross income for the period 1924-1954. In the period 1937-1942 the Andrews estimates rise relative to total income, whereas the Commerce Department estimates for that period decline relative to income; but outside that five-year period, their movements

[23] Exemptions were lowered and rates increased in 1932. In 1934 taxes were lowered slightly on "earned" income and raised, also slightly, on some property income. In 1936 taxes were again raised on dividend income, and on net incomes over $50,000. The increases in 1932 were the sharpest and most widespread among income groups.

TABLE 18

Estimated Total Philanthropic Contributions by Individuals as Per Cent of
Total Adjusted Gross Income, 1924-1954

	Estimated Contributions as Per Cent of Total AGI	
YEAR	(1)	(2)
1924	1.6	1.6
1925	1.6	1.4
1926	1.6	1.5
1927	1.7	1.6
1928	1.7	1.5
1929	1.6	1.4
1930	1.9	1.6
1931	2.7	1.6
1929	1.9	1.4
1930	2.2	1.6
1931	2.6	1.7
1932	2.7	1.9
1933	2.2	1.7
1934	1.9	1.5
1935	1.9	1.5
1936	1.7	1.4
1937	1.8	1.5
1938	1.8	1.6
1939	1.5	1.5
1940	1.5	1.5
1941	1.2	1.8
1942	1.2	2.0
1943	1.2	2.0
1944	1.3	2.0
1945	1.5	2.0
1946	1.4	1.9
1947	1.3	1.9
1948	1.3	1.8
1949	1.4	1.9
1950	1.4	1.8
1951	1.3	1.9
1952	1.4	1.9
1953	—	1.9
1954	1.6	1.9

Source: Column 1, *1924-1931*: Jenkins, Table 16, column 2. Jenkins' estimates for
1924-1928 (divided by total AGI) are: *1924*, 1,003; *1925*, 1,073; *1926*, 1,114; *1927*,
1,179; *1928*, 1,218.

1929-1954: Commerce Department and our extrapolations as in Table 16, column 1.
Column 2, *1924-1931*: Table 17, column 2. *1929-1954*: Andrews, Table 16, column
3.

are essentially parallel, that is, they show roughly identical trends. During 1940-1954, neither series shows a pronounced trend up or down, relative to income, though both are somewhat higher in 1954 than in 1940. This is of interest in view of the introduction of the standard

CHART 8

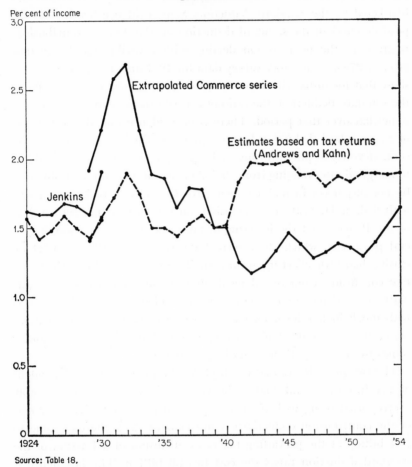

Source: Table 18.

Estimated Total Contributions by Individuals as Per Cent of Total Adjusted Gross Income, 1929-1954

deduction in the early 1940's, which severed the connection between giving and tax reduction for most taxpayers with incomes below $10,000, and also for many above that level. If there is a connection between philanthropic giving and the deductibility of gifts in the income range from which most returns with the standard deduction

71

come, a decline in the per cent of total income contributed to philanthropic enterprises might have been expected.

That, apparently, no decline has occurred is not proof of the absence of such a connection. It is also possible that the rise in tax rates of the early 1940's sufficiently stimulated contributions by taxpayers filing the itemized return to offset any possible decline in contributions blanketed by the standard deduction. Some evidence bearing on the possible effect of the standard deduction on the flow of contributions is given in the next section dealing with contributions by income groups. Briefly, consumer survey data for 1941 and 1950, in Table 23, show that for units with incomes below $5,000, most of whom choose the standard deduction, the ratio of contributions to income has risen somewhat over that period. There is no evidence that the institution of the standard deduction had a repressive effect on the share of income devoted to philanthropy. A large segment of the public, subject to marginal rates ranging from 20 to 30 per cent, may not be influenced by tax incentives in making such gifts. Our observations are in line with Sydnor H. Walker's conclusion, on the basis of tax return data of the 1920's, "that the lowering of tax rates and the increase of general prosperity, which characterized the years from 1922 to 1929 inclusive, had little effect upon the contribution rate."[24] While the tentative conclusion from our data about the contributions of taxpayers with low and modest incomes is not extended to those of taxpayers with much higher incomes, its significance is extensive. We shall see below that the bulk of philanthropic contributions by living donors comes from those with incomes below $10,000.

The two possibilities that much philanthropic giving is independent of tax incentives and that deducted contributions are considerably overreported bring us back to the question whether the revenue cost of the contribution deductions is justified. In 1954, the cost came to $1.1 billion at the prevailing tax rates; inclusion of a fraction of the standard deduction raises the cost to $1.6 billion. The last figure is one-third as large as the amount living donors contributed to philanthropy in that year, according to one estimate; 38 per cent of the total, according to another. That is, the Treasury "sacrificed" on average one dollar, at existing tax rates, for every three that individuals donated to philanthropy. Whether this is too high a price to pay for a tax subsidy that possibly stimulates contributions to some undertakings in

[24] See "Privately Supported Social Work," p. 1219.

which the national interest is high cannot be answered within the context of this study. The issue is not solely one of arithmetic. Even if we could state with certainty that the tax rebate on contributions is not responsible for gifts of an equivalent amount, the further question remains, whether the public would prefer an increase in giving smaller than the tax rebate, rather than an alternative—direct use of those funds by government or rate reduction. The community may well decide that even a small fraction of the tax rebate diverted to private philanthropic enterprises is preferable to use of the full tax equivalent of the deduction for governmental enterprises. In the areas covered by private philanthropy the value of a given amount of privately allocated funds, though smaller in dollar amount, may exceed the value to society of direct governmental expenditures somewhat larger in dollar amount.

Reported Contributions by Size of Income on Tax Returns

A glance at Table 19 is sufficient to see that for the income groups[25] shown, the average percentage of deductions claimed for contributions has been well under the allowed limits (to 1951, 15 per cent of income; 1952-1953, 20 per cent; from 1954, 30 per cent). Until 1943 the contributions reported on taxable returns were less than 3 per cent of adjusted gross income at levels below $100,000, except briefly during the deep depression years when the relative decline in incomes was much greater than that in contributions. Over this wide range of income the rates of reported contributions show only slight increases. For example, between the two income groups $3,000 to $5,000 and $50,000 to $100,000, the rates are: 1.6 and 2.3 per cent in 1925-1929; 1.9 and 3.6 in 1932-1934; 1.8 and 2.3 in 1939; 2.2 and 2.4 in 1943. Comparison of rates for the under $2,000 income group and for the higher of the two shows even smaller differences, for the curve describing the

---

[25] The reader is reminded again that our presentation by income groups has several limitations: (1) the reporting unit is the individual tax return, meaning there are fewer persons included than in the family or spending unit; (2) the income concept is adjusted gross income, which has an important bearing upon intertemporal comparisons of high incomes, since the amounts of such items as capital gains and tax-exempt interest affect the reported income of taxpayers in accordance with the current tax law definition, rather than with a consistent income concept; (3) the reported contribution figures are subject to the twin evils of the forgetfulness and fabrications of some taxpayers. We have no clue to how these offset each other by income groups. But it may be in the nature of this type of deduction that the error is more significant at low income levels than at higher.

TABLE 19

Philanthropic Contributions as Per Cent of Income, and Distribution of Total,
by Size of Income on Taxable Returns, Selected Years, 1922-1956

INCOME GROUPS[a] ($000's)	1922	1924	Average 1925-29	Average 1932-34	1937	1939	1941 Itemized	1941 All Returns	1943 Itemized	1943 All Returns
CONTRIBUTIONS AS PER CENT OF ADJUSTED GROSS INCOME										
Under 2	1.8	1.8	1.6	2.5	2.2	2.3	2.9	1.6	3.3	1.4
2-3	1.5	1.6	1.5	1.9	1.8	2.0	2.2	1.5	2.4	1.4
3-5	1.6	1.7	1.6	1.9	1.7	1.8	1.9		2.2	
5-10	2.1	1.7	1.6	2.0	1.7	1.9	2.0		2.1	
10-25[b]	1.9	1.9	1.8	2.2	1.8	2.0	1.9		1.9	
25-50[b]	2.2	2.2	2.0	2.7	2.1	1.7	2.1		2.0	
50-100	2.6	2.8	2.3	3.6	2.8	2.3	2.5		2.4	
100-500	3.5	3.4	2.6	5.0	4.0	4.3	3.4		3.0	
500 and over	6.7	5.7	3.4	5.5	6.4	6.1	5.4		4.5	
Average	2.0	2.0	2.0	2.3	2.0	2.2	2.2	1.8	2.4	1.7
PER CENT OF TOTAL CONTRIBUTIONS										
Under 2	12.7	10.2	3.7	13.8	13.7	15.1	22.8		22.6	
2-3	6.8	8.2	4.0	7.2	6.4	7.2	26.7		23.7	
3-5	19.1	24.5	10.3	18.1	18.4	20.5	18.5		29.0	
5-10	18.8	13.1	16.6	19.5	17.8	19.7	10.7		9.2	
10-25[b]	15.0	14.1	18.8	15.6	15.1	15.6	8.7		6.7	
25-50[b]	9.2	9.1	11.6	9.2	9.0	7.9	4.4		3.5	
50-100	7.3	7.7	9.9	6.7	6.2	5.3	3.2		2.4	
100-500	8.0	8.2	14.0	6.8	9.0	5.9	3.5		2.2	
500 and over	3.2	4.7	11.2	3.2	4.4	2.9	1.6		0.7	
Total[e]	100.0	100.0	100.0	100.0	100.0	100.0	100.0		100.0	

(concluded on next page)

TABLE 19, concluded

INCOME GROUPS[a] ($000's)	1945 Itemized	1945 All Returns	1947 Itemized	1947 All Returns	1949 Itemized	1949 All Returns	1954 Itemized	1954 All Returns	1956 Itemized	1956 All Returns
CONTRIBUTIONS AS PER CENT OF ADJUSTED GROSS INCOME										
Under 2	5.3	0.7	5.5	0.8	5.8	0.7	6.2	0.8	6.1	0.8
2-3	4.6	0.8	4.8	0.9	5.1	0.9	5.5	1.1	5.2	1.2
3-5	4.2	1.0	4.4	1.1	4.4	1.2	4.4	1.5	4.2	1.5
5-10	3.8	1.6	4.0	1.7	4.1	1.3	3.8	1.6	3.5	1.7
10-25[b]	3.1	2.1	3.2	2.2	3.7	1.8	3.7	1.9	3.5	2.1
25-50[b]	3.0	2.6	3.1	2.7	3.1	2.5	3.3	2.7	3.3	2.8
50-100	3.5	3.3	3.6	3.4	3.3	3.1	3.9	3.7	4.1	3.8
100-500	4.8	4.7	4.8	4.7	4.6	4.5	6.7	6.5	6.9	6.8
500 and over	6.7	6.6	6.7	6.6	6.6	6.6	11.7	11.7	11.9	11.8
Average	4.0	1.2	4.1	1.4	4.1	1.4	4.1	1.8	3.9	1.9
PER CENT OF TOTAL CONTRIBUTIONS										
Under 2	12.0			7.3		4.0		1.7		1.4
2-3	16.8			15.4		10.6		5.1		3.8
3-5	24.5			28.1		30.0		24.7		19.0
5-10	13.6			16.8		21.9		36.2		40.2
10-25[b]	13.4			13.9		13.1		10.9		16.1
25-50[b]	7.6			7.3		7.8		9.5		7.0
50-100	5.4			4.8		5.2		4.6		4.9
100-500	5.1			4.6		5.5		5.1		5.1
500 and over	1.6			1.8		2.0		2.2		2.4
Total[c]	100.0			100.0		100.0		100.0		100.0

Fiduciary returns are included in years up to and including 1949.

a Net income classes until 1948; adjusted gross income classes thereafter.

b For 1954 group limit is $20,000 instead of $25,000.

c Percentages may not add up to total because of rounding.

Source: Statistics of Income.

75

reported contribution rates is slightly U-shaped at the bottom with the trough occurring in the $2,000 to $5,000 income range (Chart 9). Above $100,000 the contributions-to-income ratio turned up appreciably.

CHART 9

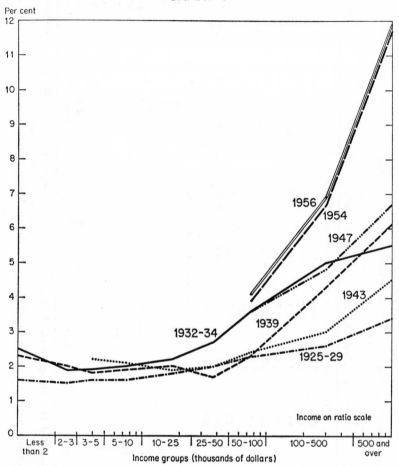

Source: Table 19.

Philanthropic Contributions Reported on Taxable Returns as Per Cent of Income Reported, by Income Groups, Selected Years, 1925-1956

As indicated in the last section, an appreciable increase is evident in the reported rate of giving after 1943. Because the standard deduction became available to all income groups, beginning with 1944, it is not possible to compare the percentages for incomes below the $10,000 level with those before that year. The ratios of contributions to income for returns with itemized deductions and for all returns constitute upper and lower limits of the "actual" reported contribution rate which must lie somewhere between them. For the lower income groups the range offered by the two extremes is too wide to be useful, but as it narrows, going up the income scale, it gives us a good idea of the actual rate of reported giving for that income group. We can see that the possible range in the $10,000 to $25,000 group was 2.1 to 3.1 per cent in 1945 and 2.2 to 3.2 in 1947, a level not previously attained except in the early '30's. The same can be observed for the other income groups above that level: the lower limit of the possible range was above the level prevailing before the mid-'40's. For the highest group, the returns with incomes over $500,000, the contribution rate stayed above 6 per cent after 1943 and reached nearly 12 per cent in 1956.

The contribution rates presented in Table 19 are for all taxable returns, regardless of whether they reported such gifts or not. If we eliminate from each group's total the incomes reported on returns with no contributions, we get the rates for taxable donors' incomes rather than for all reported taxable incomes. The percentages are shown in Table 20.[26] Since the number claiming deductions for contributions is high relative to the total (Table 21), we find that the ratios for donors are only slightly higher than the ratios for all returns with itemized deductions. In 1937 the average deduction for contributions was 3 per cent of the income of donors in the lowest income group and almost 7 per cent in the highest, with a dip to 2.1 per cent in the middle of the income range. Again, comparison with recent years is not possible except for the upper income groups. For the latter the reported rate of giving has risen sharply since prewar years: in the $100,000 to $500,000 group from somewhat less than 5 per cent prewar to 7 per cent in 1956; and for the over $500,000 group from between 5 and 7 to 12 per cent. The increase in the rate of giving among donors further down in the income scale appears to have been much milder. Apparently the spread in the reported rate of giving between high and low income donors has increased somewhat in recent years.

The above discussion and tables give little indication of how many taxpayers approach the limit on the deduction in their claim of de-

[26] We possess no data distinguishing the incomes of those who claimed contributions from those who did not. However, on the assumption that the average income in a given income group is the same for claimants as for all returns, we closely approximated the average ratio of contributions to income of donors.

TABLE 20

Contributions as Per Cent of Income on Taxable Returns with that Deduction, by Income Groups, Selected Years, 1934-1956

INCOME GROUPa ($000's)	1934	1937	1939	1941	1945	1947	1949	1950	1952	1954	1956
Under 2	n.a.	3.1	n.a.	n.a.	6.2	6.6	6.7	6.6	7.1	6.9	6.8
2-3	n.a.	2.6	n.a.	n.a.	4.6	5.3	5.5	5.5	5.8	5.8	5.6
3-5	n.a.	2.2	n.a.	n.a.	4.5	4.7	4.5	4.4	4.6	4.5	4.4
5-10	2.4	2.2	2.3	2.3	4.1	4.3	4.2	4.0	3.9	3.9	3.6
10-25b	2.4	2.1	2.3	2.2	3.4	3.5	3.8	3.7	3.8	3.8	3.6
25-50b	2.8	2.5	2.0	2.4	3.2	3.3	3.3	3.1	3.4	3.4	3.4
50-100	3.3	3.2	2.6	2.8	3.8	3.9	3.6	3.1	3.8	4.0	4.1
100-500	4.1	4.5	4.8	3.8	5.3	5.4	5.0	4.2	5.9	6.8	7.0
500 and over	5.8	6.9	6.8	6.2	7.6	8.1	7.8	6.6	10.0	11.9	12.1
Average amount of contributions reported per return (dollars)	n.a.	139	n.a.	n.a.	198	225	251	254	271	277	284

a Net income classes up to 1944; adjusted gross income classes thereafter.
b For 1952 and 1954, group limit is $20,000 instead of $25,000.
Source: *Statistics of Income.*

ductions for contributions, a point worth examining in view of the two recent extensions of the limit. Frequency distributions of tax returns by size of income and by size of contributions reported are available for the years 1949, 1954, and 1956. They include, of course,

TABLE 21

Per Cent of Taxable Returns with Deduction for Philanthropic Contributions, by Size of Income Reported, Selected Years, 1937-1956

INCOME GROUPa ($000's)	All Returns			Returns with Itemized Deductionsb				
	1937	1939	1941	1945	1947	1949	1954	1956
Under 2	72.4	—	—	87.4	86.3	90.7	90.2	89.9
2-3	71.1	—	—	92.5	92.1	94.3	93.7	93.5
3-5	76.2	—	—	94.5	94.5	96.5	96.6	96.0
5-10	79.1	83.4	85.7	95.0	94.7	97.0	97.8	97.1
10-25c	82.9	86.9	88.1	95.2	95.8	97.6	98.1	98.2
25-50c	86.4	90.5	90.8	95.7	96.1	97.7	98.2	98.3
50-100	90.5	93.0	92.5	96.3	96.4	98.0	98.5	98.7
100-500	93.0	95.7	94.9	97.0	97.4	98.6	98.6	98.9
500 and over	91.9	96.6	95.1	100.0	97.6	97.4	98.4	98.5
Average	74.9	—	—	92.0	92.5	95.6	96.6	96.3

a Net income groups for years before 1944; adjusted gross income group thereafter.
b Individual returns only. On fiduciary returns contributions are not separately reported but are included in the "amounts distributable to beneficiaries" category for the years shown, except 1954 and 1956.
c Income groups are $10-20,000 and $20-50,000 in 1954.

only returns with itemized deductions for philanthropic contributions, and no short form returns. To avoid any bias arising therefrom, we estimated how many of the returns listed contributions amounting to more than 10 per cent of the income reported, on the reasonable assumption that contributions of that relative size would be itemized. The estimated number of such returns, as a per cent of total returns in each income group, is shown in Table 22. Figures in the 20 per cent columns for 1954 and 1956 are as tabulated by the Internal Revenue Service.

TABLE 22

Estimated Per Cent of Returns with Deducted Contributions at Least Ten or Twenty Per Cent of Adjusted Gross Income, by Income Groups, 1949, 1954, and 1956

INCOME GROUP ($000's)	Total Number of Returns		Per Cent of Returns				
	1949	1956	1949	1954		1956	
	(in thousands)		10%	10%	20%	10%	20%
Under 2	19,038.4	14,974.9	1.8	2.1	0.4	2.3	0.4
2-3	12,137.6	8,043.8	2.3	3.5	0.3	3.5	0.4
3-5	14,138.4	16,327.6	2.4	3.2	0.1	3.1	0.2
5-10	4,837.8	16,339.8	2.5	4.0	0.1	3.8	0.1
10-20	802.0	2,419.3	3.1	3.2	0.3	2.8	0.3
20-50	287.7	581.3	4.2	4.6	0.7	4.5	0.7
50-100	46.1	89.2	8.2	10.5	2.2	10.8	2.6
100-500	13.3	22.0	17.3	n.a.	7.7	n.a.	8.5
500 and over	0.5	0.9	n.a.	n.a.	23.4	n.a.	26.5
Total	51,301.9	58,798.8	n.a.	n.a.	0.2	n.a.	0.3

The estimates were made on the basis of a frequency distribution of tax returns showing a deduction for contributions, by size of income and by size of contributions. See *Statistics of Income*, 1949, Part I, pp. 39-40; for 1954, p. 55; and for 1956, p. 41. The income class intervals used to estimate the frequencies shown were narrower than those in the above table. The 10 per cent level of income was set for each income class at 10 per cent of the average income in the class. For the contributions-size class into which the 10 per cent value fell, the frequencies between that value and the lower limit of the class were estimated by straight line interpolation. The number equal to or exceeding 20 per cent in 1954 and 1956 is tabulated in *Statistics of Income*.

In all three years the relative frequency of returns reporting contributions in excess of 10 per cent of income changed little with rising incomes up to the $20,000 level. Within that range the average frequency is about 3 per cent. Above that level, the relative frequency rises somewhat with income, but still remains below 5 per cent for the $20,000 to $50,000 group. It reached 17 per cent in the $100,000 to $500,000 group in 1949—the highest income group and the only year for which an estimate of the number with contributions over 10 per cent of income was possible. Above that income figure, the percentage is undoubtedly large. An unpublished Treasury Department estimate suggests that about one-third of the returns in the over-$500,000 income group reported contributions of 12 per cent or more of adjusted gross income for 1949. For 1954 and 1956 about one-fourth of returns in that group tabulated by the IRS reported contributions over 20 per cent of income.

The relatively small number of returns with contributions in excess of the biblical tithe in the income range below $50,000—which accounts for well over 90 per cent of aggregate contributions[27]—suggests that the number of taxpayers whose contributions might be affected by the ceiling imposed on the amount deductible is quite small.[28] This is borne out by the ratios of contributions to income shown for 1950 and 1952 in Table 20.[29] The rise of the ceiling from 15 to 20 per cent in 1952 appears to have had only a negligible effect on the volume of contributions below the $50,000 level. But for returns in the $100,000 to $500,000 group itemized contributions rose from 4 to 6 per cent of income, and for returns with over $500,000 from 7 to 10 per cent.

The further lift of the ceiling from 20 to 30 per cent in 1954 is again reflected only in the percentages for the two highest income groups, which rose from 6 to 7 per cent and from 10 to 12 per cent, respectively, between 1953 and 1956 (Table 20). Less than 0.5 per cent of all returns reported contributions in excess of 20 per cent of their income for 1954 and 1956 (Table 22). This is also true of returns up to the $20,000 income level. Less than 3 per cent of returns with incomes $50,000 to $100,000 and about 8 per cent of the returns in the $100,000 to $500,000 group reported contributions that high. The total amount reported for 1954 in excess of 20 per cent of income was $68 million, or less than 2 per cent of total contributions for that year.[30] Some of that amount would have been contributed even in the

[27] In Table 19 we see that 88 per cent of itemized contributions were deducted on tax returns reporting less than $50,000 income. Obviously a considerably larger percentage of total contributions must have been made by taxpayers with incomes below $50,000.

[28] On the basis of unpublished Treasury Department data for 1949 we estimated the amount of contributions itemized by taxpayers who gave in excess of 14 per cent of income at roughly $282 million in that year. If we assume all of them, in a momentary burst of generosity, had made full use of the additional 5 per cent allowance, we find that the itemized contributions would have risen by $107 million, or 5.3 per cent. Expressed as a per cent of estimated aggregate contributions (Table 16) the rise becomes even less significant, between 3.1 and 4.2 per cent.

[29] No data are available for 1951.

[30] Total contributions were estimated at $4.2 to $4.8 billion so that the amount in excess of 20 per cent came to about 1.5 per cent of the total (see Table 16).

absence of the more liberal allowance; for instance, $13 million of the total in excess of 20 per cent was reported on nontaxable returns. The effect of raising the ceiling from 20 to 30 per cent was thus slight.

While the increased maximum allowable deduction appears to have had a negligible effect on the aggregate flow of funds to philanthropy, it may have had significant effect on gifts to particular types of nonprofit activities. The changing composition of gifts with rising income is evident in percentages for American families showing the relative amounts contributed to religious and to other organizations (such as for welfare and education) by income groups (Table 23.)

According to the data from three surveys (see source note to table), philanthropic gifts reported by families and individuals with incomes up to $10,000 went primarily to religious bodies; only about one-fourth was given for other activities in 1950. In the same year, over one-half of the gifts by groups with incomes $10,000 and over was made for nonreligious purposes. Since the incidence of returns with deductions close to the 15 per cent deduction limit was greater in the higher income groups than in the lower, it is probable that the effect of raising the limit was greater for some types of philanthropy than one might surmise from the over-all figures alone.

How do the survey figures compare with the tax return data presented above (Table 19)? With the tax-return data cast into comparable income groups, the survey figures for contributions as per cent of income are somewhat lower than the tax return figures. The tax return figures are summarized below.

Net Income ($000's)	Per Cent of Adjusted Gross Income on Tax Returns[a]			
	1935	1936	1941	1950
0-2	2.2	2.2	2.5[b]	
2-3	1.7	1.8	1.9[b]	
3-5	1.6	1.7	1.9	c
5-10	1.7	1.6	2.2	
10 and over	2.3	2.2		
Total	2.0	1.9	2.1	2.4

a Fiduciary returns included in 1935 and 1936 figures; excluded from 1941 and 1950.

b Contributions estimated on basis of 1940 figures to include returns with standard deduction in 1941.

c Because of the standard deduction no estimates by income groups for all returns were attempted. A contribution rate of 1.65 per cent was attributed to returns with the standard deduction on the assumption that the 1943 rate for such returns was applicable in 1950.

TABLE 23

Survey Data on Philanthropic Gifts of Individuals by Income Groups and by Type of Gift, as Per Cent of Income, 1935-1936, 1941, and 1950

INCOME GROUP[a]	1935-36 (families)			1941 (families and single persons)			1950 (families and single persons—urban)		
	Total[b]	Religious Organizations	Other[c]	Total[b]	Religious Organizations	Other[c]	Total[b]	Religious Organizations	Other[c]
Under $2,000	1.1	1.0	0.1	1.5	1.3	0.2	2.0	1.5	0.4
2,000-3,000	1.4	1.2	0.2	1.4	1.1	0.3	1.6	1.3	0.3
3,000-5,000	1.7	1.4	0.3	1.6	1.3	0.4	1.6	1.2	0.4
5,000-10,000	1.8	1.3	0.5				1.8	1.2	0.6
10,000 and over	0.9	0.5	0.4	2.4	1.2	1.1	2.9	1.2	1.7
Total	1.3	1.0	0.2	1.7	1.2	0.5	1.8	1.2	0.6

[a] For 1935-1936, aggregate income (that is, money and non-money; for 1941, money income; for 1950, income groups for net money income after tax, with percentages shown for net money income before tax.

[b] Figures in following two columns may not add to correct total because of rounding.

[c] Other contributions include gifts to community chests and other community projects; to Red Cross, USO, and other American and foreign welfare and relief agencies; and to scholarship, memorial, and alumni funds of schools and colleges.

Source: *1935-1936*: National Resources Committee, *Consumer Expenditures in the United States, 1935-36*, Washington, 1939, Tables 24A and 27A.

1941: Bureau of Labor Statistics, *Family Spending and Saving in Wartime*, Bulletin No. 822, 1945, Tables 1, 3, and 12. Average income of those with money incomes over $5,000 was obtained from the earlier tabulation in the BLS *Spending and Saving of the Nation's Families in Wartime*, Bulletin No. 723, Washington, 1942, Table 7. Contributions for that group were obtained as a residual after assuming that average contributions of those with negative income were the same as the average for units with 0 to $500 incomes.

1950: Wharton School of Finance and Commerce, *Study of Consumer Expenditures, Incomes, and Savings*, Vol. XI, University of Pennsylvania, 1956. The sample distributions of families by income groups for nine classes of cities were blown up to correspond to the estimated total urban population in the nine classes of cities, as given on p. XIII.

For 1935-1936, the results are as expected. The survey income concept, which includes nonmoney income, is more inclusive than the tax return concept. The omission of single persons from the 1935-1936 survey figures also affects comparability, although possibly in the opposite direction. The 1941 and 1950 survey figures are for money incomes reported by families and single consumers and are therefore more, though not entirely, comparable to the tax return figures. Both sets of ratios show only moderate variation in the percentage of income given to philanthropy over the income range shown. The survey figures indicate a tendency toward rising contribution ratios with rising income (except for the over $10,000 group in the 1935-1936 survey), which is not present in the 1935-1936 and 1941 tax return figures. The latter suggest a much higher contribution ratio for low incomes than the surveys do, which may account for the higher over-all contribution rate obtained from tax returns.[31] The 1941 survey figures suggest consumers contributed 1.7 per cent of their incomes, whereas the tax returns show a 2.1 per cent rate of giving. For 1950 the respective percentages are 1.8 and 2.4, but the tax return figure for that year is, as has been explained previously, merely an estimate.

Rate Progression and the Cost of Giving

As we have seen, the rate of philanthropic giving reported on tax returns rises with the income scale. Can this be partly attributed to government's increasing share in the cost of donations as incomes rise? At the tax rates prevailing in recent years, the government's share in the deductible donations of a taxpayer may rise from one-fifth to nine-tenths at the top of the income scale. It is dependent on the highest bracket rate to which a taxpayer is subject, the net cost of a given contribution therefore diminishing as taxable income and the marginal rate of tax increase. Though it might seem that the incentive to make use of the contribution allowance among taxpayers would be greater, the higher the rate of tax, it is also frequently shown that decreases in disposable income by high rates of taxation tend to be an influence in the opposite direction; high taxes, it is said, reduce both desire and ability to contribute to philanthropy.[32] The former may be

---

[31] For further comment on the tax return and survey figures, see the last pages of Appendix F.

[32] This is the position taken by Harris (op.cit., p. 124, and pp. 32-33). Speaking of the rise in taxes over the last half century, he concludes: ". . . contributions to charity or education are affected adversely; and this is true even if it is allowed

considered the price effect of the income tax on philanthropic gifts; the latter the income effect.

On a priori grounds one might conclude that the price effect of the deduction outweighs the restrictive effect of taxes on disposable income. The reasoning would be that the cost of contributions to the taxpayer is reduced at his highest marginal rate, whereas his income is reduced by his average effective rate of tax. The marginal rate almost always exceeds a taxpayer's effective rate, and the reduction of the cost to him of his contributions is therefore relatively greater than the reduction of his income. It follows that the after-tax ratio of contributions to income is lower than the ratio before taxes.

Table 24 shows the net cost of contributions relative to net income after tax, for selected amounts of income with 1937, 1945, and 1952 tax rates. A hypothetical contribution deduction of 5 per cent of net income was used at each income level to facilitate comparison of the after-tax percentages. The so-called after-tax rate of giving tends to fall throughout most of the income range. Eventually, however, as the effective rate of tax catches up with the marginal rate (as the latter flattens out), the after-tax ratio of contributions to income rises, and at a very high level of income becomes equal to the before-tax ratio of gifts to income. At 1952 rates the hypothetical contributions of 5 per cent of income (before tax) resulted in a rate of 4.5 per cent of after-tax income for a married taxpayer with an ordinary income of $10,000; 2.9 per cent for a taxpayer with $100,000; but 4.7 per cent for one with as much as $1 million.[33]

_____

that the government through losses of taxes pays seven-eighths of the gift. With gross income cut by seven-eighths, potential donors prefer to hold on to what is left."

[33] For equivalent net incomes that include other than ordinary income, in particular capital gains, the ratios of net contributions to income after tax would often be different from those shown in Table 24. Let us assume, for example, two taxpayers, each with a statutory net income of $100,000, one of whom has $30,000 net realized capital gains taxable at the alternative rate. If both contribute 5 per cent of statutory net income, we find that for 1952 the first taxpayer contributes 2.9 per cent on an after-tax basis and the second 2.7 per cent. For 1945, the positions are reversed. The taxpayer with only ordinary income has a 1.6 per cent after-tax ratio, and the one with a realized capital gain contributes 2.3 per cent after tax.

The validity of the above treatment of the capital gains is somewhat questionable. It might be argued that the percentage for the capital gains taxpayer in our example should be compared with that of a taxpayer with $130,000 ordinary net income since under the tax law statutory net income includes only one-half of the capital gains realized. This, however, would require a different interpretation of the nature of capital gains from that implied in both the tax laws and the adjusted gross income concept underlying most of the statistics in this study.

TABLE 24

Net Cost of Hypothetical Contributions in Relation to Ordinary Net Income
After Tax, at Selected Income Levels, 1937, 1945, and 1952

NET INCOME $000's) (1)	Contributions (1)×.05 (2)	Effective Rate (per cent) (3)	Marginal Rate (per cent) (4)	Net Income After Tax (1)—[(1)×(3)] (5)	Net Cost of Contribution (2)—[(2)×(4)] (6)	Net Cost of Contribution as % of Net Income After Tax (6)÷(5) (7)
			1937a			
3	$ 150	0.3	4.0	$ 2,991	$ 144	4.81
5	250	1.6	4.0	4,920	240	4.88
10	500	4.2	9.0	9,580	455	4.75
25	1,250	10.0	21.0	22,500	987	4.39
50	2,500	17.7	31.0	41,150	1,725	4.19
100	5,000	32.5	59.0	67,500	2,050	3.04
500	25,000	60.8	72.0	196,000	7,000	3.57
1,000	50,000	67.9	76.0	321,000	12,000	3.74
			1945a			
3	150	15.8	23.0	2,526	116	4.59
5	250	19.5	25.0	4,025	188	4.67
10	500	25.9	37.0	7,410	315	4.25
25	1,250	41.2	62.0	14,700	475	3.23
50	2,500	55.2	75.0	22,400	625	2.79
100	5,000	69.4	90.0	30,600	500	1.63
500	25,000	88.8	94.0	56,000	2,000	3.57
1,000	50,000	90.0b	90.0	100,000	5,000	5.00
			1952a			
3	150	13.3	22.2	2,601	117	4.50
5	250	16.9	22.2	4,155	194	4.67
10	500	21.0	29.0	7,900	355	4.49
25	1,250	30.0	42.0	17,500	725	4.14
50	2,500	43.8	66.0	28,100	850	3.02
100	5,000	56.9	75.0	43,100	1,250	2.90
500	25,000	82.5	92.0	87,500	2,000	2.29
1,000	50,000	87.2	88.0	128,000	6,000	4.69

a Computations are for a married couple with an exemption of $2,500 in 1937, $1,000 in 1945, and $1,200 in 1952.
b Takes account of maximum effective rate limitation of 90 per cent in 1945.

The results of adjusting the actual contribution-income ratios for each income group (as given in Table 19) for the impact of the tax on both contributions and income are shown, for selected years in Table 25. For the previous hypothetical example, the curve now becomes nearly flat. Whereas the before-tax contributions ratio for 1937 rose from 2.2 to 6.4 per cent (Table 19), the after-tax percentage rose from 2.1 to only 3.5. For 1941 and 1943 the before-tax contribution ratio rose from about 2.4 to 5 per cent, but after tax there was a faint rise from 2.2 to 2.6 for 1941, and an actual decline from 2.3 to 1.3 for 1943. For the years after 1943 shown in the table, the data are for returns with itemized deductions only; this impairs comparisons with earlier years, particularly for returns below $25,000. In comparisons

TABLE 25

Net Cost of Actual Contributions as Per Cent of Income
After Tax, by Income Groups, Selected Years, 1937-1956

ADJUSTED GROSS INCOME ($000's)	1937	1941	1943	Itemized Returns Only				
				1945	1947	1949	1952a	1956a
Under 2	2.1	2.2b	2.3b	4.3	4.8	5.1	5.2	5.2
2-3	1.7	1.8b	1.8b	3.5	4.2	4.5	4.6	4.4
3-5	1.6	1.7	1.9	3.6	3.9	3.8	3.8	3.7
5-10	1.6	1.7	1.8	3.3	3.5	3.6	3.3	3.1
10-25c	1.6	1.5	1.5	2.3	2.5	3.2	3.0	2.9
25-50c	1.7	1.4	1.2	1.7	1.9	2.3	2.0	2.0
50-100	1.9	1.6	1.1	1.6	1.9	2.2	1.6	2.1
100-500	2.2	2.1	1.0	0.9	1.6	2.5	1.2	2.1
500 and over	3.5	2.6	1.3	1.0	2.0	2.5	3.0	3.2

a Excludes fiduciary returns.

b For 1941 and 1943, the 1940 before-tax contribution rate was assumed to hold for returns with $3,000 or less, to avoid the distorting effect of the standard deduction.

c For 1952, the group limit is $20,000 instead of $25,000.

restricted to returns above that level, the before-tax ratio rose from 3.0 to 6.7 per cent, whereas the after-tax ratio for 1945 declined from 1.7 to 1 per cent. In 1947 and 1949, the before-tax percentages again more than doubled, whereas the after-tax ratio for 1947 rose faintly from 1.9 to 2, and for 1949 from 2.3 to 2.5 per cent. In the 1950's the picture changed considerably. For 1956, before adjustment for taxes, the rate of giving rose from 3 to 12 per cent; the after-tax rate of giving from 2 to 3 per cent.

Such comparisons make it evident that increased taxes need not discourage the maintenance of a given relationship between philanthropic contributions and income. On the contrary, they may be an influence toward larger contributions, as long as they are deductible from income for tax purposes. While no definite conclusion may be drawn from the data here examined, on why the very rich contribute larger proportions of income to philanthropy than those with low and modest incomes, the favorable outcome of the deduction privilege to high-income taxpayers may be a partial explanation. Apart from the tax incentive, however, the "rich" may find it easier to part with a given percentage of their income for philanthropic causes than the "poor." Custom, the pressure exerted by society, and emulative display may also be of some importance.[34] The unequal tax benefit derived by deduction of an equivalent gift from taxable income by taxpayers in different income groups has many critics. One frequently suggested alternative is a tax credit, by which a fraction of contributions made could be credited against tax liability.[35] Some implications for policy of this proposal is the subject of the next section.

The Tax Credit as an Alternative Treatment of Contributions

A credit against tax is in principle the method used in Great Britain since 1946. Through it, the government's participation in a taxpayer's charitable gifts becomes equal to the standard rate of tax on an equivalent amount of his income.[36] A deduction in form of a tax credit is

[34] As far back as 1842, an Englishman travelling in the United States was struck by the extent of private finance for public purposes. "Munificent bequests and donations for public purposes, whether charitable or educational, form a striking feature in the modern history of the United States. . . . Not only is it common for rich capitalists to leave by will a portion of their fortune towards the endowment of national institutions, but individuals during their lifetime make magnificent grants of money for the same objects." Charles Lyell, *Travels in North America*, Vol. I, London, 1845, pp. 263-264.

[35] See, for instance, The President's Committee on Education Beyond the High School, *Second Report to the President*, July 1957, p. 90; Paul E. Klopsteg, "How Shall We Pay for Research and Education?" *Science*, November 16, 1956; Melvin I. White, "Deductions for Nonbusiness Expenses and an Economic Concept of Net Income," *Federal Tax Policy for Economic Growth and Stability*, Joint Committee on the Economic Report, 84th Cong., 1st Sess., 1955, p. 364; and William Vickrey, *Agenda for Progressive Taxation*, pp. 130-131.

[36] A taxpayer pays only the net sum of his contribution to a given recipient, which recovers from the Treasury, under the withholding-at-the-source system, the tax paid at the standard rate on an amount equivalent to the gross contribution. In recent times the standard rate has been 42.5 per cent, graduated by a system of so-called reliefs from the standard rate, by which a lower rate is levied on the first £360 of taxable income. The lower rate of tax for low-income taxpayers results in a lower rate of matching gifts by the government. More important to the low-income donor is the provision that a gift to be recognized as tax exempt must be made under a deed committing the taxpayer to a specified sum annually for not less than seven years. Among the effects of that provision is a probable bias of the tax deduction in favor of high-income taxpayers, whose gifts are subject to the full standard rate. The British Exchequer thus virtually matches the gifts to qualified philanthropies when made under the required deeds. For detail, see *Royal Commission on the Taxation of Profits and Income, Final Report* (Cmd. 9474), London, Her Majesty's Stationary Office, 1955, Chapter 7.

said to have two merits: (1) the relative amount of governmental participation in all gifts is the same, except where the possible amount of tax subsidy exceeds the initial amount of tax liability; and (2) it would be simple to procure the desired level of government participation, consistent with revenue requirements, by varying the rate at which taxpayers may credit their contributions against tax liability.

The tax credit accords with the reasoning that an allowance for philanthropic contributions is a deliberate instrument of public policy to encourage decentralized decision making in the allocation and administration of funds in areas commanding the public interest. In this view, the contribution allowance is not an appropriate adjustment for the determination of net income. It would be justified only if a relation between the deduction and the refinement of gross income to taxable income could be shown, and then there would presumably be little reason to limit the amounts deductible as under the federal tax.

The desirable form, if any, of a deduction depends ultimately upon acceptance of a rationale supporting the deduction. Two possible foundations, discussed previously, are: that the deduction is intended to assist by tax relief in the financing of activities in the public interest; and that its purpose is to refine income, as implied by current practice. The first interprets the deduction as an application of income, rather than as a reduction of income for tax purposes; the second interprets the deduction as a means of obtaining the best possible index of ability to pay—net taxable income. On the second premise, the argument that the cost of the gift dollar is less for the rich than the poor has little merit. The unequal tax value of the present deduction to individuals in different income classes results from the decision of Congress to impose graduated tax rates and to exclude eligible contributions from taxable income. There is nothing inherently unreasonable in this decision. The appropriate form for the allowance depends on whether Congress intended it as an indirect subsidy, or as part of the calculation of taxable net income. Arguments have been presented in favor of both views.[37]

[37] R. M. Haig wrote of the dual provision for contributions as deductible for the donor and tax exempt for the recipient that "on the ground of public policy much can be said for continuing this practice although it is also true that, speaking in terms of economic fundamentals, the man who makes a gift to some person or corporation outside his immediate family deliberately chooses that way of spending his money because it yields him a greater satisfaction than some alternative use" ("The Concept of Income," p. 26). Henry C. Simons held that "if it is not more pleasant to give than to receive one may still hesitate to assert that giving is not a

Whether the revenue cost of obtaining a given volume of contributions with a tax credit would differ from the present income deduction depends on the credit required, that is, the sensitivity of giving to tax rebates. Supposing a flat credit of 30 per cent of eligible contributions against tax liability, many taxpayers would get an increased tax abatement while a few would take drastic reductions. This might lead to a shift in the source of funds for philanthropic purposes toward the middle and low income groups, and possibly—as some authors put it[38]— a more democratic distribution of control over philanthropic institutions. It might lead also to some changes in the composition of major types of recipient institutions. If, at some time, a higher level of contributions to philanthropies should be desired, the tax credit device could easily be adapted. For instance, taxpayers might be granted a higher fractional credit allowance on contributions exceeding a given per cent of income; this method might be more effective than the recent increases in the deduction limit. The second merit claimed for the tax

---

form of consumption for the giver. The proposition that everyone tries to allocate his consumption expenditure among different goods in such manner as to equalize the utility of dollars-worths may not be highly illuminating; but there is no apparent reason for treating gifts as an exception" (*Personal Income Taxation*, pp. 57-58). Similarly, White says (*op.cit.*, p. 364): "A charitable or other such contribution by an individual is a voluntary allocation of funds, presumably more gratifying than expenditure on goods and services. Its deduction is thus not an appropriate adjustment for the calculation of net income." Sylvester Gates and John R. Hicks (a minority opinion in the recent *Final Report of the Royal Commission on the Taxation of Profits and Income*, London, 1955, p. 352) state: "We cannot find any principle to justify the total exemption of charities from income tax, except in those cases where a charity performs functions which are a well-recognized responsibility of the state."

The majority of the Commission ended up on the opposite side of the dividing line: "A charitable contribution does not appear to us to be well compared with personal expenditure or investment of income. It is more truly an act by which a man surrenders his personal decision as to the employment of that part of his income in favour of the decision of the managers of the charity. In a real sense his income is transformed into income of the charity." This reasoning forced the majority to conclude, with much hesitation and ambiguity, that an allowance against taxable income, as practiced in the United States and Canada, rather than the British tax credit, would be in order. But the Commission seemed noticeably relieved at rejecting the recommendation on "practical and administrative" grounds (*ibid.*, p. 59). The idea that contributions properly constitute diminutions of income was widely held at the time the deduction was introduced into the federal tax law. A comment inserted into the *Congressional Record* in 1917 declared: "By means of this exemption contributions to recognized religious, charitable, and educational institutions are put on the same basis as the loss of money in business, or the payment of money in taxes. Since the taxpayer, or the bad investor, or the donor does not have the use of the money, he is not asked to pay the income tax on it" (65th Cong., 1st Sess., p. 6729).

[38] White, *op.cit.*, pp. 364-365; Klopsteg, *op.cit.*, p. 968; Vickrey, *op.cit.*, p. 131.

credit is that it gives the government freedom to review periodically its own position in underwriting philanthropic gifts.[39] Only partial review is possible at present, for under the deduction-from-income provision, governmental participation is tied to the existing rate structure and therefore difficult to control. Some students in the field, however, consider frequent legislative review a distinct disadvantage, especially of a field—education, for example—that invites strong feelings against governmental interference, even though it receives some indirect public assistance. Lack of such review appears to be a point in favor of the present form of deduction from income over the tax credit.[40]

With a tax credit even the rate of benefit to different types of philanthropy could be varied at the will of Congress, and to some extent this is attempted under the federal law now. At present philanthropy encompasses a wide variety of activities and enterprises, some of which may be considered public service programs, while others affect the public interest only remotely. In both cases there occurs a redistribution of the tax load whenever deductions are taken. But when the benefited philanthropies perform functions which would alternatively be governmental, the deductible donations may be thought akin to taxes, and the taxpayer's share in the contribution dollar the price he pays for retaining some control over its allocation to projects and institutions of his choice. With smaller private contributions, the government's responsibility for the functions would increase, tax collections would have to be higher, and those who give little or nothing might have to assume more of the tax load.[41]

---

[39] Review and control of the government's action appears to have greatly concerned both the minority and the majority of the Royal Commission on the Taxation of Profits and Income. Gates and Hicks characterized the system of exempting all charities as a "blind and hidden subsidy contributed by the state [which] is never investigated or weighed" (*op.cit.*, p. 352). The majority was vexed over the lack of "public control of the object of a charity from the point of view either of importance or utility" (*op.cit.*, pp. 55, 56).

[40] This is implicit in the conclusions drawn by J. Harold Goldthorpe, in a study sponsored by the American Council on Education. He writes that "these subsidy exemptions . . . to the institutions of higher education . . . are highly desirable for the following reasons . . . (2) such indirect grants are commonly provided by government without the intrusion of undesirable and insignificant governmental controls: (3) they are a continuing type of indirect aid and do not require periodic legislative review and action. . . ." *Higher Education, Philanthropy, and Federal Tax Exemptions*, 1944, p. 32.

[41] Were the deduction privilege removed, the government's additional financial responsibilities would not necessarily exceed the added revenue accruing from the taxation of previously untaxed income. Nondonors might have no increased liability. Only a shrinking of gifts by more than the increase in tax liability might make

an increase in rates necessary for all taxpayers. Conversely, if donors reduce their gifts by less than the increase in their tax, there might even be a rate reduction and an absolute cut for nondonors.

This subject was explored earlier in discussing the severance of the connection between giving and the tax rebate for many taxpayers when the standard deduction was introduced into the tax system. It will be recalled that we found no evidence that philanthropic giving declined in the wake of the standard deduction.

CHAPTER 5

Nonbusiness Tax Payments

DEDUCTION from gross income, on individual returns, of various non-business taxes paid during the tax year has been permitted from the beginning of the federal income tax. In recent times taxes have included state income taxes, real and personal property taxes, automobile license fees, poll taxes, and state and local retail sales taxes (including special taxes on gasoline, and tobacco) that are imposed directly on the consumer. Sales taxes, collected by the retailer and paid by him to the government, may be deducted by the consumer, provided the tax is not hidden in the sales price.[1] This requirement that a tax, to be deductible, must be imposed on the person who deducts it, has been interpreted to exclude from the deductible list sales taxes that are imposed on the manufacturer or wholesaler. Until 1951 that interpretation excluded the gasoline taxes of a number of states and still excludes the cigarette taxes of several. A further requirement, that a deductible tax must be for a public nonbusiness purpose, excludes special assessments for local improvements tending to enhance the value of the property assessed, and charges that vary with a specific service rendered, such as water taxes. No taxes levied by the federal government—income taxes, estate and gift taxes, excises,[2] and social security taxes—are allowed as deductions.

Trend in Taxes-Paid Deductions

The amounts deducted on tax returns for property, income, and sales tax payments have been large as far back as our statistical record goes. The totals for the period 1927-1956 are shown in Table 26. Between 1927 and 1939 they varied from $600 million to $1 billion, and from 3.1 to 5.5 per cent of reported income (Table 27). From 1940 on the amount deducted as taxes paid exceeded $1 billion in every year.

[1] A tax is considered separately stated whenever it is clear that it was added to the sales price and charged as a separate item to the consumer, although there need be no sales statement to that effect. Before 1942, only those state and local sales taxes that were explicitly imposed on the consumer, thus legally making him the taxpayer, could be deducted in arriving at net income.

[2] Until 1943 federal excises, as for instance admissions taxes, for whose payment the individual purchasing the item was legally liable, were allowed as deductions. Changes in the law have thus moved in opposite directions, toward liberalization of deductibility for state and local excises and abolition of it for all federal excises.

92

TABLE 26

Nonbusiness Tax Payments Deducted and Estimated Total Deductible
Nonbusiness Tax Payments, 1927-1956

(dollars in millions)

YEAR	Nonbusiness Taxes Actually Deducted		Estimated Total Taxes Eligible for Personal Deductions	Amount Deducted on Tax Returns as Per Cent of Total	
	Taxable Returns (1)	All Returns (2)	(3)	(1) ÷ (3) (4)	(2) ÷ (3) (5)
1927	537	801	1,638	32.8	48.9
1928	576	889	1,723	33.4	51.6
1929	560	974	1,836	30.5	53.1
1930	499a	903a	1,894	26.3	47.7
1931	340a	834a	1,865	18.2	44.7
1932	353a	766a	1,792	19.7	42.7
1933	308	678	1,681	18.3	40.3
1934	337	605	1,942	17.4	31.2
1935	386	645	2,136	18.1	30.2
1936	532	737	2,321	22.9	31.8
1937	649	875	2,464	26.3	35.5
1938	602	861	2,555	23.6	33.7
1939	663	917	2,564	25.9	35.8
1940	901	1,289	2,793	32.3	46.2
1941	1,380	1,672	3,077	44.8	54.3
1942	1,893	2,148	3,359	56.4	63.9
1943	2,101	2,147	3,490	60.2	61.5
1944	1,152	1,194	2,858	40.3	41.8
1945	1,225	1,269	3,121	39.3	40.7
1946	1,269	1,348	3,819	33.2	35.3
1947	1,547	1,654	4,531	34.1	36.5
1948	1,500	1,649	5,227	28.7	31.5
1949	1,812	1,984	5,957	30.4	33.3
1950	2,068	2,230	6,597	31.3	33.8
1951	n.a.	n.a.	7,569	n.a.	n.a.
1952	3,034	3,186	8,476	35.8	37.6
1953b	3,453	3,647	9,159	37.7	39.8
1954b	3,826	4,085	9,833	38.9	41.5
1955	n.a.	n.a.	10,775	n.a.	n.a.
1956b	5,543	5,828	11,810	46.9	49.3

Includes fiduciaries.

a Estimates based in part on taxable returns with income of $5,000 and over.

b The tax deduction figures for these years exclude the deductions reported on fiduciary returns.

Source: Columns 1 and 2: Statistics of Income; column 3: see Appendix H.

93

TABLE 27

Deducted Nonbusiness Tax Payments as Per Cent of Income on Tax Returns, and Estimated Total Nonbusiness Tax Payments as Per Cent of Total Adjusted Gross Income, 1927-1956

YEAR	Taxes Deducted as Per Cent of AGI[a] Taxable Returns (1)	All Returns (2)	Total Deductible Taxes as Per Cent of Total AGI[a] (3)
1927	2.7	3.2	2.3
1928	2.5	3.1	2.3
1929	2.5	3.4	2.4
1930	3.2	4.3	3.0
1931	3.3	5.2	3.8
1932	3.9	5.5	4.8
1933	3.7	5.2	4.6
1934	3.6	4.2	4.4
1935	3.5	3.9	4.4
1936	3.4	3.5	4.0
1937	3.8	3.7	4.0
1938	4.3	4.1	4.6
1939	3.8	3.6	4.0
1940	3.5	3.2	4.0
RETURNS WITH ITEMIZED DEDUCTIONS			
1941	3.6	3.7	3.6
1942	3.5	3.6	3.1
1943	2.8	2.9	2.7
1944	3.5	3.6	2.1
1945	3.5	3.6	2.2
1946	3.3	3.3	2.4
1947	3.4	3.6	2.6
1948	3.4	3.6	2.8
1949	4.0	4.2	3.2
1950	3.8	4.0	3.3
1951	—	—	3.3
1952	4.2	4.3	3.5
1953	4.3	4.4	3.6
1954	4.3	4.4	3.9
1955	—	—	4.0
1956	4.6	4.7	4.0

a Income (reported on tax returns, and total) is adjusted gross income (AGI).
Source: Deductible nonbusiness tax payments from Table 26; income figures from Table 17 and Appendix Table D-2.

By 1956 it approached $6 billion. Since 1943 the amounts reported on taxable returns have been, for obvious reasons, only slightly less than those for all returns, but before that time the difference was very considerable—in 1933 only one-half the total appeared on taxable returns. According to the reported figures, the ratio of tax deductions to income was in all years except 1937-1940 higher on nontaxable than on taxable returns[3] (Table 27).

Our attempt to estimate the aggregate amount of taxes eligible for deduction involved a good deal of conjecture, since it required the division of tax collection figures as reported by federal, state, and local governments into personal and business components, in accordance with current tax laws. Since in most of them (real estate, retail sales, and gasoline) governmental reports do not distinguish between the two categories, our allocations are only approximate. The estimated total amount eligible for deduction shows an almost continuous rise over the 30-year period 1927-1956, from $1.6 to $11.8 billion. Between 30 and 50 per cent of this total was reported as deductions on tax returns in the pre-World War II period. Just before the enlargement of the standard deduction, in 1942-1943, the amounts had risen to almost two-thirds of the estimated total. Since then it has been in the range of 30 to 40 per cent until 1954. Figures for the most recent year, 1956, indicate a sharp upturn to one-half of the eligible amount (Table 26).

Unlike the similar comparisons for philanthropic contributions, the relationship between deducted taxes and income as revealed on tax returns and that between the corresponding aggregates are in close agreement (Table 27 and Chart 10). Taxes claimed as deductions on taxable returns rose from about 2.7 per cent of income reported to 4.6 per cent over the period 1927-1956. Our estimate of aggregate deductible taxes as a per cent of total income rose from 2.3 to 4 per cent over the same period. Both series show that most of the rise took place during the transition from the 1920's to the 1930's,[4] and that since the early

[3] There are probably two reasons for this. In the 1920's and 1930's nontaxable returns were filed largely by business proprietors and recipients of certain types of property income (rents, royalties, and capital gains). Gross incomes on these returns exceeded the filing requirement of $5,000, even though net incomes were often low and frequently negative. For instance, of the $370 million of nonbusiness taxes deducted on nontaxable returns in 1933, $171 million was claimed on returns with no net income after business and personal deductions. Most of these returns were in the business and property income category (*Statistics of Income for 1933*, p. 21), and it is possible that a significant part of the taxes designated as nonbusiness should have been entered as business taxes.

The second reason, probably more applicable to the years after 1940, is that many of the nontaxable returns were filed by heads of large families, whose incomes exceeded the filing requirement, but were reduced to the tax-exempt level by high exemptions and property taxes on owned homes.

[4] Our estimates of aggregate deductible taxes for years before 1927 (see Appendix H) indicate that they were in the neighborhood of 2 per cent of total adjusted gross income throughout the '20's. For the tax return series we have no figures earlier than 1927.

'30's there has been no increase in the level of deductible taxes relative to income. (The sharp decline in the first half of the '40's was caused by the wartime curtailment of state and local activities, which led to some tax reduction at those levels.) For recent years the ratios on taxable returns shown in the table and chart are consistently somewhat

CHART 10

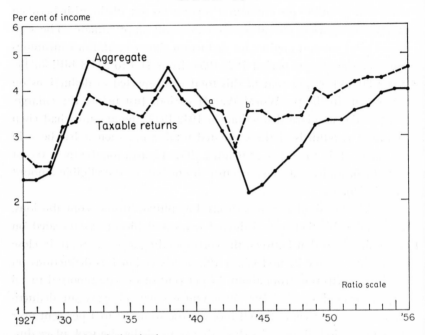

a First standard deduction introduced.
b Standard deduction enlarged.
Source: Table 27.

Deductible Nonbusiness Taxes as Per Cent of Income, 1927-1956

higher than for the underlying totals, because all the tax returns used have itemized deductions.

However, the disparity is not nearly so great as it is in the corresponding two series for philanthropic giving (Tables 13 and 18). The obvious difference between voluntary giving and compulsory tax-paying leads one to expect more dispersion in the amount per tax return in given income groups for contributions than for taxes paid. Since certain taxes are practically inescapable, and their incidence by income groups probably regressive, the difference in tax payments between those who itemize and those who choose the standard deduction is likely to be less than in some other expenditures. A further probable reason for the smaller differences in ratios between itemized returns and those of the whole population is that many homeowners do not itemize their taxes. In 1956, roughly one-half of the homeowners in the United States itemized their deductions on tax returns.[5] For that year the ratio of deductible taxes to income was 4.7 per cent for itemized returns and 4.0 per cent for the whole population. A large proportion of homeowners apparently make use of the standard deduction, and others are exempted from filing because of low incomes.[6] In addition to the ratio between deductions for taxes paid and reported income, the distribution of the deduction among taxpayers with incomes of varying size is of interest. It will now be examined.

Reported Tax Deductions by Size of Income on Tax Returns

Certain qualifications of the data must be noted at the outset. After 1943, we have only the data from returns with itemized deductions, and the information presented must therefore be viewed cautiously. Furthermore, the percentages in Tables 28 and 29 give us a clue to the incidence of the deduction allowed for taxes, not of taxes as such.[7] The figures shown are not an indication of the incidence of any group of taxes, for three important reasons: (1) They are subject to the taxpayer's understanding of the law in addition to his memory and accuracy in reporting the taxes he paid during the preceding year. Omissions and overstatements are therefore likely to occur. As we find in Table 30, many taxpayers did not claim any deductions for taxes, even

[5] In 1950 there were 23.6 million owner-occupied dwellings in the United States (Bureau of the Census, *Census of Housing, 1950*, Vol. 1, Part 1), but only 9.3 million tax returns showed a deduction for taxes and still fewer, 6 million, a deduction for interest. In 1956 the figures were about 29.5 million owner-occupied homes, 17.8 million returns with tax deductions, and 13.7 million with interest deductions (see Table 36). The number of homeowners itemizing is undoubtedly smaller than the number of taxpayers claiming deductible taxes, though possibly larger than the number deducting interest.

[6] According to the Survey of Consumer Finances, 18 per cent of the 1953 nonfarm homeowners had money incomes below $2,000 in 1952 ("Housing Arrangements of Consumers, 1955 Survey of Consumer Finances," *Federal Reserve Bulletin*, August, 1955, p. 9).

[7] The figures were misunderstood at least once. See Tax Foundation, Inc., *Federal Excise Taxes*, 1956, p. 22, where it is concluded that "according to federal income tax data for returns with itemized deductions the burden of deductible state and local taxes, a substantial part of which consists of sales taxes, is approximately proportional up to income levels over $100,000."

TABLE 28

Deductions for Taxes Paid as Per Cent of Income, and Percentage Distribution of Total, by Size of Income on Taxable Returns, Selected Years, 1928-1956

INCOME GROUP [a] ($000's)	All Returns				1941-43		1945-47		1952		1954 [b]		1956 [b]	
	1928-29	1932-34	1937	1940	Itemized returns	All returns	Itemized returns	All returns	Itemized returns	All returns	Itemized returns	All returns	Itemized returns	All returns
TAXES PAID AS PER CENT OF ADJUSTED GROSS INCOME														
Under 2	1.5	2.2	2.4	2.6	3.6	1.8	3.7	0.5	4.6	0.5	4.6	0.6	5.1	0.7
2-3	1.7	3.1	3.1	3.1	3.3	2.0	3.6	0.7	4.4	0.8	4.3	0.9	4.9	1.1
3-5	2.8	3.4	3.4	3.3		2.8	3.5	0.9	4.1	1.2	4.4	1.5	4.7	1.7
5-10	2.8	3.9	3.8	3.8		3.1	3.5	1.5	4.2	1.5	4.4	1.9	4.7	2.3
10-25[c]	2.8	4.3	4.3	4.2		3.2	3.2	2.1	4.3	2.1	4.0	2.3	4.7	2.8
25-50[c]	2.5	4.6	4.5	4.5		3.2	2.9	2.6	4.1	3.2	3.7	3.2	4.3	3.6
50-100	2.4	5.5	4.9	4.5		3.4	2.9	2.8	3.9	3.6	3.7	3.5	4.1	3.8
100-500	2.1	6.2	5.6	4.4		3.4	3.0	3.0	4.0	3.9	3.7	3.6	4.3	4.3
500 and over	1.7	4.7	4.3	3.7		2.9	2.3	2.3	3.1	3.1	3.0	3.0	3.4	3.4
Average	2.4	3.8	3.8	3.4		2.4	3.4	1.1	4.2	1.5	4.3	1.8	4.6	2.2
PER CENT OF TOTAL AMOUNT DEDUCTED														
Under 2	2.4	7.7	8.0	14.4	20.4		7.3		1.9		1.2		1.0	
2-3	3.4	7.1	5.9	17.3	26.2		14.4		5.2		3.9		3.0	
3-5	12.7	20.1	19.6	21.3	24.0		25.4		23.9		23.7		17.8	
5-10	22.6	23.6	20.9	17.2	10.7		16.8		34.7		40.2		45.1	
10-25[c]	22.7	18.9	19.7	14.6	9.0		17.0		12.0		12.5		18.2	
25-50[c]	11.3	9.5	10.5	7.0	4.5		9.1		12.5		11.0		7.6	
50-100	8.5	6.3	7.2	4.1	2.8		5.3		5.4		4.2		4.1	
100-500	10.4	5.2	6.6	3.2	2.1		3.8		3.8		2.7		2.7	
500 and over	5.9	1.7	1.6	0.9	0.4		0.7		0.7		0.5		0.6	
Total [d]	100.0	100.0	100.0	100.0	100.0		100.0		100.0		100.0		100.0	

a Net income groups until 1943; adjusted gross income groups thereafter.

b Excludes fiduciary returns.

c For 1952 and 1954, group limit is $20,000 instead of $25,000.

d Totals do not always equal 100 per cent, due to rounding.

TABLE 29

Deductions for Taxes Paid as Per Cent of Income on Taxable Returns with
That Deduction, by Income Groups, Selected Years, 1934-1956

INCOME GROUP[a] ($000's)	1934	1937	1939	1941	1945	1947	1949	1952	1954	1956
Under 2	n.a.	4.3	n.a.	n.a.	5.1	4.8	4.7	5.5	5.4	5.9
2-3	n.a.	4.2	n.a.	n.a.	3.9	4.0	4.2	4.8	4.7	5.2
3-5	n.a.	4.1	n.a.	n.a.	3.9	3.9	4.1	4.3	4.5	4.9
5-10	4.5	4.5	4.5	4.1	3.6	3.9	4.2	4.3	4.4	4.8
10-25[b]	4.4	4.8	4.8	4.1	3.4	3.6	4.5	4.5	4.5	4.8
25-50[b]	4.3	4.9	5.0	4.0	3.2	3.2	4.1	4.2	4.1	4.3
50-100	4.4	5.2	5.0	4.1	3.2	3.2	3.9	4.0	3.8	4.1
100-500	4.8	5.7	5.0	4.0	3.4	3.2	4.0	4.2	3.8	4.4
500 and over	3.8	4.5	5.0	3.7	2.9	2.3	3.4	3.3	3.1	3.5
Average deduction per return (dollars)	n.a.	268	n.a.	n.a.	182	195	244	278	289	336

a Net income classes for years before 1944; adjusted gross income classes thereafter.
b For 1952 and 1954 the percentages are for returns in the $10-20,000 and the $20-50,000 income groups.

before the introduction of the standard deduction, although it is unlikely that as many as 15 per cent of those who filed returns in the
$5,000 to $10,000 income group incurred no deductible taxes. (2) We
have no knowledge of the actual composition of the taxes deducted,
even though we know the list of legally deductible taxes. (3) The

TABLE 30

Per Cent of Taxable Returns with Deductions for Taxes Paid,
by Size of Income Reported, Selected Years, 1937-1956

INCOME GROUP[a] ($000's)	All Returns			Returns with Itemized Deductions					
	1937[b]	1939	1941	1945	1947	1949	1952	1954	1956
Under 2	57.0	—	—	74.2	75.6	81.5	84.3	86.0	86.1
2-3	74.0	—	—	87.0	87.0	90.9	92.8	93.0	93.5
3-5	81.9	—	—	91.3	91.8	96.0	97.1	97.0	97.3
5-10	84.3	87.3	87.0	92.2	92.7	96.2	98.3	98.3	98.2
10-25[c]	89.5	91.8	90.6	93.7	94.3	96.9	97.7	98.2	98.4
25-50[c]	92.7	94.8	93.3	95.2	95.5	97.4	98.1	98.1	98.4
50-100	94.9	96.4	95.3	95.5	96.0	97.6	98.3	98.4	98.8
100-500	97.0	98.4	97.1	97.2	97.8	98.3	98.5	98.3	99.0
500 and over	95.7	100.0	97.5	96.6	99.3	98.0	98.8	97.2	97.8
Average	71.9	—	—	85.5	87.9	93.6	96.1	96.7	97.1

a Net income groups for years before 1944; adjusted gross income groups thereafter.
b Fiduciary returns included in 1937 only.
c Income groups are $10-20,000 and $20-50,000 in 1952 and 1954.

legally deductible items are not suitable for use in a study of tax incidence. The income tax law has too many omissions for such a purpose; for example, it permits deduction of sales taxes imposed at the retail level but not those collected from the manufacturer or wholesaler.

The figures in Tables 28 and 29 show that, as a percentage of income reported on all taxable returns, the deduction tends to rise slightly up to the $100,000 level. The figures for years before 1944 show this clearly. For later years it is not certain, but the higher percentage on low-income than on high-income returns after 1943 can be mostly, if not altogether, explained by the standard deduction. From the figures shown in Table 28 we can say with some confidence that, had there been no standard allowance, the deduction for state and local taxes in the 1950's would have amounted to between 3 and 4 per cent of all income reported on tax returns; and this percentage would have varied only little by size of income reported.

Among returns with deductions for taxes paid (omitting itemized returns with no tax deductions) there is little variation in the percentage deducted, by size of income reported (Table 29). Even for the years after 1943, the significant variations are confined to the two extremes of the income scale. Between the income groups $2,000 to $3,000 and $100,000 to $500,000 they remain within one percentage point. Between those income levels, in 1945, the percentage deducted declined from 3.9 to 3.4 per cent; in 1949, from 4.2 to 4 per cent; in 1953, from 4.7 to 4.2 per cent; and in 1956, from 5.2 to 4.4 per cent. For selected years in the 1930's our figures show increases in percentage to the same upper level. The reversal occurred apparently for reasons besides the standard deduction, as shown by the figures for 1941.

The distribution of the tax deduction is not surprising in view of two characteristics of the taxes eligible for deductions. First, the deduction is heavily weighted with property taxes of homeowners and state personal income taxes—both usually well recorded in the minds and files of taxpayers. Second, state and local excises and sales taxes are not all deductible, and are paid in such small amounts and so frequently that some taxpayers tend to forget part or all of them. This seems to be true especially of low-income taxpayers (see Table 30). Other taxpayers resort to such rule-of-thumb estimates as a percentage of income corresponding to the local rate of sales tax. Thus the relation to income of tax deductions can hardly be taken as indicative of the actual incidence by income groups of state and local taxes.

Tax Deductibility as a Coordination Device

The rationale behind the deductibility of taxes paid in computing taxable net income has undergone some change over the years. In our earliest income tax acts, the idea that net income after taxes is the true measure of taxpaying ability seems to have been implicit. Accordingly all taxes, including the federal income tax, paid in the tax year, were deductible. Developments following the United States' entry into World War I suggested that continuation of this practice would force tax rates to very high levels, and eventually only state and local taxes remained eligible.[8] Today tax deductibility appears to be regarded as primarily a coordination device.[9] It is held that without it the states would find it difficult to continue to use the income tax since, first, the combined rates might easily become confiscatory and, second, interstate competition might force a retreat from income taxation by states whose tax rates are now relatively high. The same justification is, of course, not advanced for the other state and local taxes, but their deductibility has probably been continued to avoid discrimination against states without income taxes.[10]

From a look at Table 31 it becomes evident that the states could at present raise their income tax rates appreciably without thereby seriously increasing the combined state and federal tax liability of high-income taxpayers. We have chosen the 1956 New York State income tax, with its top rate then at 7 per cent, as typical for illustration. In 1953, 28 out of the 33 states with income taxes had top rates not exceeding 7 per cent and none had a rate higher than 11 per cent.[11] From the table it is evident that the increase in the marginal rate of tax, on account of the state tax, is progressive only at the lower part of the income scale. As net income rises, any progression in state marginal

[8] See p. 7 for more detail.

[9] See Herbert E. Klarman, "Income Tax Deductibility," National Tax Journal, September 1948, pp. 241ff, and also the comment by Byron L. Johnson and Klarman's, rejoinder, in National Tax Journal, March 1949, pp. 88-90; L. L. Ecker-Racz, "Intergovernmental Tax Coordination: Record and Prospect," National Tax Journal, September 1952, p. 254; Joseph A. Pechman, "The Individual Income Tax Base," Proceedings of the National Tax Association, Detroit, 1955, p. 306; William Vickrey, Agenda, pp. 93-100.

[10] Vickrey (op.cit., p. 95), however, appears to argue in favor of such outright discrimination to encourage the use of income taxes by the states.

[11] See U.S. Treasury Department Tax Analysis Staff, Overlapping Taxes in the United States, January 1, 1954, Table 12.

rates is easily swamped by the effect of the high federal marginal rates. Thus for a married taxpayer with $25,000 net income, although the nominal top marginal rate of New York tax was 7 per cent, deductibility reduced it to an actual 4.3 per cent. But at the $50,000 net income level, the same nominal rate becomes 2.9 per cent, and at $500,000,

TABLE 31

Effect of Deductibility on Combined Marginal Rates of Federal and New York State
Individual Income Tax at Selected Income Levels, 1956 Rates
(*married couple, no dependents*)

NET INCOME ($000's) (1)	Marginal Rate Federal (2)	Marginal Rate N.Y. State (3)	Federal and State Rates Combined (4)	Increase in Marginal Rate due to State Tax[a] (4) — (2) (5)
3	20	2	21.6	1.6
5	20	3	22.4	2.4
10	26	6	30.4	4.4
25	38	7	42.3	4.3
50	59	7	61.9	2.9
100	72	7	74.0	2.0
500	91	7	91.6	0.6
1,000	91	7	91.6	0.6

[a] This equals $S(1-F)$, when $S =$ state marginal rate, and $F =$ federal marginal rate.

a mere 0.6 per cent.[12] For more than half of the income-tax states which in turn grant deductibility for the federal income tax paid, this effect is considerably reinforced. But to deal with reciprocal deductibility at this point would complicate unnecessarily the discussion of the effect of deductibility under the federal tax law.

The preceding exposition needs qualification to take account of the many taxpayers who choose the standard deduction offered by the

[12] The increases in the effective rate of tax due to the New York income tax were as follows:

Net Income ($000's)	Without Deductibility	With Deductibility
5	1.30	1.04
10	2.90	2.15
25	5.30	3.28
50	6.15	2.53
100	6.58	1.84
500	6.92	0.64
1,000	6.96	0.63

federal income tax law, and who therefore can make no specific deduction for taxes paid to their states and localities. The type of computation shown in Table 31 is not strictly applicable to that group of taxpayers. But the fact that a taxpayer makes use of the standard deduction may be considered presumptive evidence that he has obtained all, if not more than, the benefit the law was intended to bestow. Nevertheless, for those who have not "used up" all of their standard deduction, a rise in state or local tax rates would not be mitigated by deductibility. In any immediate sense, the amount of an increase in state and local taxes paid for by the federal government is (1) less in the aggregate and (2) even more unequally distributed among income groups than is apparent from a consideration of the federal marginal tax rates separately (column 2, Table 31).

The first point is amply illustrated by the figures in Table 32. The

TABLE 32

State and Local Taxes Deducted on Taxable Returns, Cost of the Deduction to Federal Government, and Net Cost to Taxpayers, 1952-1956
(amounts in millions of dollars)

	Estimated Total Amount Eligible for Deduction	Amount Itemized (taxable returns)	Cost to Federal Government	Net Cost to Taxpayers Itemizing	Cost to Government as Per Cent of:	
					Taxes Itemized	Taxes Eligible for Deduction
	(1)	(2)	(3)	(4)	(5)	(6)
2	8,476	3,004	1,021	1,983	34.0	12.0
3	9,159	3,453	1,122	2,333	32.5	12.2
4	9,833	3,826	1,106	2,720	28.9	11.2
5	10,775	n.a.	—	—	—	—
6	11,810	5,543	1,598	3,945	28.8	13.5

Source, by column

1) Table 26.
2) *Statistics of Income* (individual returns only).
3) See Appendix G.

(4) Column 2 — column 3.
(5) Column 3 ÷ column 2.
(6) Column 3 ÷ column 1.

cost to the federal treasury of itemized deductions for state and local nonbusiness taxes in terms of current federal rates was $1 billion in 1952 and $1.6 billion in 1956. This constituted 34 per cent of the nonbusiness taxes itemized on taxable returns in 1952, and 29 per cent of the amount itemized for 1956. But of the estimated total of nonbusiness-connected taxes paid by individuals, the amount absorbed by the federal income tax was 12 per cent in 1952, and 14 per cent in 1956. The second point, relating to the fraction of an increase in state or local taxes that is passed on to the federal government at various income levels, is illustrated in Table 33 and Chart 11. That fraction is initially set by the marginal federal rates of income tax to which the

TABLE 33

Estimated Fraction of an Increase in State and Local Nonbusiness Taxes Passed on to Federal Government in the Form of Deduction, 1956

ADJUSTED GROSS INCOME GROUP ($000's)	Average Marginal Rate of Federal Tax (1)	Taxable Returns with Deduction for Taxes as per cent of All Returns (2)	Per Cent of Nonbusiness Taxes Shifted to Federal Government (1) × (2) (3)
0.6-1	0.20	1.6	0.3
1-1.5	.20	4.7	0.9
1.5-2	.20	9.4	1.9
2-2.5	.20	13.5	2.7
2.5-3	.20	17.7	3.5
3-3.5	.20	22.2	4.4
3.5-4	.20	28.4	5.7
4-4.5	.20	33.1	6.6
4.5-5	.20	37.8	7.6
5-6	.20	46.2	9.2
6-7	.21	48.8	10.1
7-8	.21	49.0	10.5
8-9	.21	48.1	10.3
9-10	.23	47.3	10.9
10-15	.26	51.3	13.6
15-20	.32	65.5	20.7
20-25	.40	74.2	30.0
25-50	.54	83.2	45.0
50-100	.66	92.4	61.4
100-150	.77	96.5	74.3
150-200	.84	97.2	81.7
200-500	.88	97.4	86.1
500-1,000	.87	96.3	84.0
1,000 and over	.87	94.5	82.2

Source: Column 1: *Statistics of Income*, 1956. Change in average tax liability between two income groups divided by change in average taxable income. For income groups above the $15,000 level, the amount of income subject to alternative long-term capital gains rate was subtracted before computing average taxable income. Similarly the amount of long-term capital gains tax was subtracted before computing average tax liability.
Column 2: *Statistics of Income*, 1956.

various income groups are subject (column 1 of the table). But because the proportion of taxpayers who itemize is small at the bottom of the income scale and large at the top, the fraction of an increase in deductible taxes passed on to the federal government is further reduced—

greatly for low income groups and slightly for high income groups. That is, the average marginal rate for each income group must be weighted by the per cent of all returns in the group that are taxable and itemize their deductible taxes (column 2 of the table). The result is column 3 of Table 33: the fraction of an increase in deductible taxes

CHART 11

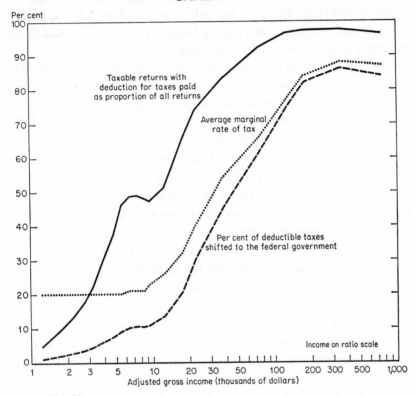

Per cent

Taxable returns with deduction for taxes paid as proportion of all returns

Average marginal rate of tax

Per cent of deductible taxes shifted to the federal government

Income on ratio scale

Adjusted gross income (thousands of dollars)

Source: Table 33.

Fraction of an Increase in State and Local Nonbusiness Taxes Passed on to Federal Government, 1956

that is likely to be passed on to the federal government rises from 1 per cent at the bottom to over 80 per cent near the top.[18]

[18] The above discussion, based on Table 33 and Chart 11, follows closely and owes much to James N. Morgan, "The Federal Personal Income Tax and the Incidence of Deductible Costs," *American Economic Review*, September 1958. However, Morgan overlooks that it is not the proportion of taxpayers who *itemize* deductions that influences the shiftability to the federal government of an increase in any particular deductible expense, but the proportion of taxpayers who itemize that *particular* expense. With respect to deductible state and local taxes, this point is unimportant.

The fraction of returns with deductions for taxes paid is only an accurate indicator of the proportion of an increase in state and local taxes that will be deducted when we deal with small changes in a particular tax. Such small changes in one tax would not significantly affect the proportion of taxpayers itemizing. Moreover, this proportion is merely an average for all deductible taxes. If the increase in question is one in property taxes, a larger proportion than that suggested in Table 33 would be shifted to the federal government, because generally a greater proportion of property taxpayers than of state and local taxpayers itemize their deductible taxes.

From the discussion of coordination of federal and state tax rates by deduction of taxes, two conclusions clearly emerge. The deductibility feature of the federal law lessens the actual cost to the taxpayer of a state income tax from what might appear on inspection of the rate schedule per se. Further the actual cost to the taxpayer is not progressive with income in the sense in which nominal state rate schedules are conceived to be progressive. After a certain point in the income scale, the cost of a state income tax as an addition to federal income tax, measured as a per cent of income, declines rather than rises. Thus the states have for some time been able to divert tax revenue from the federal treasury to the state treasuries at little cost to the taxpayer. But the taxpayer must itemize his tax deductions to accomplish it. That it has not occurred to any significant extent may be partially ascribed to lack of understanding of the effect on combined tax rates of deductibility of state income taxes. A large section of the public continues to think of nominal rates separately, rather than of the complexities of combined rates emerging from the action of deductibility devices.

The effect on combined rates of deductibility, as summarized above, has been stated several times in one form or another by students of the income tax.[14] Nevertheless, several of these authorities uphold the deductibility device for state income taxes solely on the ground that it enables states to maintain otherwise unobtainable progressive rate

---

But with respect to medical expenses and interest paid it makes a great difference which set of percentages is used. Because of the 3 per cent exclusion, the fraction of returns itemizing medical expense is as large at the $6,000 level as it is at the $100,000 level (see Table 44). Morgan also ignores the fact that the proportion of taxpayers who itemize is an average with different meaning for different deductible taxes.

[14] See those cited in footnote 9, and a particularly explicit statement in Richard Goode, *The Corporation Income Tax*, 1951, p. 91.

schedules.[15] This inevitably begs the question whether such progressive rate schedules are worth maintaining if indeed they cause the combined federal and state rates to be less progressive than the federal schedule is now, and if their nominal existence serves to mislead many taxpayers on the true impact of state income taxes.

From a national viewpoint one may be inclined to think progressivity of state taxes—if they must be coupled with the current form of tax deductibility—not worth maintaining. But from the states' point of view it may be argued that without deductibility they might be forced to adopt less progressive income tax rate schedules, with the possible result that revenue losses might be replaced by enlarging existing sales taxes, or adopting new ones. It may be countered that a move toward sales taxes is only one of several possible adjustments. The federal government, gaining a somewhat larger tax base if tax deductibility were abandoned, could reduce its rates accordingly, which might help the states toward maintaining some progressivity in their rate structure. But this reduction in federal rates would be of minor significance. In the main, the states might simply raise the same amount of revenue by income taxation as before, but with less progressive rate schedules, leaving progressivity mainly to the federal government. Here it can be objected that the states should have some share in progressivity. Thus deductibility as a coordination device may be one answer to the question of how progressivity is to be shared between the states and the federal government since, as we have seen, over-all progressivity can hardly be increased by the deductibility device.

As the progressivity of state income taxes is reduced or turned into regressivity by the deductibility feature, in the same sense, the deductibility also accentuates regressivity in other state and local taxes. The deductibility of general and selective sales taxes, provided they are imposed by law on the consumer in the sense described above, is based on a partial acceptance of traditional incidence theory.[16] The acceptance is only partial because sales taxes or excises imposed at levels other than the retail stage are not deductible by the consumer-pur-

---

[15] See Klarman, *op.cit.*, pp. 248-49; Pechman, *op.cit.*, p. 306; Vickrey, *op.cit.*, pp. 95-96. An exception is the article by Morgan, *op.cit.*, p. 657.

[16] Opinion in recent years has been considerably less than unanimous on the incidence of sales taxes. For two significant attempts to revise the theory of sales tax incidence, see H. G. Brown, "The Incidence of a General Output or a General Sales Tax," *Journal of Political Economy*, April 1939, pp. 254-62; and E. R. Rolph, "A Proposed Revision of Excise-Tax Theory," *Journal of Political Economy*, April 1952, pp. 102-17.

chaser (but they are by the manufacturer or wholesaler), and also because deductibility of the full amount of such taxes assumes that they are fully borne by the consumer.

As frequently pointed out, deductibility of a sales tax depends on form rather than incidence. The law, in permitting the deduction of taxes that the consumer can "segregate," discriminates against those whose consumption patterns encompass a relatively large amount of taxes that cannot be segregated.[17] Most frequently cited cases are the tax treatment in favor of automobile owners over bus and taxi riders, and owner-occupants of houses over tenants. Fare-paying riders and rent-paying tenants pay the motor vehicle and property taxes indirectly, but cannot claim them as tax deductions because they are not paid explicity. To the extent that motor vehicle and property taxes are justified on the grounds of benefits received, the question arises why they should be treated differently in any way from a locality's special property assessments, which are not deductible for precisely that reason. These special taxes and several others may be viewed as payments to the government for services rendered, and hence are like any other payments made for personal consumption purposes.

Finally, a recurring criticism about the deduction for excises and sales taxes is that it suffers from haphazard administration, owing largely to the many vexing differences in practice depending on what state the taxpayer makes his purchase in.[18] It is difficult for taxpayers to keep accurate records of such tax payments, and not a few are unable to determine what is deductible and what is not. The result, as pointed out above, is that many a taxpayer simply indulges his own fancy, which may partly explain why the distribution of taxes-paid deductions, by size of income, has little resemblance to other distributions of state and local taxes.

[17] Vickrey, *op.cit.*, p. 95.

[18] For example, the tax on cigarettes purchased in a state which imposes it on the wholesaler is not deductible, whereas for those who buy their cigarettes in a state where the tax is legally imposed on the consumer, it is deductible.

CHAPTER 6

Personal Interest Payments

DEDUCTION of interest paid, as of nonbusiness tax payments, has been allowed by the federal income tax laws from the very beginning. To this day, all interest paid on personal as well as business indebtedness has been deductible, with the single exception of interest incurred for carrying tax-exempt securities. Currently, the only distinction drawn is by the method of deduction. Interest expenses incurred for business or professional reasons are deducted in computing adjusted gross income; nonbusiness interest, if the taxpayer chooses to itemize, is deducted from adjusted gross income in computing taxable income. This distinction has been important since 1944, when the amount allowed for philanthropic contributions and medical expenses as well as the amount of the standard deduction became dependent upon the size of adjusted gross income. This chapter deals with nonbusiness interest only.

Nonbusiness interest is defined by the law as interest on loans contracted neither for the production of taxable income nor in connection with taxpayers' trade or business, but for personal or family purchases and expenses. Probably a major share of deductible personal interest is paid for mortgages on owner-occupied residences. Since 1939 tenant stockholders in cooperative apartment buildings have also been able to deduct their proportionate share of interest paid on the cooperative's indebtedness. Interest on personal loans includes that paid in discount form; that incurred in installment buying if separately stated; and if not separately stated, an amount equal to six per cent of the average unpaid balance under an installment contract may be deducted.

Trend in Deductions Claimed

Total personal interest in the category deductible[1] from adjusted gross income to compute taxable income was nearly constant in abso-

---

[1] For 1936-1939 Copeland's estimate of cash interest expenditures by households—families and single persons, estates, personal holding companies and trusts—was used here as a measure of total deductible personal interest (see Morris A. Copeland, *A Study of Moneyflows in the United States*, National Bureau of Economic Research, 1952, pp. 66-67). For 1939-1953 we used the Federal Reserve Board's figures for monetary interest payments of consumers, which cover "natural persons and personal trusts" (see Board of Governors of the Federal Reserve System, *Flow of Funds in the United States, 1939-1953*, Washington, D.C., 1955, p. 239).

lute amount during the period 1936-1945. It varied only between $1.3 and $1.6 billion during these ten years owing to consistently low interest rates and the wartime restrictions on residential construction and the output of consumer durables. As a per cent of income, total personal interest declined steadily from 2.4 in 1936 to less than 1 per cent in 1945. But beginning with 1946 the trend was reversed. The absolute and relative amounts rose in every year—from the low of $1.3 billion in 1945 to $8.5 billion in 1956, or from 1 per cent to nearly 3 per cent of income.

The amount of this interest appearing as itemized deductions on tax returns rose from 42 per cent of the total in 1936 to 82 per cent in 1943, when it exceeded $1 billion. Since then the standard deduction has held the amount of itemized interest deductions to roughly one-half of estimated total personal interest (Table 34). Like the ratios of deductible nonbusiness taxes to income, the ratio of personal interest deductions to income on tax returns has shown the same pattern of change as the ratio of total personal interest to total income (Chart 12). Again, mainly because of the operation of the standard deduction, the tax-return ratios since 1941 have been consistently higher than the ratios for the underlying totals. But the relative difference in the ratios is considerably greater for interest than for taxes. For 1944 interest deducted on taxable returns was 2.1 per cent of income reported, whereas the corresponding countrywide percentage was only 0.9 per cent; for 1956 the percentages were 3.8 and 2.9, respectively (Table 35).

Interest Deductions and Homeownership

One probable reason for the high ratio of interest to income on tax returns is that the returns with itemized personal interest expenditures are largely those of homeowners with mortgages, who tend to have sizable outlays for interest.[2] The available evidence suggests that many

[2] See, for instance, 1956 Survey of Consumer Finances, "Consumer Indebtedness," *Federal Reserve Bulletin*, July 1956, p. 691: "About two-thirds of all mortgage debts outstanding exceed $3,000. Spending units rarely have personal debts in excess of $3,000 . . . and more than half of all units with such debt owe less than $500." And it is reported that about two-thirds of spending units with mortgage debt also have some kind of personal debt (p. 702), the latter being defined as all short-term and intermediate-term consumer debt other than charge accounts and mortgages. The interest cost per dollar of debt is of course greater on personal loans than on home mortgages, but the difference is not large enough to offset the great disparity in the amounts of principal involved.

TABLE 34

Personal Interest Payments Deducted on Tax Returns and Estimated
Total Deductible Personal Interest Payments, 1927-1956

YEAR	Personal Interest Deducted Taxable Returns (millions) (1)	All Returns (millions) (2)	Total Deductible Interest Payments[a] (billions) (3)	Amount Deducted as per cent of Total 1 ÷ 3 (4)	2 ÷ 3 (5)
1927	827[b]	1,131[b]			
1928	927	1,368[b]			
1929	922	1,439[b]			
1930	640	1,250[b]			
1931	371	940[b]			
1932	352	796[b]			
1933	296	643			
1934	313	606			
1935	327	572			
1936	397	593	1.4	28.4	42.4
1937	405	606	1.4	28.9	43.3
1938	340	557	1.3	26.2	42.8
1939	383	583	1.3	29.5	44.8
1939	383	583	1.4	27.4	41.6
1940	467	751	1.5	31.1	50.1
1941	754	956	1.6	47.1	59.8
1942	1,010	1,168	1.5	67.3	77.9
1943	1,038	1,066	1.3	79.8	82.0
1944	696	719	1.3	53.5	55.3
1945	683	704	1.3	52.5	54.2
1946	694	749	1.6	43.4	46.8
1947	855	928	2.0	42.7	46.4
1948	903	1,014	2.5	36.1	40.6
1949	1,106	1,238	3.0	36.9	41.3
1950	1,372	1,511	3.6	38.1	42.0
1951	—	—	4.2	—	—
1952	2,095	2,240	4.8	43.6	46.7
1953[c]	2,585	2,739	5.7	45.4	48.1
1954[c]	2,985	3,205	6.3	47.4	50.9
1955	—	—	7.3	—	—
1956[c]	4,544	4,810	8.5	53.5	56.6

a *1936-1939*: Morris A. Copeland, *A Study of Moneyflows in the United States* (NBER, 1952), pp. 66-67; *1939-1952*: Board of Governors of the Federal Reserve System, *Flow of Funds in the United States, 1939-1953*, Washington, D.C., 1955, p. 239.

b Estimates.

c The interest deduction figures for these years exclude those reported on fiduciary returns.

of them itemize their deductible interest (and property taxes).[3] As Table 36 shows, there were an estimated 13.6 million nonfarm home-owners with mortgage debt in 1956; there were also 13.7 million tax returns with itemized deductions for interest expense. This means that all nonfarm homeowners with mortgage debt could have item-

CHART 12

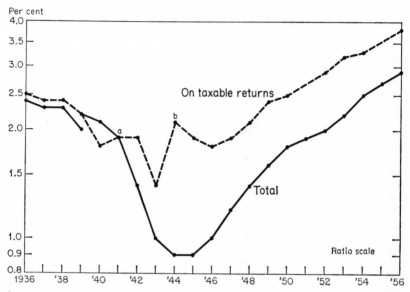

a First standard deduction introduced.
b Standard deduction enlarged.
Source: Table 35.

Deductible Personal Interest as Per Cent of Adjusted Gross Income, 1936-1956

ized their deductions in that year. If owner-occupied mortgaged farm homes were included in the comparison, the percentages on line 5 would be lower. However, it is probable that the majority of such farmers filing tax returns treat mortgage interest as business expense rather than prorating it between residential and business purpose. Most of such interest, even if properly prorated, is business interest.

Table 36 also shows that, of the nearly 26 million nonfarm home-owners, only a possible maximum of 18 million, or somewhat less than seven-tenths, itemized their taxes in 1956. Since it can be assumed that all who itemize mortgage interest also itemize tax deductions, it is likely that the number of nonmortgage homeowners who itemize de-

[3] See the end of the next section.

ductions is relatively small. If, for example, nearly all the returns with interest deductions in 1956 were those of homeowners, then only about 4 million out of the 12 million debt-free nonfarm homeowners, or about one-third, could have itemized. It is of course unlikely that all the 13.7 million returns with deductible interest are those of home-

TABLE 35

Deducted Personal Interest Payments as Per Cent of Income on Tax Returns, and Estimated Total Personal Interest as Per Cent of Total Adjusted Gross Income, 1936-1956

| | Interest Deducted as Per Cent of AGI | | Total Deductible Interest as Per Cent of Total AGI |
| | Taxable Returns | All Returns | |
YEAR	(1)	(2)	(3)
1936	2.5	3.8	2.4
1937	2.4	3.6	2.3
1938	2.4	3.9	2.3
1939	2.2	3.3	2.0
1939	2.2	3.3	2.2
1940	1.8	2.9	2.1
RETURNS WITH ITEMIZED DEDUCTIONS			
1941	1.9	2.1	1.9
1942	1.9	2.0	1.4
1943	1.4	1.4	1.0
1944	2.1	2.2	.9
1945	1.9	2.0	.9
1946	1.8	1.9	1.0
1947	1.9	2.0	1.2
1948	2.1	2.2	1.4
1949	2.4	2.6	1.6
1950	2.5	2.7	1.8
1951	—	—	1.9
1952	2.9	3.0	2.0
1953	3.2	3.3	2.2
1954	3.3	3.5	2.5
1955	—	—	2.7
1956	3.8	3.9	2.9

Source: Deductible interest payments from Table 34; income figures from Table 17 and Appendix Table D-2.

owners, but it is even less likely that all the 17.8 million returns with tax deductions are those of homeowners. Thus probably fewer than one-third of the debt-free homeowners itemized deductions.

Many regard deductions allowed for taxes and personal interest to be in line with, if not specifically designed for, encouragement of homeownership. The figures presented above suggest that in recent years probably more than one-half of homeowners with mortgages have benefited to some extent from interest deductions, but that a

TABLE 36

Number of Tax Returns with Deductions for Interest and Taxes Compared with Total Number of Owner-Occupied Residences and Number of Mortgaged Owner-Occupied Residences, 1950, 1952, 1953, and 1956

	1950	1952	1953	1956
	(in millions)			
1. Owner-occupied dwelling units	23.6	25.8	26.6	29.5
2. Nonfarm	19.8	22.0	22.8	25.6
3. Farm	3.8	3.8	3.8	3.8
4. Mortgaged owner-occupied dwellings	9.9	—	—	—
5. Nonfarm	8.7	10.3	10.7	13.6
6. Farm	1.2	—	—	—
7. Tax returns with itemized deduction for interest	6.0	8.1	9.5	13.7
As per cent of line 5	69.0%	78.6	88.8	100.8
8. Tax returns with itemized deductions for taxes	9.3	11.8	13.4	17.8
As per cent of line 2	47.0%	53.6	58.8	69.3

1950: lines 1 to 3: Census of Housing: 1950, Vol. I, Part 1, Table L;
line 4: lines 5 + 6;
line 5: line 2 multiplied by 0.44, the ratio of dwelling units (in one- to four-dwelling unit structures without business) for which mortgages were reported to total nonfarm owner-occupied units for which mortgage status was reported. *Census of Housing,* Vol. I, Part 1, Table T;
line 6: number of owner-occupied farms (fully owned and partly owned), which were mortgaged in 1950. 1950 Census of Agriculture, *1950 Farm Mortgage Debt,* 1952, p. 11.
1952 and 1953: line 1: Number of households in the United States multiplied by estimated per cent of owner-occupied dwelling units. The latter were obtained for 1952 and 1953 by straight interpolation between the percentages for 1950 and 1956. *Statistical Abstract of the United States, 1956,* Tables 47 and 972;
line 2: line 1 — line 3;
line 3: Farm dwellings were 16 per cent of the total in 1950, and 14 per cent in mid-1954 (for latter figure, see Bureau of the Census, *Housing and Construction Reports,* Series H-101, No. 1). The 1952 and 1953 percentages were obtained by interpolation, and were multiplied by line 1 to obtain line 3;
line 5: line 2 multiplied by 0.47 to obtain figures for 1952 and 1953, and by 0.53 to obtain them for 1956. See Survey of Consumer Finances, "Housing and Durable Goods," *Federal Reserve Bulletin,* June 1957, Supplement, Table 2. To obtain a ratio for 1956 the average for early 1956 and early 1957, (that is, of 0.50 and 0.44) was used. For 1957, see above source. For 1956, "Durable Goods and Housing," *Federal Reserve Bulletin,* August 1956, Supplement, Table 20.

much smaller fraction of homeowners without mortgages have benefited from a specific deduction for taxes paid. Inasmuch as those with mortgages are presumably newer homeowners, the deduction has been consonant with the subsidy objective. Two-thirds, at the most, of nonfarm homeowners with mortgages were subsidized via the income tax in 1950, three-fourths in 1952, and four-fifths in 1953. By 1956, as we have seen, the number of returns with deductions for interest had risen to include (conceivably) nearly all homeowners with mortgage debt. The number of returns with itemized interest deductions has risen from 6 million in 1950 to 14 million in 1956, while the estimated number of mortgaged nonfarm houses rose over the same period from 9 to 14 million. For 1954 and 1956, the tax equivalents of the interest deduction, and therefore the extent of any implied subsidy, are shown below.

	Total deductible interest paid	Amount itemized, taxable returns	Tax cost to federal government	Cost to government as per cent of	
				amount itemized	total deductible
	(dollar amounts in millions)				
1954	6,346	2,985	762	25.5	12.0
1956	8,499	4,544	1,176	25.9	13.8

Comparison of the number of returns showing interest deductions with the total number of itemized returns suggests that homeowners with mortgage debt may be a sizable proportion of the total, but not so overwhelming a proportion as commonly supposed. Of 18.5 million returns with itemized deductions in 1956, 13.7 million had deductions for interest. This is three-fourths of itemized returns.[4] However, since not all returns with interest deductions are necessarily those of homeowners, the true number of returns with mortgage interest deductions is a lower percentage of the total of itemized returns.[5] There is a greater possibility that a preponderance of itemized returns with personal deductions are filed by homeowners (with or without mortgage debt), for we have also observed that 17.8 out of 18.5 million returns reported deductible taxes. Undoubtedly many of these—although how many is unknown—were returns of debt-free homeowners. But as nearly all taxpayers incur some deductible taxes, a significant number of returns may have been itemized because of other sizable personal deductions, such as philanthropic contributions or medical expenses. All we can say is that, since homeowners probably constitute a large proportion of the group that itemizes, they are also likely to be the

[4] In the $5,000 to $10,000 income group, however, the number of returns with deductible interest rose as high as 86 per cent (Table 38).

[5] Here, too, the trend has been upward. In 1950 the number of returns with interest deductions was 58 per cent of the total number itemizing; in 1953, 66 per cent deducted interest, and in 1956, 74 per cent.

major beneficiaries of personal deductions which make provision for sudden personal hardship, such as medical expenses and uninsured losses. Those who do not itemize already when personal hardship occurs must first exhaust the unused part of their standard deduction before they can benefit from the medical expense and casualty loss allowances.

Deductions by Size of Income on Tax Returns

Deductions for interest paid decline as a percentage of income above the $5,000 to $10,000 level (Table 37). This contrasts with deductions

TABLE 37

Deductions for Interest Paid as Per Cent of Income on Taxable Returns with that Deduction, by Income Groups, Selected Years, 1934-1956

INCOME GROUPa ($000's)	All Returns				Returns with Itemized Deductions Only					
	1934	1937	1939	1941	1945	1947	1949	1952	1954	19
Under 2	—	5.0	—	—	6.9	6.3	6.1	7.4	6.2	6.
2-3	—	5.7	—	—	4.7	4.8	5.0	5.8	5.2	5.
3-5	—	5.9	—	—	4.4	4.4	4.9	5.0	5.3	5.
5-10	8.1	5.7	5.4	4.3	4.0	3.7	4.4	4.5	4.9	5.
10-25b	7.0	4.8	4.5	3.5	2.9	2.8	3.3	3.7	3.9	4.
25-50b	6.0	3.9	3.6	2.7	2.3	2.4	2.5	2.7	2.8	3.
50-100	5.0	3.3	3.0	2.4	2.3	2.2	2.3	2.3	2.5	2.
100-500	4.0	2.8	2.6	1.9	2.4	2.5	2.0	2.5	3.0	3.
500 and over	3.7	3.3	1.5	1.0	1.4	1.1	1.0	1.1	1.8	2.
Average amount of interest deducted (dollars)	—	353	—	—	194	199	242	274	300	35

a Net income groups until 1943; adjusted gross income groups thereafter.

b For 1952 and 1954 the percentages are for returns in the $10-20,000 and the $20-50,000 incom groups.

taken for philanthropic contributions (larger percentages deducted at the top of the income scale than at the bottom) and for taxes paid (deductions almost proportional to income). In 1934 the decline in interest deductions was from 8 to 4 per cent; in 1941, from 4 to 1 per cent over the same income range; and in 1956, from 5 to 2 per cent. For returns with incomes below $5,000, the figures for 1937 show a slight rise in the ratio of deductible interest to income; the figures for the most recent years show declines, but this may have been caused by the standard deduction.

Since these interest payments are made in connection with various types of personal consumption, such as housing, installment purchases of durable goods, and personal expense loans, it is not surprising to find that after a certain level of income they are a declining percentage of income as income rises. The decline in proportion to income reported, however, is not duplicated in the fraction of taxpayers claiming interest deductions, which has grown larger with income up to the $5,000 to $10,000 level. Above that level the relative frequency of interest deductions declined somewhat but did not fall to the low frequency for taxpayers with incomes under $3,000 (Table 38). Between 1944

TABLE 38

mber of Taxable Returns with Deductions for Personal Interest as Per Cent of All Taxable eturns Itemizing Deductions and as Per Cent of Total, by Size of Income Reported, 1934-1956

INCOME GROUPa ($000's)	Per Cent of All Returns			Per Cent of Returns with Itemized Deductions					
	1934b	1937b	1941	1945	1947	1949	1952	1954	1956
s than 2	—	19.1	—	25.1	23.6	24.8	30.4	33.7	34.3
-3	—	27.3	—	46.1	44.2	45.7	47.1	49.2	51.3
-5	—	44.8	—	58.1	58.5	65.4	68.8	72.3	73.1
-10	53.0	51.7	51.9	60.0	59.1	70.4	80.0	83.9	85.8
-25c	57.0	55.7	53.4	49.8	50.8	59.8	69.8	74.3	79.3
-50c	60.4	60.1	55.3	47.4	48.9	53.5	58.8	63.9	64.4
-100	64.2	65.4	59.0	50.6	52.4	54.7	56.8	60.0	62.2
-500	68.2	74.8	64.8	55.7	58.8	60.2	60.9	61.7	65.6
and over	71.4	79.6	76.2	68.5	63.5	69.6	67.4	64.8	71.8
Average	—	34.0	—	45.0	47.7	57.7	67.0	72.5	76.0
	PER CENT OF TOTAL CLAIMING INTEREST								
s than 2		22.4		16.0	9.2	4.6	3.3	2.3	1.9
-3		10.8		27.4	24.2	15.3	8.5	6.6	5.3
-5		33.9		36.6	42.4	47.6	39.1	36.9	28.8
-10		21.2		12.6	16.0	24.6	40.7	45.4	52.7
-25c		8.7		5.4	6.1	5.6	5.5	6.0	9.3
-50c		2.0		1.4	1.5	1.6	2.3	2.3	1.5
-100		0.7		0.5	0.4	0.5	0.5	0.4	0.4
-500		0.3		0.1	0.1	0.2	0.1	0.1	0.1
and over		d		d	d	d	d	d	d
Totale		100.0		100.0	100.0	100.0	100.0	100.0	100.0

Net income groups until 1943; adjusted gross income groups thereafter.
Fiduciary returns included in 1934 and 1937 only.
For 1952 and 1954, group limit is $20,000 instead of $25,000.
Less than 0.05 per cent.
Total may not equal 100 because of rounding.

and 1956, there was a substantial rise in the proportion of returns with deductions for nonbusiness interest in the $5,000 to $10,000 group—from 61 to 86 per cent. For the most part this appears to be a reflection of the growth of mortgage and consumer debt in the middle income range during the postwar period.[6]

The bulge since 1944 in the relative frequency of returns with interest deductions among those itemizing in the $3,000 to $25,000 income range tells us something about the identity of "itemizers." In 1956 four out of five taxpayers in this group had interest deductions. We may take this as indirect evidence that a high proportion of those who benefit from itemizing in this middle income range are homeowners with mortgage debt.[7] The fact that over 90 per cent of those with interest deductions in 1956 reported incomes in the $3,000 to $25,000 range (Table 38) further strengthens the supposition that a large proportion of the tax returns with interest deduction are those of homeowners.

Interest Paid Out and the Income Concept

The question whether all interest, not only that incurred in the production of taxable income, should be allowed as a deduction relates to the very essence of the income concept underlying the tax. It is generally agreed that the question would not arise if the statutory concept of taxable income included consumption income derived from the ownership of property. Possession of durable consumer goods allows a short-circuit of the market economy upon which a modern income tax, based on money income, depends. Widespread avoidance of the market economy would indeed seriously undermine the possibilities for a workable income tax. Those who own durables—a residence, a washing machine, or an automobile—and consume the services of their property in preference to obtaining the same services through the market, thereby secure a tax advantage. They lower their money income if they choose to own durable consumer goods rather than a

6 See 1956 Survey of Consumer Finances, *op.cit.*, Supplementary Table 2, where the frequency of spending units with some debt is shown to rise continuously from 37 per cent of all units in the under $1,000 money income group to 76 per cent in the $7,500 to $9,999 group. For those with $10,000 and over, it drops back to 65 per cent.

7 The 1956 Survey of Consumer Finances notes that "Total debts of less than $500 were reported with greatest frequency in income brackets under $3,000. On the other hand, debts of $5,000 or more were most frequent among incomes of $7,500 and over." *Ibid.*, p. 691. Debts of that size may be presumed to be primarily mortgage debts. At the income level cited, the standard deduction is fairly high relative to the deductible expenditures that a taxpayer might have, except if he is a homeowner with debt. It seems reasonable to conclude from the high frequency of interest on returns with itemized deductions in the $3,000 to $25,000 income range that a majority of this group are homeowners.

118

financial asset of equivalent value; but they presumably also lower their money expenditures for housing, laundry services, or transportation by not obtaining equivalent services through the market. Other things remaining the same, the investor in consumer durables has lowered his money income, though not his total income, by an amount equal to the current rate of return on an investment in some financial asset. This amount escapes the income tax.[8] The two methods of consumption correspond to those of the outright owner of durable goods and the so-called renter, or pay-as-you-go consumer.

Between these two cases falls that of the debtor-owner who pays interest on the sum borrowed to obtain services from the ownership of one or more durable goods. His interest is deductible under the

[8] This applies in full only to the modern United States income tax. Since the inception of the income tax in Great Britain, the net rental value of an owner-occupied house has been imputed and included in the owner's income. It seems to have caused no great difficulties of administration. A neat summary of the British position is given by Alfred Marshall: "The Income Tax Commissioners count a dwelling house inhabited by its owner as a source of taxable income, though it yields its income of comfort directly. They do this, not on any abstract principle; but partly because of the practical importance of houseroom, partly because the ownership of a house is commonly treated in a business fashion, and partly because the real income occurring from it can easily be separated off and estimated" (*Principles of Economics*, 8th ed., London, 1938, p. 77).

The only serious attempts made in the United States to cope with the problem of rent occurred in connection with the Civil War income tax and during the early years of the Wisconsin tax. In the Civil War law a solution was attempted by permitting tenants to deduct their rent payments from income to put them on an even footing with owner-occupants, who were not required to include any imputed rentals. In 1863 the Commissioner of Internal Revenue began to argue for a more clear-cut solution. "It will, I think, contribute to fairness if the provision allowing a deduction for rent paid for dwelling-houses be stricken from the law, and that owners of such houses, residing in them, be charged with their rental value as income" (*Report of the Secretary of the Treasury on the State of the Finances for the year ending June 30, 1863*, Washington, 1863, p. 70). The Commissioner's drive was soon seconded in a report of the Special Revenue Commission of 1865, which recommended "that in assessing the income tax no allowance whatever be made for house rent, or at least that the amount allowed to be deducted for rental should not in any case be allowed to exceed three hundred dollars." The commissioners apparently had both tenants and owner-occupants in mind, but they stressed primarily the very sizable revenue losses that resulted from the "excessive and unreasonable" deductions claimed for rental payments (House Executive Documents, Vol. 7, No. 34, 39th Cong., 1st Sess., pp. 27-28; the commission consisted of David A. Wells, Stephen Colwell, and S. S. Hayes). Subsequently only the allowance for rental payments was repealed by Congress.

The Wisconsin income tax, from its inception in 1911, followed the British practice and that suggested by the Commissioner in 1863, until 1917. The provision was repealed in that year because of the difficulties encountered in obtaining an "estimated rental" figure with the then existing property tax information, and because of a widespread practice of overstating expenses, which could be offset against gross imputed rent.

income tax, which places him roughly in the same favorable tax position as the clear-owner. If his interest were not deductible he would be moved closer to the position of the renter; the thinner his equity in a residence or appliance, the smaller the disparity between borrower-owner and renter, but the greater that between borrower and clear-owner.

In the absence of imputation of a return on the equity in durable goods, the interest deduction is thus ambiguous, as recognized by at least two previous writers.[9] Because of the ambiguity, neither has come to a firm conclusion about policy in the absence of a system of income imputation. Their views, which tend toward opposite conclusions, merit analysis in our discussion of the problem.

Vickrey concludes that there is no clear-cut equity case for or against an interest deduction, but that there are other reasons making the elimination of the deduction desirable. First, with an increase of the tax base rates could be decreased correspondingly. "This may be a distinct advantage insofar as it decreases the intensity of such other inequities as cannot be eliminated and reduces the effect of the tax on incentives to production."[10] Second, abolition of the interest deduction might accelerate the further step toward complete inclusion of imputed rent and interest in the tax base.[11]

White's reasoning favors retention of the interest deductions, although he holds that the only wholly satisfactory solution would be imputation of return on durable goods to the owner-user. Indeed, for owner-occupied houses, he refrains from any recommendation for treatment of interest under the present system, concluding simply that "without the inclusion of an imputed net rental there is no clear-cut equity criterion for the treatment of mortgage interest."[12] However, when the proceeds of a loan are for the purpose of acquiring consumer goods other than houses, he considers that greater equity results

[9] See William Vickrey, *op.cit.*, pp. 22-26; and Melvin I. White, "Deductions for Nonbusiness Expenses," pp. 357-360.

[10] *Op.cit.*, pp. 23-24. In the above quotation, he was discussing mortgage interest only, but later on he clearly implied that his recommendations cover all nonbusiness interest.

[11] Earlier, Robert M. Haig, in dealing more briefly with the tax treatment of homeowners, stated a similar view: "The present position is anomalous, particularly when one remembers that such owners, while they may not deduct insurance and upkeep, may, nevertheless, deduct the taxes on the property and the interest on any money they may have borrowed to carry the property. The way to remove the anomaly is to approach the definition of income more closely in practice." See "The Concept of Income—Economic and Legal Aspects," p. 24.

[12] *Op.cit.*, p. 359.

when the interest incurred is deductible. Unlike the case for residential housing where all three categories—renters, mortgagors, and clear-owners—are significant, for other durables, particularly automobiles, "the renter population is comparatively small," and imputation impractical in most cases. Hence, by allowing the debtor-owner of an automobile a deduction for his interest paid, a significant measure of equity is achieved between the two principal types of owner-users of consumer durables. The renters, that is, the users of taxis and public transportation services and of laundry services outside the home, continue, of course, to be at a disadvantage. He argues further that interest incurred for current household expenses should be deductible. For such outlays everyone falls into the role of the renter, who pays as he consumes (uses). Of two who consume at a given level, the one with "sufficient receipts or a cash balance" from which to finance spending without borrowing has a higher income than one who does not. "Therefore," White concludes, "treatment consistent with the income concept permits the deductibility of personal interest where the funds are used for ordinary current expenses."[13]

The income concept referred to is that proposed for the income tax by Henry C. Simons, who defines income simply in terms of the dual objectives of consumption and accumulation over a specified time interval, measured in market prices.[14] White at the outset adopts that definition of income for his analysis of personal deductions. Finding it impracticable to compute directly the sum of each taxpayer's consumption and the changes in cash balances and other asset holdings, he proceeds "to translate the definition, to reformulate it in familiar accounting 'income' categories," in the manner we outlined above. For housing, automobiles, and appliances, he compares three individuals with equal incomes and assets: the "renter," the borrower-owner, and the clear-owner. Each has clearly the same income under both methods of accounting, but the mortgagor and clear-owner have

---

[13] *Ibid.*, p. 360.

[14] See note 7, Chapter 1. While Simons does not address himself to the problem of the proper treatment of interest expenses under the income tax, his forerunner Georg Schanz, who apparently influenced Simons considerably, argued—though without much explanation—for the deduction of all interest: "We include, then, in income all net proceeds and receipts in kind (*Nutzungen*), money's worth of services of third persons, all gifts, inheritances, legacies, lottery winnings, insurance settlements (*Versicherungskapitalien*), annuities, speculative gains of any kind; we exclude all interest on debts and capital losses." See "Der Einkommensbegriff und die Einkommensteuergesetze," *Finanz Archiv, XIII* (1896), p. 24; also pp. 3 and 7. (Translation ours.)

imputed incomes arising from their investments in consumer durables, which gives them an advantage under the income tax.

For cases in which debt is incurred to finance current household expense, White seems to depart from this method of comparison, and compares two individuals whose consumption is the same, but whose incomes, however defined, differ. If the source of disparity in consumption is higher "receipts or a cash balance" for person A than for B, wherein does B's disadvantage under the tax law lie? If higher receipts allow A to consume at a given level without borrowing, then the disparity is obviously taken care of under current tax law and requires no compensating interest deduction for B. But if the reason is the possession of a cash balance, then White's case appears to have more merit. It would then rest on the argument that a taxpayer who possesses a cash balance has an imputable income in the sense that he would not need to borrow at interest when in need of additional funds. But this has really no connection with the manner in which the cash balance is eventually employed.[15] The designation of this case as that of "recurrent household expenses," in which every one assumes the role of the tenant, appears somewhat beside the point. For it is the investment in a cash balance rather than in household expenses that gives rise to imputable income at present not included in the tax base. It is the fact that a taxpayer invests in a residence, from which there is no explicit monetary return, that raises an equity problem—not the fact that he borrowed for residential use.

The distinction we stress is important because White's emphasis on household expenses leads to his conclusion that in this case "everyone falls in the role of the tenant—that is, is on a pay-out-as-you-consume basis," and that the interest deduction is therefore an unambiguous correction of an inequity, whereas in the case of durables the renters were given no relief and the deduction accordingly was ambiguous. But if we apply the same frame of analysis to the cash balance case as White (and Vickrey) employed for housing and other durables, we find the same ambiguity as before. Let A, B, and C each come into the possession of $1,000. A and B invest in interest-bearing securities; C prefers to hold it as cash. Now assume B and C decide to increase their consumption temporarily by $1,000; B, rather than selling his securities, borrows $1,000 at interest, and C uses his cash

---

[15] Indeed the cash balance is employed at all times, for presumably the very act of holding it idle, with the attendant sacrifice of explicit interest return, is compensated by liquidity and a feeling of security.

balance, that is, borrows so to speak from himself. Now, by allowing B to deduct his interest payments, which he incurs on his debt, he is put on the same tax basis as C. But A, who continues to keep his $1,000 invested in securities, is now at a disadvantage. Without the interest deduction A and B are in the same position; C is favored. With the interest deduction B and C are on the same basis; A is discriminated against.

But entirely aside from the fact that it does not seem possible to achieve completely equitable treatment, through an interest deduction, between all who consume the same services with different financial arrangements, it also seems questionable whether equity within certain consumption categories is the goal to be achieved.[16] Even if we grant that for automobiles, washing machines, dishwashers, and so forth, the corresponding renter populations are comparatively small, it is not clear that a gain in equity between different types of users of long-lived appliances is one of the tests of a good income tax. It is evident that such an equity goal would widen the disparity in treatment between those whose consumption patterns do not lean toward the direct employment of capital and those who delight in the accumulation of consumer durables.[17] Nor would it be enough to show that nearly everyone owns an automobile, with or without debt; even here the interest deduction will increase the advantage of those who, with given incomes and assets, own two or three automobiles over those who own only one because they happen to prefer fine foods and the theatre to a second or third car. What seems desirable is a tax law that is neutral with respect to all consumption, rather than neutral within particular categories of consumption. The issue is thus between owners and renters in a larger sense, renters being those with relatively small investments in property that yields consumption services, and owners those with relatively large investments in such property.

As noted above, probably the major beneficiaries of the interest

[16] White is not the only one who seems to imply that equity can be achieved by treating the consumers of given services equally. Vickrey also, in passing, gives evidence of subscribing to it: "All forms of durable consumer goods give rise to an imputed income . . . although the discrimination is not so patent if the item in question is not commonly rented, and the services derived by the owner are of a type not comparable to any service commonly furnished separately." *Op.cit.*, p. 25.

[17] Essentially this point is embodied in Simons' treatment of the problem of income in kind: "The direct employment of capital is far from equally feasible for different kinds of consumption or for different people with similar consumption tastes" (*op.cit.*, p. 114). See also Donald B. Marsh, "The Taxation of Imputed Income," *Political Science Quarterly*, December 1943, p. 532.

deduction in recent years have been homeowners with mortgage interest. For this group the allowance is in effect an incentive-subsidy, which encourages home ownership over tenancy. However, we found no evidence that the law's partiality was deliberate. Congress simply did not choose to attempt a distinction between interest as a business expense and interest as a personal consumption expenditure.[18] It may be argued that the distinction is not always possible, or even valid. If the proceeds of a residential mortgage loan are used in business, the security for the loan cannot designate the interest paid as nonbusiness. A nominal business loan may be put to personal uses. A person with a business or investments in securities, when borrowing on a residence, could nominally invest his own money in a home and borrow, to repay himself, on his inventory or securities as collateral. These are difficulties which would complicate the administration of the law if personal interest expenses were disallowed as deductions. To some extent a difficulty exists even now, since personal interest cannot be deducted from gross income in arriving at adjusted gross income, but only from the latter to calculate taxable income.

One suggestion has been that deductibility of interest helps those likely to find home ownership financially most difficult—the mortgagors. Whereas home mortgagors are helped (the debt-free owners having an offsetting tax advantage through nonimputation), it does not follow that the interest deduction constitutes an effective form of assistance. For a given amount of interest the amount of the subsidy rises with rising taxpayer income, owing to the progressive rate schedule of the income tax. In addition, the data presented in Tables 37 and 38 show that the frequency and size of interest deductions have had some tendency to rise with income. For these and other reasons, some students view the deduction as a somewhat awkward instrument for encouragement of home ownership.[19]

In conclusion, the standard deduction has in some measure succeeded in counteracting the disparity in tax treatment between homeowners

[18] When the matter was debated in the Senate in 1913, Senator Cummins gave the following reply to a colleague's complaint that the law as it stood discriminated against the renter: "I think the conclusion of the Senator from Utah is correct. It is simply another illustration of the fact that the bill was composed to meet the conditions of organized business, such as merchants and manufacturers, and is not well fitted to meet the situation as it actually exists" (*Congressional Record*, 63rd Cong., 1st Sess., p. 3848).

[19] See, for instance, White, *op.cit.*, pp. 359-360.

and renters.[20] But it is only a rough and incomplete type of adjustment, and above all its effects move toward granting relief through extension of an allowance which itself appears to some as questionable. Once a deduction is found of questionable value, from the standpoint of preserving the tax base, its removal rather than its extension might be preferable.

[20] Somewhat paradoxically an argument to the contrary may, and indeed has been made, that increases in interest rates can be passed on in part to the federal government by those who itemize their deductions, but not by those who use the standard deduction. Since there is a positive relationship between the number of itemized returns and size of income, not only the rising marginal rates of income tax but also the rising proportion of itemized returns tend to result in favored treatment of high-income taxpayers (see note 13, chapter 5). However, it should be stressed that, in the case of interest, the effect of the standard deduction can be gauged only if one uses the ratio of those who itemize an interest deduction to all persons with deductible interest rather than the ratio of those who itemize to all taxpayers as proposed by J. N. Morgan. For lack of comparable data we have therefore refrained from presenting a chart for personal interest payments comparable to Chart 10 for taxes paid.

CHAPTER 7

Medical Expenses and Casualty Losses

THE medical expense allowance was added to the list of personal deductions in 1942. Its initial form has endured to the present, although its scope has been considerably enlarged. Its limits—upper and lower—make the provisions for its calculation more complex than those for the other deductions. The lower limit, or floor, is a given percentage of adjusted gross income which must be excluded from the sum of medical expenses to be deducted. The exclusion is therefore in proportion to size of income. The upper limit is a ceiling on the amount of medical expenses that can be deducted per return. The ceiling varies with the family status of the taxpayer, having a larger maximum for those with dependents.

Almost all medical and dental expenditures made on behalf of the taxpayer and his immediate family qualify for deduction. Included are payments made during the year for diagnosis, treatment, and prevention; for medical supplies, drugs, and equipment (eyeglasses, dentures, and other prosthetic devices); for hospitalization and clinical care; and premiums for accident and health insurance. To offset the inclusion of insurance premiums, only amounts not reimbursed may be included as deductions.

Quantitative Restrictions and the Rationale of the Medical Deduction

The quantitative restrictions placed on this allowance have been relaxed from time to time. Initially, 5 per cent of the taxpayer's income[1] was excluded from the medical expenses, and the maximum amount deductible was $1,250 for single persons and married persons filing separate returns, $2,500 for heads of families and married persons filing joint returns. By 1948 the deduction had evolved to a $1,250 upper limit per exemption claimed, with a maximum of $2,500 on separate returns, but the upper limit for joint returns could now reach $5,000 if there were as many as four exemptions. Beginning with 1951, the exclusion of 5 per cent of income was removed if the taxpayer,

[1] Net income (including medical expenses) before 1944; adjusted gross income from then on.

or his spouse, had reached the age of 65 (but the exclusion for medical expenses made on behalf of his dependents and the ceiling provisions remained). Recently, under the Internal Revenue code of 1954, the floor was lowered and the ceiling raised for all taxpayers. The floor was divided into two parts. For all medical, dental, and drug expenses the minimum exclusion became 3 per cent of income. But before being included with other expenses, drugs became subject to a separate floor of 1 per cent to exclude the large variety of ordinary drugstore purchases, such as bandages and aspirins, which have long been regular household expenses for American families. The floor varies at present by exclusion of between 3 and 4 per cent of income, depending on the amount spent for drugs per return. The ceilings were uniformly doubled, the upper limit now ranging from $2,500 to $10,000.

The form in which the medical deduction was cast suggests that it was intended only for taxpayers with unusually large medical expenditures in relation to their incomes. It is the only deduction for which there is strong evidence of the intent behind its enactment. On the part of the Treasury it stated: "A deduction should be allowed for extraordinary medical expenses that are in excess of a specified percentage of the family's net income. The amount allowed under such a deduction should, however, be limited to some specified maximum amount."[2] The objective appears to have been greater differentiation between taxpayers than that obtained through economic net income alone. At the same time the Treasury seems to have feared unwelcome extensions of the underlying principle, unless the deduction was confined to the unpredictable and emergency component of medical expenditures. It is not evident that the ordinary, predictable amount of such expenses, which can be budgeted like all others, affect individuals' capacity to pay taxes differently from outlays for food, clothing, and shelter. Hence, the emphasis on "extraordinary" medical expenses.[3]

[2] Statement of Randolph E. Paul at Hearings before the Committee on Ways and Means, *Revenue Revision of 1942*, 1942, 77th Cong., 2nd Sess., p. 1612.

[3] For a somewhat different point of view, see James E. Jensen, "Rationale of the Medical Expense Deduction," *National Tax Journal*, September 1954, p. 275. Jensen appears to hold that if refinement of the tax base "to correspond as closely as possible with individuals' ability to pay" is to be the objective, then "personal differences, such as medical expenses, which affect ability to pay should give rise to deductions, irrespective of the size of gross income. Of the several plans available, the full deduction plan best satisfies the differentiation objective." See also, by the same author, "Medical Expenditures and Medical Deduction Plans," *Journal of Political Economy*, December 1952, p. 504. Jensen's concept of ability to pay is not made

Of course, the mere provision of a floor is no evidence that a desire for more interpersonal equity motivated the medical deduction. A subsidy device, calculated to expand medical expenditures, could conceivably have such a feature also. Indeed, the ceiling on the amount deductible seems to contradict the interpersonal-equity rationale, for if the extraordinary, "catastrophic" element of medical expenses was to be singled out for better differentiation between taxpayers, a ceiling on the amount deductible would be in conflict with this purpose. But, judging from the words of the Treasury's spokesman at the time of enactment, a medical care subsidy through the medium of the income tax was not the primary intent. "We have to think of the revenue as well as the considerations of equity, and we do not want to open the door to a deduction for the ordinary medical expenses which go along in ordinary course in the average family. But we do think there should be some allowance, and we think of the allowance in terms of medical expenses in excess of 5 per cent of the income, but not to exceed $2,500. . . . We do not want to extend this deduction to families with chronic invalids who spend a great deal of money and perhaps enjoy their illnesses. In other words it seemed to us that $2,500 was a reasonable maximum limitation."[4] Thus the Treasury's professed interest was increased "equity,"[5] and the upper limit was proposed for administrative and revenue purposes although, as we shall see presently, the imposition of an upper limit has had only a slight effect on the amount deductible.

The minimum exclusion of 5 per cent of income, on the other hand, had a very important effect on the amount that could be deducted,

---

explicit, but it seems to require the deduction of all medical expenses. By extension, it might be necessary to add a large number of other deductions with a consequent drastic shrinkage of the tax base.

[4] *Revenue Revision of 1942*, pp. 1613, 1623.

[5] However, the Senate Finance Committee's report made no mention of such fundamental considerations. It recommended enactment "in consideration of the heavy tax burden that must be borne by individuals during the existing emergency and of the desirability of maintaining the present high level of public health and morale" (*The Revenue Bill of 1942*, Senate Report No. 1631, 77th Cong., 2nd Sess., 1942, p. 6). One may infer from this somewhat cryptic statement that the deduction was intended as a device to affect the volume of medical expenditures rather than one to refine the tax base in line with some concept of taxable income. But if a subsidy is desired, a tax credit of the type discussed in the chapter dealing with philanthropic contributions (pp. 87ff.), rather than an income offset, might be more appropriate. Such a tax credit, varying only with the size of medical expense, and not with income, has been proposed by Harold M. Groves to the President's Commission on Health Needs of the Nation (see Vol. 4 of the Commission's Report to the President, *Financing a Health Program for America*, Washington, 1953, p. 145).

and even on the distribution of the deduction by size of income. The 5 per cent floor was decided on when the data compiled by the National Resources Committee on consumer expenditures in 1935-1936 had already been well digested, and when figures from the Bureau of Labor Statistics' *Study of Family Spending and Saving in Wartime* were just appearing. It is therefore fair to assume that the general effect of the minimum exclusion on the amount and distribution of the deduction was understood from the outset. The data showed that, like expenditures for food and shelter, medical outlays rose as income rose, but not in proportion. They were generally close to 5 per cent of money income for families and single individuals with incomes below $2,000 and about 3 per cent of income for those with $5,000 and over (Table 39). The average for all groups was around 4 per cent. Since the figures showed that the percentage of income spent on medical care tends to vary inversely with income, it was fairly evident that medical hardship, as defined by the tax law, would be most likely to occur among persons in the lower part of the income distribution.

An inspection of the 1935-1936 and 1941 figures must have revealed from the start that under the new medical allowance (1) only a modest fraction of total medical expenditures would be deductible, and (2) the distribution, by size of income, of the medical deductions would differ appreciably from the distribution of medical expenditures themselves. The higher the 5 per cent exclusion relative to taxpayers' average medical expenditures, the less would be the deduction in the aggregate and the more concentrated in the lowest income groups.

The 1950 and 1952-1953 patterns were similar to those for the earlier years. The increase in medical expenditure continued to be in lower proportion than the increase in income, but the percentage of income spent for medical care in given income groups appears to have been much higher than before. As we see from the table, however, the rise in medical outlays at given income levels was greatly offset by the upward shift in incomes, which had taken place in the intervening years. For example, the group with less than $2,000 per annum is reported to have spent almost 12 per cent of its income for medical care in 1952-1953, as against roughly 5 per cent in the years before 1950. But it also comprised only one-fifth of the reporting units, as against two-thirds a decade earlier. The same is more clearly shown in Table 40, where families and single individuals are ranked by quintiles rather than by income groups with fixed class limits. The amount spent for

TABLE 39

Per Cent of Consumer Money Income Spent for Medical Care,
by Income Groups, 1935-1936, 1941, 1950, and 1952-1953

MONEY INCOME ($000's)	Medical Expense as Per Cent of Income (1)	Per Cent of Families and Single Individuals in Income Group (2)
1935-1936 (NATIONAL RESOURCES COMMITTEE)		
Under 1	5.2 ⎫	53.0 ⎫
1-2	4.3 ⎬ 4.7	31.0 ⎬ 84.0
2-3	4.3	9.7
3-5	4.1	4.0
5 and over	3.2	2.3
All Groups	4.0	100.0
1941 (BUREAU OF LABOR STATISTICS)		
Under 1	7.5 ⎫	33.9 ⎫
1-2	5.0 ⎬ 5.6	30.5 ⎬ 64.4
2-3	4.2	21.1
3-5	4.1	10.5
5 and over	2.7	4.0
All Groups	4.3	100.0
1950 (BLS—WHARTON SCHOOL: URBAN U.S.)[a]		
Under 2	7.5	18.6
2-3	5.4	18.7
3-5	5.0	40.9
5-10	4.2	19.4
10 and over	2.4	2.4
All Groups	4.6	100.0

1952-1953 (ANDERSON-FELDMAN)

MONEY INCOME ($000's)	Based on Totals	Median Percentages	
Under 2	11.8	6.2	19
2-3.5	6.1	4.0	22
3.5-5	5.4	3.9	24
5-7.5	4.7	3.6	21
7.5 and over	3.0	3.3[b]	13
All Groups	4.8	4.1	99[c]

[a] The percentages for 1950 are for net money income before tax, but are arrayed by net money income after tax.

[b] Because the exact incomes of families whose stated incomes were greater than $10,000 was not available, the income of each family in this group was taken to be $10,000 for this computation. The median presented for the $7,500-and-over group may conceivably be one-half of 1 per cent too high, "although the actual error is probably smaller than that." The median for all units is not likely to be too high by more than one-tenth of 1 per cent. See Anderson, *op.cit.*, p. 115.

[c] Income of 1 per cent of units unknown.

Source, by dates

1935-1936: National Resources Committee data, adjusted for comparability with

1941 BLS data (see Bureau of Labor Statistics, *Family Spending and Saving in War-time*, Bulletin No. 822, Washington, 1945, p. 201).
1941: Bureau of Labor Statistics, *op.cit.*, pp. 68-75.
1950: Wharton School of Finance and Commerce, *Study of Consumer Expenditures, Incomes and Savings*, Vols. xi, xvi, University of Pennsylvania, 1956. The sample distributions of families by income groups for nine classes of cities were blown up to correspond to the estimated total urban population in the nine classes of cities as given in Vol. xi, p. xiii.
1952-1953: Odin W. Anderson with Jacob J. Feldman, *Family Medical Costs and Voluntary Health Insurance: A Nationwide Survey*, New York, 1956, pp. 114, 231.

medical care by all groups rose from 4.3 per cent of income in the 1941 survey to only 4.8 per cent in the 1952-1953 survey. Since the surveys were conducted under different auspices and with some differences in technique and concepts, we are not in a position to say that the figures in Table 39 indicate an upward trend.[6] In short, the percentage of

TABLE 40

Per Cent of Consumer Money Income Spent for Medical Care, by Quintiles of Consumer Units, 1935-1936, 1941, 1950, and 1952-1953

QUINTILES	1935-1936	1941a	1950	1952-1953
Lowest	6.9	12.9	7.3	11.6
Second	5.1	5.3	5.4	6.5
Third	4.5	5.0	5.3	5.4
Fourth	4.3	4.3	4.7	4.9
Highest	3.9	3.4	3.7	3.4
Total	4.0	4.3	4.6	4.8

a When negative income recipients are excluded for 1941 the percentages are as follows:

Lowest	7.9
Second	5.3
Third	5.0
Fourth	4.3
Highest	3.4
Total	4.2

Source: Same as Table 39 for 1935-1936, 1941 and 1950. For 1952-1953 the figures are not strictly comparable to those in Table 39. To obtain estimates by quintiles, the incomes of families in each income group had to be estimated. This was done by dividing mean gross medical charges as given by Anderson and Feldman (*op.cit.*), in Table A-15 by the ratio of medical outlay to income in Table A-16. The income figures thus obtained are only approximately correct.

[6] Other estimates of total personal medical care expenditures, such as that made by the Department of Commerce as part of the Personal Consumption Expenditure series, suggest that there has been no upward trend in direct personal medical care expenditures relative to income over the past quarter-century. See Table 45 and note 24 below. Louis J. Paradiso and Clement Winston have found that for the years 1947-1954 medical care and burial expenditures of consumers have, on average, varied in proportion to changes in disposable personal income (see "Consumer Expenditure-Income Patterns," *Survey of Current Business*, September 1955, p. 29).

income spent for medical care in any one (current dollar) income group has risen, but the distribution of income has shifted upward as well, and the over-all ratio of medical expenditures to income has not changed much. The first fact is probably strongly connected with the second and third: the decade separating the 1941 and 1952-1953 data was one of inflationary price rises. The cost of medical care goes up with other costs during inflation. Hence, for persons in the same income group at the beginning and at the end of the period, the ratio of medical expenditures to income is likely to rise.

Had medical expenditures not risen in proportion to incomes, the percentage exclusion would probably have lowered progressively the fraction of the public's total medical expenses that could be deducted. That lowering has so far not occurred, as we shall see later. If it should occur over a sustained period of time, the question of periodic downward revisions of the percentage exclusion (that is, the standard of medical hardship) would probably arise.

Even without a decline in the over-all ratio, there were nevertheless strong popular demands in the early 1950's to lower the percentage exclusion. In part the demands may have arisen from the realization, during a decade of experience, that while the exclusion was only a little above the ratio of average expenditures to income, the unequal distribution of medical expenditures left many more taxpayers' medical outlays below the exclusion than the ratio of average expenditures to income might suggest. This is illustrated by the juxtaposition in Table 39 of median percentages and percentages based on total expenditures and income for 1952-1953. One-half of consumer units in the survey reported medical expenses under 4 per cent of their income while total outlays were 4.8 per cent of total income.[7] These facts were, of course, not necessarily out of line with the aim of the deduction, which was presumably to make allowance for "extraordinary" expenses. Yet the deduction's adequacy is largely a matter of opinion, and both the House and Senate committees concerned found "general agreement that limiting the deduction only to expenses in excess of 5 per

[7] The same is also suggested by the statistics discussed below, showing that in 1956 18 per cent of all tax returns reported medical expenses amounting to 46 per cent of the Commerce Department's estimate of personal medical care outlays for that year (Tables 42 and 43). Emily H. Huntington, in a study entitled *Cost of Medical Care: The Expenditures for Medical Care of 455 Families in the San Francisco Bay Area, 1947-1948* (University of California Press, 1951), notes that for the 455 urban families surveyed, medical and dental expenditures were on average 7.6 per cent of income and the corresponding median percentage 5.5 per cent.

cent of adjusted gross income does not allow the deduction of all 'extraordinary' medical expenses."[8] Previously, in his budget message of January 1954, President Eisenhower had urged Congress to lower the minimum exclusion. "The present tax allowance for unusual medical expenses is too limited to cover the many tragic emergencies which occur in too many families. I recommend that a tax allowance be given for medical expenses in excess of 3 per cent of income instead of 5 per cent as at present."[9]

Three years earlier the floor had been removed entirely for a taxpayer and his spouse if either had reached the age of 65. The reasons for this move were the generally lowered earning capacity and increased medical expenses of people aged 65 and over. Therefore, it was thought that the percentage exclusion would accentuate their hardship.[10] Some may question, with Pechman,[11] whether our system of differentiating tax liabilities on the basis of income and personal exemptions does not adequately reflect any existing differences between older and younger persons' ability to pay taxes. It is true that older persons tend to have lower incomes than others, but size of income is automatically taken into account by a progressive rate schedule (and some may argue even by a flat rate income tax!). Above-average medical expenses are also allowed for, in the type of deduction available to all taxpayers. One may indeed argue that if the aged have much higher medical expenses than the rest of the population, the removal of the ceiling rather than the floor provision might be more appropriate. On the other hand, one may defend the removal of the floor for the aged, on the ground that even with incomes comparable to those of younger persons, the aged operate under peculiar handicaps: their prospects for income and ability to recuperate from illness are less favorable, and they find it frequently more difficult than younger persons to obtain medical insurance.[12]

[8] *Internal Revenue code of 1954*, House Report 1337 to accompany H.R. 8300, 83rd Cong., 2nd Sess., March 9, 1954, p. 20.

[9] *The President's Budget Message for 1955*, Washington, 1954, p. 17.

[10] See Senate Report 781, *The Revenue Act of 1951*, 82nd Cong., 1st Sess., 1951, p. 51.

[11] Joseph A. Pechman, "Individual Income Tax Provisions of the 1954 Code," *National Tax Journal*, March 1955, p. 122.

[12] "Persons 65 years of age and over are hospitalized more often than any other age group (except females 18 to 34), and they stay in the hospital longer. At the same time it is difficult for them to obtain insurance because of their age." Odin W. Anderson with Jacob J. Feldman, *Family Medical Costs and Voluntary Health Insurance: A Nationwide Survey*, New York, 1956, p. 88.

Finally, we have to consider that taxpayers with health insurance tend to get relatively less benefit from the medical deduction than those without, their precise position varying with the breadth and amount of insurance coverage.[13] The insured benefit less from the deduction because their medical outlays tend to be less erratic than those of the uninsured. The percentage exclusion was intended to make allowance for the erratic element in medical expenses. For the year 1956, data show that 70 per cent of the United States population was covered by some voluntary hospital insurance, 61 per cent by some surgical-services insurance, and 39 per cent by some medical-services insurance.[14] Among the family units in the survey for 1953 (Anderson and Feldman, sponsored by the Health Information Foundation), 41 per cent of those with income under $3,000 were enrolled in some kind of health insurance, but the proportion rose to 71 per cent for those with $3,000 to $5,000, and to 80 per cent for those with $5,000 and over.[15] Of the total amount of medical expenses incurred during 1955, an estimated 22 per cent was covered by insurance benefits.[16] While not a large proportion, all signs point toward a higher rate currently and continued growth in future years. Furthermore, the 22 per cent figure just cited probably somewhat understates the importance of the overlap between insurance benefits and the medical deduction, since a large part of these benefits are paid for the so-called extraordinary medical expenses for which most insurance plans, as well as the medical deduction, are designed.

There is, however, another aspect of the relation between insurance and the deduction. It has been found that for given income levels the

[13] The deductibility, without limitation, of all costs of voluntary health insurance plans received considerable support during the House Ways and Means Committee Hearings on the Revenue act of 1954. (See Hearings before the Committee on Ways and Means, *General Revenue Revision*, 83rd Cong., 1st Sess., Part 1, 1953.) Representatives Oliver P. Bolton (p. 79), Robert W. Kean (p. 81), Paul B. Dague (p. 82), and Kenneth B. Keating (pp. 117ff.) each made strong pleas for complete deductibility of health insurance premiums on the ground that it would be an effective answer to demands for a compulsory health insurance program. Representative Keating introduced a bill to provide an offset against tax liability itself, on a sliding scale, for voluntary insurance premiums paid. The general tenor of the hearings was in favor of liberalization of the medical deduction in the direction of a subsidy, rather than a device to relieve extraordinary medical expenses of those who find it temporarily difficult to carry their ordinary share of the tax load.

[14] *Statistical Abstract of the U.S., 1958*, p. 481.

[15] Anderson with Feldman, *op.cit.*, Tables A-1 and A-4.

[16] See Health Insurance Council, *The Extent of Voluntary Health Insurance Coverage in the United States*, October 1956, p. 27. Benefit payments for 1955 are given as $2,530 million, or 22 per cent of the total shown in Table 41.

insured generally incur higher medical expenses (including reimbursed expenses but excluding premium payments) than the noninsured. Thus it is possible—though we possess no adequate information[17]—that the insured at given income levels obtain as large an absolute amount of medical deduction (although a smaller proportion of total expenditures) as the noninsured. This follows from the deliberate bias of the deduction in favor of medical expenses that are large relative to income, whereas medical insurance tends to even out an individual's or family's medical outlays over time. In its treatment of medical insurance, the Canadian income tax law excludes premium payments from deduction, but allows deduction of insurance benefits paid to the insured. This automatically evens the advantage in deduction between insured and uninsured taxpayers. A revenue problem may be created by insurance plans that provide full coverage for some or all types of medical expenditures. Deductibility would then encourage the taxpayer to incur medical bills as large as possible.

[17] The survey conducted by Anderson and Feldman shows, by income groups, that average medical expenses are larger for families with some health insurance than for those without insurance (*op.cit.*, Tables A-15 and A-16). Insurance benefits as per cent of gross medical charges (all charges incurred for hospital, medical, and dental services and goods, but excluding costs of voluntary health insurance) for families who received insurance benefits averaged 52 per cent in 1952-1953 for families with incomes under $2,000, and 30 per cent for those with incomes over $7,500 (Table A-72). However, information on the size of this groups' gross medical charges is not given, nor would this information, in the absence of data on the cost of insurance for those families, give an adequate idea of the size of their possible medical deductions.

A study by Emily H. Huntington of expenditures of salaried workers in the San Francisco Bay area in 1950 (*Spending of Middle Income Families*, University of California Press, 1957) suggests that among those who had medical care expenditures in connection with hospitalization, the amount paid for such care by individuals, aside from insurance premiums, if any, was on average considerably lower for the insured than the uninsured. But figures for expenditures for nonhospitalized care, suggest the opposite comparison: the cost of care not paid for by prepayment plans was generally greater for those with insurance than for those without. Huntington's figures are not sufficiently refined by size of income (though they are for middle-income salaried families), nor sufficiently representative geographically and occupationally, to support more than a vague surmise on the effect of insurance on the pattern of medical deductions. Thus tentatively, the figures suggest that, for illnesses involving hospitalization, the insured are less likely to be able to claim medical deductions than the uninsured, but for nonhospitalized medical care, the insured have an equal or better chance for deductions (see Huntington, pp. 125-131, particularly Tables 67-69).

Further relevant information is presented by George A. Shipman and others in an unpublished study of medical service corporations in the state of Washington (sponsored by the Health Information Foundation). The data, from a sample survey of insured rural and urban families in two Washington counties for 1956, suggest that families and individuals tend to spend more "out of pocket" for health goods and services, the higher their premium payments.

Some writers on the subject have looked on the medical deduction as something akin to a social health insurance scheme, a protection within the income tax framework against involuntary risk, similar to the deduction allowed for casualty losses.[18] The higher taxes, incurred in years when taxpayers can claim no commensurate deductions, may be viewed as premiums, and the tax reduction obtained when a deduction can be claimed may be likened to benefit payments. Of course, the fact that some taxpayers pay "premiums," that is, higher taxes, without much likelihood of receiving direct benefits, makes the medical deduction an insurance plan with a subsidy element. Those who do not purchase available private medical insurance may benefit at the expense of those who do.

Briefly, the medical deduction allowance as now constituted appears to favor those over 65 years old, those with relatively low incomes, and those with little or no insurance—three groups that overlap considerably. A qualification for all three groups is the standard deduction. Those who can claim significant amounts for other deductible expenses are more likely to be able to claim medical deductions than are those who cannot. Evidence on this relationship will be presented in the next section.

Trend in Medical Deductions, 1942-1956

Personal medical care expenses, as estimated by the Department of Commerce, have risen from $3.7 billion in 1942 to $12.1 billion in 1956.[19] Of the 1942 total, $0.7 billion, or 18 per cent, was reported

---

[18] White, for instance (op.cit., pp. 362-63), considers the medical expense and casualty loss deductions a reflection of society's dual concern with risk: protection of persons and property against the involuntary risk of loss from sudden, unforeseen illness and destruction; and protection of the rewards, often spectacularly high, resulting from voluntary risk taking. See also Jensen, "Medical Expenditures," p. 503. Jensen notes that "a full medical deduction at the federal level would achieve partial compulsory health insurance without inciting the controversy aroused by the latter proposal." Comparison of the medical deduction with the casualty loss deduction is discussed in the last section of this chapter.

[19] The Department of Commerce estimates of total medical care expenses of consumers are used in Tables 41 and 42 as rough approximations of medical expenses in the deductible category. They include some outlays not made by consumers themselves, such as payments by government and philanthropy for hospital care and employer contributions to insurance. Herbert E. Klarman, taking these items into account, obtained estimates of $9.3 for 1953 and $9.5 billion for 1954, compared to $10 and $10.6 billion in our tables. (See Klarman, "Changing Costs of Medical Care and Voluntary Health Insurance," Journal of Insurance, September 1957, pp. 23-41.) On the other hand the tax return concept of medical expense is in some ways considerably more liberal than that underlying the Commerce estimates, as for instance the

as deductions on all tax returns, and $3.5 billion, or 29 per cent, in 1956. From 1942 to 1950, the last year before the percentage exclusion was abolished for those over 65 years of age, the amount deducted on all returns fluctuated between 17 and 20 per cent of the estimated total (Table 41). By 1952 and 1953 it had risen to 23 and 24 per cent,

TABLE 41

Estimated Total Deductible Medical Expenses and Amounts
Deducted on Tax Returns, 1942-1956
(dollars in millions)

	Total *Deductible* (1)	*Amounts Deducted on*		*Amount Deducted as* *Per Cent of Total*	
AR		*Taxable* *Returns* (2)	*All Returns* (3)	(2) ÷ (1) (4)	(3) ÷ (1) (5)
42	3,735	534	656	14.3	17.6
43	4,189	773	800	18.5	19.1
44	4,705	722	803	15.3	17.1
45	5,042	836	936	16.6	18.6
46	6,104	906	1,100	14.8	18.0
47	6,817	1,156	1,398	17.0	20.5
48	7,385	1,040	1,304	14.1	17.7
49	7,702	1,170	1,488	15.2	19.3
50	8,276	1,260	1,560	15.2	18.9
51	8,780	n.a.	n.a.	—	—
52	9,397	1,843	2,138	19.6	22.8
53	10,107	2,043	2,397	20.2	23.7
54	10,603	2,482	2,975	23.4	28.1
55	11,273	n.a.	n.a.	—	—
56	12,106	2,993	3,473	24.7	28.7

Source, by column

(1) Department of Commerce, *Survey of Current Business.*
(2) and (3) U.S. Treasury Department, *Statistics of Income* for years 1942 to 1956.

respectively. The lowering of the floor for the medical expense deduction by the 1954 Revenue act further increased the amounts deducted to 28 per cent of the total. The above percentages suggest that of the increase in medical deductions, from $1.56 billion in 1950 to $2.14 billion in 1952,[20] about $350 million was due to the additional allowance for those over 65.

The $3.5 billion claimed as medical deductions in 1956 may be viewed in one sense as a federal government participation of $700

---

inclusion of transportation costs to and from clinics and physicians. The direction of bias in the figures we use below is thus difficult to assess.

20 No data were tabulated for 1951.

million in private medical expenditures via the income tax. Roughly 90 per cent of this amount was for so-called expenses of extraordinary size (that is, expenses exceeding the floor), and about 10 per cent constituted participation in the ordinary expenses of taxpayers over 65 years old, that is, the expenses of the aged which did not exceed the 3 per cent floor.[21]

The data in Table 41 show the relationship between medical deductions and estimated total personal medical expenses of all individuals. Since the deductions are only those medical expenses that fell between the floor and ceiling, the table does not tell us the total medical expenses of those who received tax abatements. The total is approximated in Table 42. For 1942-1953, only the amounts below the floor were included since there was too little information on amounts above the ceiling, except for 1949. Figures for that year indicate that the amounts shown in Table 42 would have been only 1 per cent higher without the ceiling for 1948-1950.[22] In contrast, the amounts

[21] A breakdown of the $2,993 million of medical deductions on taxable returns, in millions of dollars, follows:

| | Itemizers' Medical | | Tax Cost to Government | Percentage Cost to Government |
	Expenditures (1)	Deductions (2)	(3)	(3) ÷ (1) (4)
Taxpayers under 65	4,381	2,542	567	12.9
Taxpayers over 65	542	452	133	24.5
	4,923	2,993	699	14.2

Of the $452 million deducted by taxpayers over 65, medical expenses of ordinary size amounted at most to 3 per cent of the adjusted gross income of those taxpayers, giving us this possible breakdown for taxpayers over 65, in millions of dollars:

| | Itemizers' Medical | | Tax Cost to Government | Percentage Cost to Government |
	Expenditures (1)	Deductions (2)	(3)	(3) ÷ (1) (4)
Ordinary size	262	228	82	31.3
Extraordinary size	280	223	50	17.9
	542	452	133	25.5

Thus at most $82 million, out of $699 million, was the tax cost to the government of the deductions representing ordinary sized medical expenses of the aged. Since not all the aged who itemized medical expenses actually had deductions equal to 3 per cent of their income, our estimate overstates their ordinary sized deductions and understates their extraordinary sized ones. We can therefore say with some confidence that not more than one-tenth of the total estimated tax cost of the medical allowance arises from exemption of the aged from the 3 per cent exclusion.

[22] As shown in Table 50 below, 1 per cent of those with medical deductions had expenses equal to, or exceeding, the upper limit in 1949 according to data in *Statistics of Income* for 1949. Jensen's data for Wisconsin (*op.cit.*, p. 510), also for 1949,

TABLE 42

Estimated Amount of Medical Expenses of Individuals Claiming Deductions
Compared to Total Amount Deductible, 1942-1956
(*dollars in millions*)

| YEAR | Total Deductible (1) | Medical Expenses[a] of Those Reporting on | | Per Cent of Total | |
		Taxable Returns (2)	All Returns (3)	(2) ÷ (1) (4)	(3) ÷ (1) (5)
)42	3,735	944	1,102	25.3	29.5
)43	4,189	1,393	1,415	33.3	33.8
)44	4,705	1,161	1,253	24.7	26.6
)45	5,042	1,329	1,442	26.4	28.6
)46	6,104	1,462	1,705	24.0	27.9
)47	6,817	1,875	2,174	27.5	31.9
)48	7,385	1,740	2,079	23.6	28.2
)49	7,702	1,957	2,356	25.4	30.6
)50	8,276	2,148	2,530	26.0	30.6
)51	8,780	n.a.	n.a.	—	—
)52	9,397	3,024	3,379	32.2	36.0
)53	10,107	3,428	3,848	33.9	38.1
)54	10,603	3,873	4,470	36.5	42.2
)55	11,273	n.a.	n.a.	—	—
)56	12,106	4,923	5,505	40.7	45.5

[a] Estimated by adding to the amounts shown in Table 41 the equivalent of 5 per cent of the income reported on returns with medical deductions for years before 1954. For 1952 and 1953, the 5 per cent exclusion applied only to taxpayers below 65 years of age, and therefore the correction was made on the basis of the estimated income of only that group. No adjustment was made for medical expenses that exceeded the upper limit for the years 1942-1953, so that strictly speaking the heading for those years should read "medical expense below upper limits, etc." On the basis of Wisconsin data for 1949, the totals shown above for the years 1948-1950 would be raised by only 1.2 per cent in the absence of the upper limit. See Jensen, "Medical Expenditures and Medical Deduction Plans," *Journal of Political Economy*, December 1952, p. 510. For 1954 the figures are as given in *Statistics of Income*. For 1956, drug expenses as reported in *Statistics of Income* do not include expenses of less than 1 per cent of AGI. The amount was therefore estimated n the basis of 1954 data, and this figure is included in the totals shown above.

below the floor accounted for well over one-third of the medical expenses of taxpayers claiming the deduction (Table 43). So estimated, the amount of medical expenses incurred by those able to claim a deduction came to 30 per cent of the aggregate in 1942, 31 per cent in 1950, and upwards of 45 per cent in 1956. These are sizeable percentages when we consider that those who claimed the deduction had to over-

show that after correction for the upper limit the expenditure figures in columns 2 and 3 of Table 42 would be raised by only 1.2 per cent. This would raise the medical expenses of those reporting on all returns in 1949 from 30.6 to 31 per cent of the total. The same approximate relationship holds for the other years. This is suggested by the figures for 1956, shown in Table 47. In that year the amount above the ceiling was 1.8 per cent of the amount reported below the ceiling.

come the barrier of the standard deduction as well as that of the floor. In fact, the impediment of the standard deduction was greatest in the income range where the floor alone would have been less an obstacle than at higher ranges.

The combination of these two percentage exclusions, moreover,

TABLE 43

Ratio of Deductions for Medical Expenses to Estimated Total Medical Expenses of Individuals Claiming the Deduction, 1942-1956

| | Amount Deducted as Per Cent of Total | |
| | Taxable Returns | All Returns |
YEAR	(1)	(2)
1942	56.6	59.5
1943	55.5	56.5
1944	62.2	64.1
1945	62.9	64.9
1946	62.0	64.5
1947	61.7	64.3
1948	59.8	62.7
1949	59.8	63.2
1950	58.7	61.7
1951	—	—
1952	60.9	63.3
1953	59.6	62.3
1954	64.1	66.6
1955	—	—
1956	60.8	63.1

Source, by column
(1) Column 2, Table 41 ÷ column 2, Table 42.
(2) Column 3, Table 41 ÷ column 3, Table 42.

makes it difficult to predict a priori the incidence of the medical deduction by size of medical expense. As we have seen, the medical deduction was designed for taxpayers whose medical expenses are large relative to their income, not necessarily to those with large absolute medical expenses. Moreover, the standard deduction prevents many with relatively and absolutely large medical expenses from claiming the deduction for lack of other deductible expenses. This makes it the more significant that what was evidently a small percentage of the population—the taxpayers with medical deductions—reported a large share of total private medical expenses. We estimate that for 1950 medical expenses equal to 31 per cent of the total were reported on 9 per cent of all tax returns filed; for 1956 (with the greatly reduced floor provision in effect) 46 per cent of the total were reported on 18 per cent of the returns filed (Tables 42 and 44). This is a rough, though adequate, indication that on average medical expenditures were much higher for the group claiming the deduction than for the population as a whole.[23] That recent changes in the floor provision, and its aboli-

TABLE 44

Number of Tax Returns with Itemized Medical Expense Deduction as Per Cent of All Tax Returns, 1942-1956

YEAR	Taxable (1)	All Returns (2)
1942	12.0	10.5
1943	11.8	11.1
1944	7.1	6.9
1945	7.8	7.2
1946	8.9	7.4
1947	10.0	8.7
1948	9.5	7.9
1949	10.8	8.9
1950	10.8	9.2
1951	—	—
1952	13.2	11.4
1953	14.4	12.5
1954	17.9	15.2
1955	—	—
1956	20.7	17.9

Source: *Statistics of Income.*

tion for the aged, have made deductions available to persons with relatively smaller medical expenditures than before, is borne out by the fact that the fraction of those with medical deduction doubled, from 9 to 18 per cent, whereas the fraction of medical expenditures thus covered rose from only 31 to 46 per cent. That is, the additional

[23] The inference is somewhat strengthened if we consider that the group taking the deduction is an even smaller percentage of the total population than of the tax return universe. On the other hand, not all families (or single persons) have medical expenses in a given year, as we seem to imply above. The tax return population was 89 per cent of the total United States civilian population in 1950 and 94 per cent in 1952. According to the survey for 1952-1953 by Anderson and Feldman (*op.cit.*, p. 135), 5 per cent of families and single individuals had no net medical expenses (after insurance benefits) in that period. Similarly, the Bureau of Labor Statistics' 1950 survey of urban consumer units shows about 4 per cent of the units reporting no medical care expenditures (Wharton School of Finance and Commerce, University of Pennsylvania, *Study of Consumer Expenditures, Incomes and Savings, 1950*, University of Pennsylvania Press, 1956, Vol. VIII, p. 3). These facts modify, but do not alter materially, the relationships cited in the text.

9 per cent of returns added only 15 per cent of total medical expenditures.

Table 45 shows the size of medical expenses relative to income. Nationwide personal medical expenses have been about 4 per cent of income since 1946 and slightly less in the four earlier years (Chart 13).[24] Medical deductions on tax returns have been between 6 and 9

TABLE 45

Medical Expenses as Per Cent of Income, 1942-1956
(dollars in billions)

YEAR	Total Adjusted Gross Income (1)	Total Medical Expense as Per Cent of Total AGI (2)	AGI Reported on Returns With Medical Deduction (3)	Medical Expense of Taxpayers as Per Cent of AGI (3)	
				Deducted (4)	Total (5)
1942	107.2	3.5	9.6	6.8	11.5
1943	129.0	3.2	12.8	6.2	11.1
1944	137.5	3.4	9.0	8.9	13.9
1945	140.2	3.6	10.1	9.3	14.3
1946	156.1	3.9	12.1	9.1	14.1
1947	171.6	4.0	15.5	9.0	14.0
1948	184.8	4.0	15.5	8.4	13.4
1949	184.3	4.2	17.4	8.6	13.5
1950	201.4	4.1	19.4	8.0	13.0
1951	226.6	3.9	—	—	—
1952	240.6	3.9	31.6	6.8	10.7
1953	254.4	4.0	36.1	6.6	10.7
1954	253.0	4.2	45.8	6.5	9.8
1955	272.7	4.1	—	—	—
1956	292.5	4.1	61.6	5.6	8.9

Source, by column

(1) Department of Commerce personal income figures adjusted for differences in concept.

(2) Column 1, Table 41 ÷ column 1 of this table.

(3) 1944-1950, 1954, and 1956 from Statistics of Income. 1942-1943 and 1952-1953 are our estimates obtained by multiplying average AGI of all taxpayers in each income class by the number of returns with medical deductions.

(4) Column 3, Table 41 ÷ column 3.

(5) Column 3, Table 42 ÷ column 3.

per cent of the income reported by those claiming the deductions. But total medical expenses of this group have been over one-tenth of its income in every year before 1954. In the period 1944-1947 total

[24] There was, however, no upward trend in personal medical expenditures relative to income. Medical care expenditures were well over 4 per cent of income during the latter half of the 1930's (for example, 4.3 per cent of adjusted gross income in 1936) and apparently declined only during the war years.

expenses were as high as 14 per cent of income, while the amounts actually deducted were 9 per cent in each of those four years. In 1948, when income-splitting between spouses was inaugurated and the ceil-

CHART 13

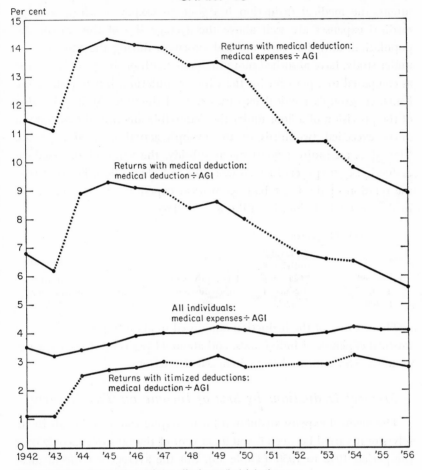

Per cent

Returns with medical deduction:
medical expenses ÷ AGI

Returns with medical deduction:
medical deduction ÷ AGI

All individuals:
medical expenses ÷ AGI

Returns with itimized deductions:
medical deduction ÷ AGI

Note: Dotted lines indicate changes in law affecting medical deduction.
Source: Table 45 and bottom line from column (3) Table 41 ÷ column (5) Table 13.

Medical Deductions and Expenses as Per Cent of Adjusted Gross Income, 1942-1956

ing on the standard deduction raised from $500 to $1,000, the ratios fell to a slightly lower level. For the three years 1948-1950 medical expenses were somewhat above 13 per cent of income of the group itemizing them, and the corresponding medical deductions exceeded 8 per cent of income. When, in 1951, the minimum exclusion for the aged was removed, there was another decline in the ratios reflecting the addition of taxpayers with medical expenses of ordinary size. By 1956 medical expenses were 9 per cent, and the deductions less than 6 per cent of the income of taxpayers with medical deductions.

The figures in Tables 42 to 45 show that, in line with the provision's intent, the medical deduction has gone to taxpayers whose average medical expenses are well above the average size of the rest of the population, and that such medical expenses, during the fifteen years under study, have absorbed more than one-tenth of the group's income as compared to 4 per cent for the whole population. But not all of the benefited group's medical expenses were deductible. Mainly because of the provision of a floor under the deductible amount, the deduction never exceeded two-thirds of the group's actual medical expenses. Viewed as an indirect government subsidy, the value of the medical deduction to taxpayers in 1956 was close to $700 million. For that year the relation of the tax rebate to medical expenditures is summarized in the next tabulation, in millions of dollars.

Medical Expenses			Tax Equivalent as per cent of:	
	Of taxable Individuals			
Estimated total	Claiming Deduction	Tax Equivalent of Deduction	Total	Expenditures of claimants
12,106	4,923	699	5.8	14.2

The tax cost of the deduction amounted to about 6 per cent of total medical expenses of individuals, and about 14 per cent of the expenses of those who benefited from itemized deductions.

Medical Deductions by Size of Income on Tax Returns

The medical expense deduction for taxpayers who could avail themselves of it varied between 6 and 9 per cent of that group's income over the period 1942 to 1956 (Table 45). But the average for the medical allowance gives less indication than that for any of the three previously discussed deductions of how taxpayers fare at various levels of income. As Table 46 shows, the differences are striking. On returns with a medical deduction and less than $2,000 income, the deduction has been well over 10 per cent of income in all years, except 1942. Moving up the income scale, the decline in the percentages has been smooth and steep. In the $5,000 to $10,000 income range the deduction has been close to 5 per cent of income in recent years; in the

$50,000 to $100,000 income group it has been less than 3 per cent; and for incomes over $100,000 it has been less than 1 per cent.

On the low income returns the deduction has been a relatively large proportion of a taxpayer's total medical expense. As the income scale

TABLE 46

Medical Deduction as Per Cent of Income on Taxable Returns with That Deduction, by Income Groups, Selected Years, 1942-1956

INCOME GROUP[a] ($000's)	1942[b]	1945	1947	1949	1952[b]	1953[b]	1954	1956
Under 2	8.7	12.4	12.2	11.7	12.9	12.6	11.3	11.7
2-3	5.5	9.4	9.5	9.7	9.7	10.0	9.7	9.3
3-5	4.5	7.5	7.7	7.2	7.2	7.1	7.0	6.7
5-10	5.1	7.0	6.9	6.8	5.6	5.3	5.3	4.6
10-25[c]	4.5	5.4	5.5	6.3	5.5	5.3	5.0	4.4
25-50[c]	3.0	3.5	3.6	4.4	3.5	3.5	3.8	3.5
50-100	1.8	2.2	2.2	2.9	1.8	1.8	2.3	2.2
100-500	1.0	0.9	1.0	1.4	0.8	0.8	1.1	1.0
500 and over	0.1	0.1	0.4	0.3	0.1	0.1	0.2	0.2
Average	6.1	8.5	8.0	7.4	6.2	6.0	5.7	5.1

a Net income groups for 1942; adjusted gross income groups for all other years.
b For 1942, 1952, and 1953, the income of taxpayers with medical deductions was computed by multiplying the average income reported on all returns with itemized deductions in a given income group by the frequency of returns with medical deduction in that group. A slight downward bias in the percentages shown in the table resulted from this method. Thus had computed, instead of actual, incomes been used for 1947, 1949, and 1954, the average percentages would have been 7.9, 7.2, and 5.7, respectively.
c Income groups are $10-20,000 and $20-50,000 in 1952, 1953, and 1954.

rises, the proportion declines. In Table 47 estimates by income groups of the total medical expenses of taxpayers with medical deductions are presented for 1949 and 1956. In 1956 the deduction amounted to $3.5 billion on all returns, the amount below the floor to $1.9 billion, and that beyond the ceiling to a little less than $0.1 billion. Nearly two-thirds of the medical expenses of those claiming the deduction was deductible from income, a proportion close to the average for those in the $3,000 to $5,000 income group. For those with less than $2,000, over four-fifths was deductible, and for the group with $100,000 and over slightly less than half. It is thus once more evident that but for the upward shift in the medical expense-to-income ratios for given money incomes (a shift suggested by the figures in Tables 40 and 45), the rise over time in taxpayers' incomes with a given percentage floor,

TABLE 47

Total Medical Expenses and Income Reported on Returns with Medical Deductions, by Income Groups, 1949 and 1956

(dollars in millions)

INCOME GROUP ($000's)	AGI on Returns With Medical Deduction (1)	Amount Deducted (2)	Amount not Deducted — Below Floor[a] (3)	Amount not Deducted — Above Ceiling (estimate)[b] (4)	Total (2)+(3)+(4) (5)	Amount Deducted as % of Total[d] (6)	Group's Total Expenses as % of Income[e] (7)
			1949				
Under 2	1,142.3	209.3	57.1	1.4	267.8	78.2	23.4
2–3	2,776.0	310.7	138.8	2.7	452.1	68.7	16.3
3–5	7,281.9	575.9	364.1	11.5	951.5	60.5	13.1
5–10	4,176.0	283.6	208.8	6.9	499.3	56.8	12.0
10–25	1,337.6	84.2	66.9	4.0	155.1	54.3	11.6
25–50	421.1	18.3	21.1	1.3	40.7	45.0	9.7
50–100	165.8	4.8	8.3	0.5	13.5	35.2	8.2
100–500	63.7	0.9	3.2	0.1	4.2	21.8	6.7
500 and over	4.6	c	0.2	c	0.2	4.9	5.3
Total	17,369.1	1,487.8	868.5	28.4	2,384.6	62.4	13.7
			1956				
Under 2	1,088.3	197.6	33.6	4.5	235.7	83.8	21.7
2–3	2,941.3	343.9	93.3	2.8	439.9	78.2	15.0
3–5	14,162.5	1,049.7	479.6	20.3	1,549.6	67.7	10.9
5–10	29,240.2	1,370.2	1,022.3	14.4	2,407.0	56.9	8.2
10–25	8,588.2	373.9	243.3	23.5	640.7	58.4	7.5
25–50	2,637.8	92.6	44.6	15.8	153.0	60.5	5.8
50–100	1,479.4	32.9	13.7	8.7	55.3	59.5	3.7
100–500	1,131.9	11.5	5.9	4.6	22.0	52.4	1.9
500 and over	364.8	0.6	1.1	0.6	2.3	26.9	0.6
Total	61,634.4	3,472.9	1,987.3	95.2	5,505.5	63.1	8.9

Figures may not add to totals because of rounding.

[a] For 1949, the figures in column 3 were obtained by multiplying column 1 by 0.05. For 1956, the reported adjusted gross income of taxpayers under 65 was multiplied by 0.03. The adjusted gross income of those with a deduction for drugs was estimated by using the information published for 1954. The estimated income of those with drug deductions was then

of $28.4 million among income groups in the same proportions as the frequency of taxpayers who had medical deductions equal to, or exceeding, the upper limit (see Table 50 below). The total was obtained by applying Jensen's ratio (see footnote 22, above) to the sum of columns 2 and 3.

[c] Less than $0.1 million.

[d] Column (2) ÷ (5).

[e] Column (5) ÷ (1).

146

would lead to a gradual decline in the deductible proportion of their medical expenses.[25]

The effect of the exclusion was, however, much more pronounced before it was lowered from 5 to 3 per cent and eliminated for persons over 65. The figures for 1949 show that the proportion that could be deducted declined from four-fifths at the lower end of the income distribution to one-fifth for taxpayers with reported incomes in excess of $100,000. Taxpayers in the $25,000 to $50,000 income group deducted 45 per cent of their medical expenses in 1949, and 60 per cent in 1956. Table 48 confirms the rise in the deductible proportion of medical expenses between 1949 and 1956, for taxpayers both under and over

TABLE 48

Medical Expenditures Deducted by Persons Under and Over 65 Years of Age as Per Cent of Total Medical Expenses and of Adjusted Gross Income, 1956

(dollars in millions)

ADJUSTED GROSS INCOME GROUP ($000's)	*Medical Expenses*			*Amount Deducted as Per Cent of*	
	Total Outlay (1)	*Deducted* (2)	*AGI* (3)	*Total Outlay* (4)	*AGI* (5)
TAXPAYERS UNDER 65					
Under 2	177.7	145.6	870.1	81.9	16.7
2-3	348.4	258.0	2,409.5	74.1	10.7
3-5	1,342.6	869.9	12,620.4	64.8	6.9
5-10	2,231.9	1,216.0	27,350.0	54.5	4.4
10-25	510.8	270.2	6,746.8	52.9	4.0
25-50	93.8	49.8	1,229.4	53.1	4.1
50-100	25.7	12.8	360.4	49.6	3.5
100-500	6.5	2.3	110.6	35.4	2.1
500 and over	0.1	a	1.4	14.0	0.6
Total	4,737.6	2,824.6	51,698.5	59.6	5.5
TAXPAYERS OVER 65					
Under 2	57.9	52.0	218.2	89.7	23.8
2-3	91.6	85.8	531.8	93.7	16.1
3-5	207.0	179.8	1,542.1	86.9	11.7
5-10	175.1	154.3	1,890.3	88.1	8.2
10-25	129.9	103.7	1,841.4	79.8	5.6
25-50	59.2	42.8	1,408.3	72.3	3.0
50-100	29.6	20.1	1,119.0	68.1	1.8
100-500	15.4	9.2	1,021.3	59.5	0.9
500 and over	2.3	0.6	363.4	27.2	0.2
Total	767.9	648.3	9,935.8	84.4	6.5

Figures may not add to totals because of rounding.

a The medical deduction in this income group amounted to $8,000.

Source: *Statistics of Income.*

25 See the discussion relating to this on pp. 129-132.

65. Whereas the decline in percentage deductible, from the bottom to the top of the income scale, was from 78 to 5 per cent in 1949—when the 5 per cent exclusion was in effect—the decline was from 82 to 14 per cent for taxpayers under 65 in 1956, when the 3 per cent exclusion was in effect.

On returns filed for 1956 by persons over 65 the deduction declined over the income range from 90 to 27 per cent of total medical expenses. For this group the 1 per cent exclusion of drug expenditures and the ceiling on the deduction were retained, preventing deduction of all medical expenses. Up to about the $25,000 income level, the medical deductions were on average a greater proportion of income for taxpayers who itemized and were over 65 than for taxpayers who itemized and were under 65. Above the $25,000 level, the opposite is the case: the deduction was a smaller fraction of the income of those over 65 than of the income of those under 65. The tabulation below shows the range for 1954 and 1956, from lowest to highest income group, of medical deductions as per cent of income for the two age groups.

	Over 65	Under 65
1954	28 to 0.2	17 to 0.4
1956	24 to 0.2	17 to 0.6

The explanation lies in the way the standard deduction and the 3 per cent exclusion interact in "selecting" taxpayers who can take medical deductions. Even though the aged are not subject to a percentage exclusion of 3 per cent, up to the $10,000 level, they generally require a much larger medical deduction than those under 65, to enable them to reduce their tax liabilities by itemizing (as an alternative to the standard deduction). The reason is probably that younger persons can claim larger amounts of other deductions, especially property taxes and mortgage interest, and are less dependent upon large medical expenses in order to profit by itemizing. After a certain income level, apparently around $25,000, the respective effects of the two floors become reversed: the standard deduction, because it is limited to $1,000, becomes less important relative to income, and more of those over 65 find it advantageous to itemize; but the exclusion from medical expenditures, from which that age group is exempt, assumes increasing importance because medical expenses do not rise in proportion to income, and fewer taxpayers under 65 find it possible to itemize medical expenses as income rises. Table 49 shows this strikingly. The frequency of re-

TABLE 49

Number of Returns with Deduction for Medical Expenditures as Per Cent of All Returns, by Income and Age, 1956

(numbers in thousands)

ADJUSTED GROSS INCOME GROUP ($000's)	Under 65 Years			65 Years or Over		
	Number of Returns With Deduction for Medical Expense (1)	Total Number of Returns (2)	Per Cent With Deduction (1) ÷ (2) (3)	Number of Returns With Deduction For Medical Expense (4)	Total Number of Returns (5)	Per Cent With Deduction (4) ÷ (5) (6)
Under 2	605.7	13,389.8	4.5	147.7	1,983.2	7.4
2-3	952.6	7,216.0	13.2	212.3	827.8	25.6
3-5	3,088.3	15,250.8	20.3	396.4	1,076.9	36.8
5-10	4,150.9	15,659.6	26.5	282.6	683.6	41.3
10-25	506.0	2,426.5	20.9	118.8	224.7	52.9
25-50	37.7	293.5	12.9	40.5	52.7	76.7
50-100	5.6	69.9	8.0	16.4	19.2	85.1
100-500	0.8	15.2	5.3	6.0	6.7	89.9
500 and over	a	0.5	0.4	0.3	0.4	89.7
Total	9,347.7	54,321.8	17.2	1,220.9	4,875.2	25.0

Figures may not add to totals because of rounding.
a Only 2 returns in this income group.

Source: *Statistics of Income.*

turns with medical deductions of taxpayers over 65 rose steadily from 7 per cent in the less-than $2,000 group to 90 per cent in the over-$100,000 group, whereas for those under 65 the frequency rose from 5 per cent in the less-than $2,000 group to 26 per cent in the $5,000 to $10,000 group, returning to 5 per cent in the group reporting $100,000 and over.

While the ceiling limitation on the medical deduction has been quantitatively unimportant in relation to the aggregate, it has been of importance to taxpayers with incomes over $10,000 whose medical expenses exceeded the floor. Of the taxpayers in this group 11 per cent reported medical expenses for 1949 large enough to make their specific upper limit effective (Table 50). In the income group $25,000

TABLE 50

Number of Returns Reporting Medical Expense Deduction Equal to or Exceeding Specific Ceilings on Amount Deductible, by Income Groups, 1949

ADJUSTED GROSS INCOME GROUP ($000's)	Number of Returns With Medical Deduction (1)	Number With Deduction Limited by Ceiling (2)	Per Cent of Total (2) ÷ (1) (3)
	TAXABLE RETURNS		
Under 2	485,820	200	0.04
2-3	864,470	3,810	0.44
3-5	1,718,330	6,510	0.38
5-10	668,732	13,574	2.03
10-25	93,920	7,928	8.44
25-50	12,772	2,641	20.68
50-100	2,555	963	37.69
100-500	437	255	58.35
500 and over	5	4	80.00
Total	3,847,041	35,885	0.93
	NONTAXABLE RETURNS		
Total	736,966	20,024	2.72

Source: Statistics of Income, 1949.

to $50,000, one-fifth of the taxpayers had deductions of that size, and at the very top four-fifths fell into that category. This may be taken as evidence that for high-income taxpayers with extraordinarily large medical expenses, in the tax-law sense, the deduction allowance was inadequate because of its rigid ceiling provision, at least when judged by the established criterion that extraordinary, unbudgeted medical expenses affect the taxpayer's capacity to carry his ordinary share of the tax load. The ceilings were generous in relation to the income and expenditure patterns of the low- and middle-income taxpayers. They were apparently not so for high income taxpayers, assuming that their medical expenditures are reported in good faith and do not include such borderline items as expensive prescribed vacations. But the latter problem might more appropriately be handled through administrative enforcement rather than the rough justice of a ceiling; unlike the lower limit, the ceiling bears no recognizable relation to income or expenditures, although it varies with family size.

Since 1949, the year to which the data in Table 50 pertain, the ceilings have been doubled. From 1954 on they varied from $2,500 to $10,000 instead of from $1,250 to $5,000. For many, particularly in the low- and middle-income range, the increase has undoubtedly removed the effect of the ceiling as a limitation on medical deductions. For high-income taxpayers the situation is less clear cut because the floor applicable to all taxpayers was also reduced—a measure which tends to move taxpayers closer to their ceilings. For those over 65 the floor was lowered to 1 per cent of income for expenditures on drugs, and for others to between 3 and 4 per cent of income. Hence, while these changes have increased the amount of medical deduction available to everybody, they have not necessarily made the ceiling less effective for high-income taxpayers.[26] Indeed Table 47 showed us that for persons who itemized the relative amount of medical expense over the ceiling was slightly larger in 1956 than in 1949.

The relationship between medical deductions and size of reported income so far discussed characterizes only a group of taxpayers filing— in the period 1942 to 1950, little over one-tenth of the number of taxable returns; in 1953, 14 per cent; and in 1956, 21 per cent. The increasing size of this group after 1953 reflects the lower minimum exclusion. Until 1950 the number of taxable returns with medical deductions in any of the income groups shown never exceeded 14 per cent of the total (Table 51). In the low- and middle-income groups the 10 per cent standard deduction effectively limited the number of taxpayers who could profit by itemized medical deductions, and the floor limited the number able to claim them. For a taxpayer with

---

[26] For example, a single taxpayer with an income of $100,000 and medical expenses of $7,000 could not, with the former 5 per cent floor and $1,250 upper limit, deduct all of the $2,000 by which his medical expenses exceeded the floor. Now the new upper limit is $2,500, but his medical expenses above the new floor—probably 4 per cent of income—come to $3,000, which is still more than he is allowed to deduct.

adjusted gross income of $10,000 or less in 1950, medical expenses had to be anywhere from 5 to 15 per cent of his income, depending on what other deductions he was able to claim, before he could benefit from itemizing.[27] Since 1954, the effective floor for the same income range

TABLE 51

Number of Taxable Returns With Medical Deductions as Per Cent of
All Taxable Returns, by Size of Income Reported,
Selected Years, 1942-1956

INCOME GROUP[a] ($000's)	1942	1945	1947	1950	1952	1954	1956
Under 2	11.0	5.9	6.7	6.0	6.1	6.6	6.9
2-3	13.0	8.7	10.0	9.2	11.0	12.8	14.6
3-5	14.7	10.0	12.3	13.3	15.6	20.0	21.5
5-10	10.5	10.9	14.0	13.5	16.0	23.0	27.0
10-25[b]	6.4	7.9	10.3	9.9	14.7	20.7	23.6
25-50[b]	3.7	4.6	6.3	7.5	16.6	22.5	22.6
50-100	2.3	3.0	4.3	5.4	20.7	25.0	24.6
100-500	1.0	1.7	2.1	3.2	27.6	30.9	31.2
500 and over	0.4	0.3	0.2	0.7	36.2	37.0	36.8
Average	12.0	7.8	10.0	10.8	13.2	17.9	20.7
				DOLLARS			
Average deduction	161	251	279	304	322	325	312
Average medical expense	276	399	453	509	559	507	514

Figures for all taxable returns exclude fiduciary returns.
a Net income groups for 1942; adjusted gross income groups all other years.
b For 1952 and 1954, the class limit is $20,000 rather than $25,000.

can vary anywhere from 0 to 14 per cent of income depending now on age, size of drug expenses, and other deductions.

The estimates presented in Table 52 show that in 1949 there were indeed a large number, probably over 1.6 million, of returns with medical expenses over 15 per cent of reported income. This is more than one-third of the returns with medical deductions and about 3 per cent of

27 In other words, for a taxpayer with an income of $10,000 or less, medical expenses, if the only deductible expense, had to be as large as 15 per cent of income before an itemized deduction could exceed the standard deduction. The proverbial big-city dweller who rents his home and leads an anonymous life of no borrowing and no giving to philanthropy exemplifies this extreme. For the community-minded homeowner whose taxes, mortgage interest, and contributions may be high, medical expenses barely over 5 per cent of income sufficed for a specific deduction. Since 1954 the limits within which a taxpayer under 65, with income of $10,000 or less, may decide to claim medical expenses, have been 3 to 4 per cent at one end and 13 to 14 per cent at the other. The taxpayer with an income exceeding $10,000 needs a combination of medical expenses over 3 to 4 per cent of income and total deductions exceeding $1,000 in order to profit by itemizing.

TABLE 52

Estimated Number of Tax Returns with Medical Deductions of Ten Per Cent
or More of Adjusted Gross Income, by Income Groups, 1949 and 1956

(numbers in thousands)

ADJUSTED GROSS INCOME GROUP ($000's)	Number of Returns			Returns as Per Cent of:	
		With Medical Deduction		Total Returns (3) ÷ (1)	Total with Deductions (3) ÷ (2)
	Total (1)	Total (2)	Over 10 per cent of income[a] (3)	(4)	(5)
		1949			
Under 2	19,550.6	824.4	489.8	2.5	59.4
2-3	12,137.6	1,099.5	456.8	3.8	41.5
3-5[b]	14,138.4	1,889.5	514.9	3.6	27.3
5-10	4,837.8	668.7	139.7	2.9	20.9
10-25	918.4	93.9	22.3	2.4	23.7
25-50	171.3	12.8	1.5	0.9	11.7
Total under $50,000	51,754.1	4,588.8	1,625.0	3.1	35.4
		1956			
Under 2	14,974.9	753.4	446.5	3.0	59.3
2-3	8,043.8	1,164.9	494.6	6.1	42.5
3-5	16,327.6	3,484.7	800.9	4.9	23.0
5-10[b]	16,339.8	4,433.5	567.2	3.5	12.8
10-25	2,654.3	624.8	68.6	2.6	11.0
25-50	346.4	78.2	6.8	2.0	8.7
50-100	89.2	22.0	1.2	1.3	5.5
Total under $100,000	58,776.0	10,561.5	2,385.8	4.1	22.6

a The estimates were made on the basis of a frequency distribution of tax returns with medical deduction by size of income and by size of medical deduction. See *Statistics of Income*, 1949 and 1956. For each income class the number of returns with medical deductions greater than 10 per cent of income was estimated. The 10 per cent level was set for each income class at 10 per cent of the average income for the class. For the medical deduction size class into which the 10 per cent value fell, the frequencies between that value and the upper limit of the class were estimated by straight line interpolation.

b Includes all nontaxable returns with adjusted gross income exceeding the lower class limit.

all returns.[28] In the group with incomes less than $2,000, over one-half
of the returns with medical deductions showed medical expenses exceeding 15 per cent of income; in the $25,000 to $50,000 group, close
to 12 per cent of the returns showed the same.

[28] This percentage appears conservative in view of the statistics presented in the
Health Information Survey for 1952-1953 (Anderson and Feldman, *op.cit.*, p. 136).
The authors report that 18.4 per cent of the families in their sample spent more than
10 per cent of income for personal health services, and 6.3 per cent spent more than
20 per cent for this purpose. A large part of the seeming discrepancy may arise from
inclusion of persons with very low incomes who do not file tax returns. Omission of
families with less than $1,000 income from the Health Information tabulation re-
duces the percentages to 14.1 with medical expenses exceeding 10 per cent of income, and 3.3 with 20 per cent of income.

Similar estimates were possible for 1956. To make the figures for the two years as comparable as possible, we estimated the number of returns with medical *deductions* exceeding 10 per cent of reported income for 1949 and 1956. The difference in the two years is that for 1949 a medical deduction of 10 per cent means in effect a medical *expense* of 15 per cent of income, because the 5 per cent exclusion applied to all taxpayers. In 1956 a deduction equal to 10 per cent of income may indicate an actual expense between 10 and 14 per cent of income. As the table shows, slightly over 4 per cent of all returns showed deductions exceeding 10 per cent of income for that year, which may mean expenses of about 12 per cent, on average. Thus there has been little significant change in this respect between 1949 and 1956. The figures suggest that many taxpayers' medical expenses may have to surmount a large proportion of the standard deduction, as well as the floor, before itemized medical expenses are advantageous and possible.

The changes in the medical deduction allowance since 1951 have, however, altered the direction of the curve describing the proportion of increased medical expenses that is passed on to the federal government at each level of income. The amount that can be passed on at a given level of income depends, first, on the marginal rate of tax at that level and, second, on the fraction of returns itemizing medical deductions (columns 2 and 3 of Table 53). The decline in proportion of itemized returns was so sharp before 1951 (because of the percentage exclusion applicable to all taxpayers) that it offset the rise with income in marginal tax rates. A larger amount of an increase in medical expenses was passed on to the federal government at low income levels than at higher levels.[29] The curve for 1956, in Chart 14, shows that the reverse now holds: an increase in medical expenses at high income levels brings with it, on average, more government participation than an increase at modest levels of income. The qualification "on average" is even more important here than when dealing similarly with deductible state and local taxes. The bottom curve in Chart 14 rises because taxpayers over 65 are not subject to the exclusion of 3 per cent of income. However, as Table 49 shows, the percentage for those under 65 still declines after the $10,000 income level; for those over 65 it rises throughout. The effect of the difference in degree of government participation in the expenses of persons under and over 65 is clear in the

[29] This is in sharp contrast to the curve showing relative amounts of an increase in deductible taxes that could be passed on to the federal government. See Table 33 and Chart 11, Chapter 5.

figures shown in footnote 19 above: 13 per cent of the amount of medical expenditures by those under 65, and 25 per cent of the amount by those over 65, was absorbed by tax abatement.

TABLE 53

Estimated Fraction of an Increase in Medical Expenses Passed on to Federal Government in the Form of Deduction, 1956

ADJUSTED GROSS INCOME GROUP ($000's)	Average Marginal Rate of Tax (1)	Taxable Returns with Medical Deduction as per cent of all Returns (2)	Per Cent Increase in Medical Expenses Shifted to Federal Government (1) × (2) (3)
0.6-1	0.20	1.0	0.2
1-1.5	0.20	3.2	0.6
1.5-2	0.20	6.5	1.3
2-2.5	0.20	9.6	1.9
2.5-3	0.20	12.2	2.4
3-3.5	0.20	14.6	2.9
3.5-4	0.20	18.7	3.7
4-4.5	0.20	21.0	4.2
4.5-5	0.20	23.8	4.8
5-6	0.20	27.9	5.6
6-7	0.21	27.8	5.8
7-8	0.21	26.5	5.7
8-9	0.21	23.0	4.9
9-10	0.23	22.7	5.2
10-15	0.26	23.3	6.2
15-20	0.32	24.7	7.8
20-25	0.40	22.9	9.3
25-50	0.54	22.6	12.2
50-100	0.66	24.6	16.4
100-150	0.77	28.7	22.1
150-200	0.84	33.6	28.3
200-500	0.88	36.9	32.6
500-1000	0.87	36.9	32.2
1000 and over	0.87	35.7	31.0

Source: Column 1: *Statistics of Income*, 1956. Change in average tax liability between two income groups divided by change in average taxable income. For income groups above the $15,000 level, the amount of income subject to alternative long-term capital gains rate was subtracted before computing average taxable income. Similarly the amount of long-term capital gains tax was subtracted before computing average tax liability.

Column 2: *Statistics of Income*, 1956.

Students and critics of the medical expense deduction, as formulated, frequently compare it, favorably or unfavorably, with the personal casualty loss deduction, pointing to either similarities or incongruities between them. A brief discussion of the comparisons follows.

CHART 14

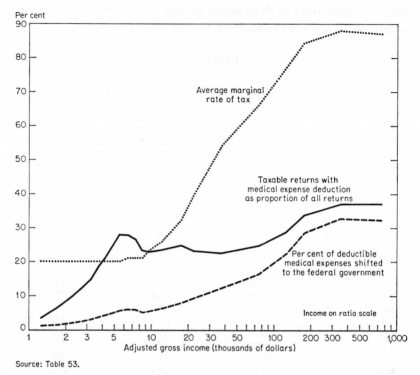

Per cent

Fraction of an Increase in Medical Expenses Passed on to Federal Government, 1956

Source: Table 53.

Medical Expenses and Casualty Losses

Two aspects of the medical expense deduction have been most frequently compared with the personal casualty loss deduction, one of the deductions in the earliest federal income tax law, which is still in its original form. They are the upper and lower limitations on the deductible amount of medical expenditures, and the deductibility of health insurance premiums. The two are so interrelated in this comparison that they cannot be entirely separated.

Compared with the medical expense allowance, in which, as we have seen, an attempt is made to differentiate among taxpayers by size of income, size of family, and age, the allowance for personal casualty losses is almost unrefined. Taxpayers have been permitted since the inception of the income tax to deduct the net loss of personal property caused by fire, flood, windstorm, theft, and the like, to the extent that such losses are not covered by insurance. At first glance, this allowance deals with impairment of personal property much as the medical deduction deals with impairment of personal health, and the similarity has been stressed frequently in recent times by advocates of a more liberal tax treatment of medical expenses.[30] In the case of two taxpayers, one of whom suffers a broken leg and the other an explosion on his yacht,[31] the similarity is so great that it seems to demand equal tax treatment of the two losses. If the first taxpayer has no other medical outlays, the chances are that he will obtain little or no deduction for his expenses because of the percentage exclusion. The person who experiences the property loss, on the other hand, is not subject to any quantitative limitations other than the size of his income. However, the premium payments for insurance against such losses are not deductible, while medical insurance premiums are.

The exclusion of insurance premiums from the casualty loss deduction points up some consistency in the two allowances, which is frequently overlooked and easily obscured by the citation of polar cases as the above example. Medical expenditures, particularly when insurance premiums are included, encompass a wide variety of fairly routine, and hence budgetable, expenses like periodic visits to the family doctor and dentist, eyeglasses, and a host of preventive medicines that could hardly be classified under the rubric of casualties. Expenses of an emergency or casualty character are comparable to much of what is included in the casualty loss allowance. It follows that the percentage exclusion from the medical deduction need not imply inconsistency with the casualty loss deduction as long as the exclusion effects a separation of the routine from the sudden and unforeseen, especially since insurance premiums are excluded from the casualty loss deduction but not from the medical expense allowance.

The percentage exclusion does not strictly separate the routine from the sudden, casualty-type medical expense. Such a distinction is essentially a qualitative one, and the percentage exclusion was intended, as we have seen above, to quantitatively separate expenses of ordinary from those of extraordinary size. The consistency between the two deductions is, after all, probably only rough, and ready. The percentage floor will often exclude some casualty-type medical expenses, whereas under the allowance for property losses all casualties, however small,

30 For instance, Hearings before the Committee on Ways and Means, House of Representatives, *General Revenue Revision*, 83rd Cong., 1st Sess., Part 1, 1953, pp. 74, 108, and 110.
31 *Ibid.*, Representative Carl T. Curtis, p. 74.

are deductible. Indeed it might be argued that many of the personal property losses deducted are also likely to be routine, as in broken window panes and minor automobile mishaps. Another basic difference is that one is concerned with loss and the other solely with expenditures. Thus under the casualty loss deduction, expenditures to prevent loss are not deductible, but all actual losses incurred, whether or not replaced, are deductible. Under the medical expense allowance, some expenditures to prevent loss of health qualify for deduction, but loss of health as such is dealt with only as it manifests itself in actual expenditures.[32]

The question of insurance persists for both deductions. To the extent that it is available, the occurrence of large, unforeseen expenses and losses is avoidable, and the attendant hardship becomes more or less a matter of choice. Those who buy insurance, as pointed out above, tend to benefit less from both deduction allowances, and their tax payments tend to subsidize the uninsured, who assume for themselves that part of the risk not absorbed via the tax system. For a taxpayer subject to a high marginal rate of tax, that risk is greatly reduced for all personal property losses, and with regard to medical expenses above the floor for those under 65 years old. Indeed for property losses, high-income taxpayers who rationally compare alternatives can hardly afford to purchase insurance. They can save the expense of insurance premiums, and in case of loss the Treasury shares the cost at a rate equal to the taxpayer's marginal rate of tax.[33] The argument that the deductions are intended for those unable to afford the cost of insurance would transfer the rationale for medical and property loss deductions from the area of interpersonal equity to that of subsidy. And it is question-

[32] It would take little ingenuity to construe expenditures preventing loss of health to include better food and vacations. Borderline cases have many times dealt with vacations prescribed by physicians.

[33] In connection with personal property casualty losses, Vickrey comments: "This is at least one case in which . . . the tax law actually encourages the taxpayer to take risks. Ironically, in this particular case there is no special social advantage in having the taxpayer assume a risk, as there is in the case of investment in a new field." (Op.cit., pp. 60-61) "The present law certainly tempts the wealthy to refrain from insuring and even to neglect to protect property adequately against fire, theft, or other casualty: in the event the casualty occurs the tax deduction will absorb such a large part of the loss that the protection may cost more than it is worth to the taxpayer as an individual. . . ." (p. 62) There is, however, no evidence so far to indicate widespread neglect of personal property. Our figures in Table 55 do show some rise in the relative frequency of returns with casualty loss deductions, particularly on returns with high incomes, but this may be attributed to the sharp rise, during the period, of ownership of automobiles, residences, and other consumer durables.

able whether the present deductions constitute an efficient device for a tax subsidy.

Critics of the medical expense deduction have used the personal property allowance to support arguments against the ceilings imposed. There is no upper limit on personal property loss deduction. They argue also that the stated intent of the medical allowance is to relieve those with expenses of extraordinary size, and that a ceiling on the deductible amount seems to be a contradiction in terms. Some would go in the other direction and allow a carry-forward or carry-back, or both, for medical expenses.[34] Such carry-forwards and carry-backs have been allowed for casualty losses and thefts since 1951.

In defense of the ceiling the usual argument is that medical expenditures beyond a generous maximum are often hard to distinguish from ordinary living expenses, and would therefore create an audit problem. While that particular difficulty may not exist so much for property losses, there seems to be some inconsistency of treatment between medical expenses and personal property losses. The number of returns with medical expenses exceeding the ceiling is relatively small (Table 50) suggesting that additional auditing in the interest of increased consistency might be worth its cost.

So far the deductions claimed for personal property losses resulting from theft, fire, storm, and various other accidents have never amounted to much over 1 per cent of total personal deductions (Table 9). In 1954, a year of serious floods, they amounted to $444 million on all tax returns, or less than 0.2 per cent of income reported. Because of their quantitative unimportance, no attempt is made here to present as detailed a statistical picture of the casualty loss deductions as for the four major personal expense allowances. The main features of this deduction are revealed in Table 54, showing the amounts claimed since 1939 in relation to income reported, and in Tables 55 and 56, where relative frequencies and the relation to income are presented by size of income reported.

The amount deducted on taxable returns for casualty loss was only 0.08 per cent of income in 1939 and 0.12 per cent in 1956. Since 1944, when the percentage was 0.13, there has been no rise in the amount reported relative to total reported income. However, as previously noted, the relative frequency of returns showing casualty losses has

[34] Hearings before the Committee on Ways and Means, op.cit., pp. 80, 114.

TABLE 54

Amount of Casualty Loss Deductions Reported on Tax Returns
As Per Cent of Total Income Reported, 1939-1956

| | Casualty Losses Reported on: | | Per Cent of AGI on: | |
YEAR	Taxable Returns (1)	All Returns (2)	Taxable Returns (3)	All Returns (4)
	(millions)			
1939	14	26	.08	.10
1940	22	40	.09	.10
1941	44	70	.09	.11
1942	91	133	.13	.16
1943	116	140	.11	.13
1944	149	179	.13	.15
1945	128	153	.11	.13
1946	137	179	.12	.13
1947	193	254	.14	.17
1948	179	244	.13	.15
1949	171	229	.12	.14
1950	248	308	.16	.17
1951	n.a.	n.a.	—	—
1952	293	368	.15	.17
1953	326	393	.15	.17
1954	359	444	.17	.19
1955	n.a.	n.a.	—	—
1956	295	348	.12	.13

Source, by column

(1) and (2): *Statistics of Income.*
(3): (1) ÷ (3), Appendix Table D-2.
(4): (2) ÷ (6), Appendix Table D-2.

TABLE 55

Per Cent of All Taxable Returns Reporting Casualty Loss,
by Size of Income Reported, Selected Years, 1939-1956

INCOME GROUP[a] ($000's)	1939	1941	1945	1947	1949	1952	1954	1956
Under 2	n.a.	n.a.	0.6	0.8	0.8	0.8	1.0	0.8
2-3	n.a.	n.a.	1.4	1.6	1.5	1.7	1.9	1.7
3-5	n.a.	n.a.	2.5	3.1	3.3	3.8	4.1	3.2
5-10	2.7	4.6	3.8	5.4	4.9	6.4	7.6	5.8
10-25[b]	3.0	4.7	4.4	6.2	5.1	7.1	9.0	7.7
25-50[b]	3.8	5.0	5.1	7.4	7.1	8.9	12.2	9.3
50-100	4.6	5.8	6.0	8.8	9.6	12.2	16.5	11.7
100-500	6.3	7.6	6.8	12.0	12.5	15.6	23.9	14.3
500 and over	14.4	17.3	12.5	28.6	22.8	19.9	35.7	16.8
Average	n.a.	n.a.	1.4	2.2	2.6	3.7	4.6	3.9

a Net income groups for 1939 and 1941; adjusted gross income groups for other years.
b For 1952 and 1954, class limit is $20,000 instead of $25,000.
Source: *Statistics of Income.*

TABLE 56

Deductions for Casualty Loss as Per Cent of Income on Taxable Returns with
That Deduction, by Income Groups, Selected Years, 1939-1956

INCOME GROUP[a] ($000's)	1939	1941	1945	1947	1949	1952	1954	1956
Under 2	n.a.	n.a.	9.1	8.3	7.7	8.1	6.9	7.1
2-3	n.a.	n.a.	6.1	5.8	5.0	5.1	5.6	5.3
3-5	n.a.	n.a.	4.8	4.7	4.0	3.8	3.2	3.4
5-10	4.1	2.8	4.4	3.8	3.1	2.8	2.4	2.2
10-25[b]	3.4	2.3	3.5	2.9	2.3	2.1	2.2	1.5
25-50[b]	1.9	1.4	2.5	2.5	2.1	1.7	2.0	1.4
50-100	1.6	1.4	2.1	2.4	1.6	1.4	2.1	1.0
100-500	1.2	0.5	1.6	2.1	1.2	1.0	1.6	0.7
500 and over	0.6	1.1	0.5	1.1	0.8	0.3	0.7	0.3
Average loss reported (dollars)	n.a.	n.a.	208	212	185	184	183	162

a Net income groups for 1939 and 1941; adjusted gross income groups for other years.

b For 1952 and 1954, class limit is $20,000 instead of $25,000.

Source: *Statistics of Income.*

increased. Less than 2 per cent of returns listed such loss in 1944 but almost 4 per cent did so in 1956 (Table 55).[35]

In contrast to the medical expense deductions, the relative frequencies rise sharply with size of income reported. In recent years, casualty losses were reported on only 1 per cent of returns in the lowest income group, and on between one-fifth and one-third in the highest. But for those who did report such losses, the relation to income resembled that for medical expenses, that is, the ratio of reported losses to income varied inversely with size of income (Table 56).

35 This, and an upward shift in the percentage breakdown of the total by income groups, explains the sharp decline in the average ratio of loss to income on returns reporting casualty losses, observable in Table 56, even though the ratio did not decline when income on all taxable returns was used (Table 54).

CHAPTER 8

The Standard Deduction

WHEN the federal income tax became a mass tax in the early 1940's, the ever-present demand for simplification of the tax return, for the benefit of both the majority of taxpayers and the auditing authorities, became more insistent. The first serious attempt at simplification was made in 1941. Through it, the majority[1] of taxpayers with gross incomes of $3,000 or less could choose to compute their taxes with itemized deductions or to determine the amounts from a simple table, in which the tax due at each income level had been computed, allowing for varying personal exemptions and for a minimum personal deduction in the form of a 10 per cent tax reduction. The latter was equal to a deduction of about 4 per cent of gross income for the group as a whole, but less for those whose gross incomes were only a little more than the exemptions, and they were usually better off itemizing their deductions. The initial result was that 45 per cent of the returns with income below $3,000, and 40 per cent of the total filed were in the standardized form. The percentages rose somewhat in the following two years after the standard allowance had been revised to 6 per cent of gross income. For 1943, 56 per cent of the returns with less than $3,000 income were the short form with standard deduction.

Failure of this method to achieve the desired shift of most taxpayers with small incomes to the simplified return, and the difficulty encountered in use of gross income as the basis for the simplified schedule, led to the adoption of a new system in 1944. The adjusted gross income concept became the means of placing all taxpayers on an equal basis for the purpose of applying a standard personal deduction.[2] The new minimum was set at 10 per cent of adjusted gross income with an upper limit of $500 per return, with the result that in 1944 over 80 per cent of tax returns filed were on the short form with the standard deduction. A further liberalization in 1948, when the "split-income" provision for married couples was enacted, extended the minimum 10 per

[1] From 1941 to 1943 the optional standard deduction was available only to taxpayers with gross incomes up to $3,000 and derived from wages and salaries, dividends, interest, and annuities.
[2] See p. 8 for a somewhat more detailed explanation.

cent optional deduction to almost all returns in the $5,000 to $10,000 income group and raised the upper limit from $500 to $1,000.[3]

Trend in Choice of the Standard Deduction

While the introduction of the 10 per cent minimum allowance in 1944 caused most taxpayers to shift from itemized deductions to the new standard deduction, and the number has remained high since then, its proportion of the total has nevertheless steadily declined. By 1956, it had slipped to 69 per cent of all returns and 63 per cent of taxable returns (Table 57). The decline was much more pronounced in the

TABLE 57

Number of Tax Returns with Standard Deduction as Per Cent of All Returns, 1941-1956
(numbers in millions)

	Number of Returns with Standard Deduction		*Total Number of Returns Filed*		*Per Cent with Standard Deduction*	
					Total	*Taxable*
YEAR	*Total* (1)	*Taxable* (2)	*Total* (3)	*Taxable* (4)	(1)÷(3) (5)	(2)÷(4) (6)
1941	10.3	6.2	25.9	17.5	39.6	35.4
1942	16.1	11.3	36.6	27.6	44.0	40.9
1943	20.3	18.2	43.7	40.2	46.5	45.3
1944	38.7	34.6	47.1	42.4	82.1	81.7
1945	41.5	34.8	49.9	42.7	83.0	81.5
1946	44.1	30.3	52.8	37.9	83.4	79.9
1947	44.7	32.6	55.1	41.6	81.1	78.4
1948	43.2	29.1	52.1	36.4	83.0	79.9
1949	42.1	27.7	51.8	35.6	81.3	77.8
1950	42.7	29.5	53.1	38.2	80.5	77.2
1951	43.9	31.6	55.4	41.6	79.1	76.0
1952	43.7	31.6	56.5	42.8	77.3	73.7
1953	43.4	31.4	57.8	44.2	75.1	71.2
1954	41.0	28.9	56.7	42.6	72.3	67.8
1955	41.4	29.3	58.3	44.7	71.0	65.5
1956	40.7	29.3	59.2	46.3	68.8	63.3

Source: *Statistics of Income.*

amounts of deductions taken. Of the 1944 total of $12.5 billion personal deductions on taxable returns, $7.9 billion or 63 per cent con-

[3] The extension applied to all joint returns, and returns of single persons and heads of families. Only married couples filing separate returns were held to the old $500 upper limit per return; but few did from 1948 on, since few of those choosing the standard deduction also found it advantageous to file separately.

sisted of standard deductions. In 1956, the total had risen to $33.5 billion, but only $12.5 billion or 37 per cent was in the form of the standard deduction (Table 58). The change in relative positions of standard and itemized deductions is further brought out in Chart 15, which shows each as a per cent of total adjusted gross income for the period 1941-1956.

There is reason to expect this trend to continue, in view of the previously mentioned factors influencing taxpayers to revert to the itemized form. These influences are widening of the scope of existing deductions, particularly the 1954 increase in the medical deduction; the more generous allowance of installment interest; the addition of the child care allowance; the growth of homeownership; and the rise in incomes. The rise in incomes is important because taxpayers are apparently less impressed with the convenience of the standard deduction as their incomes rise. We find in Table 58 that the decline in proportion of deductions in standard form during 1944-1956 is not attributable in any significant sense to the gradual movement of some taxpayers into the income range where the standard deduction's upper limit becomes effective. Most of the decline occurred within the group eligible for the flat 10 per cent of income deduction, that is, on returns with incomes up to $10,000. Within that income range the decline was from 65 to 43 per cent of deductions taken between 1948 and 1956. Assuming that the proportion in the below-$10,000 income group had remained at 65 per cent during 1948-1956, the over-all ratio of standard deductions to total deductions would have declined only from 58 to 54 per cent instead of the actual decline from 58 to 37 per cent shown in Table 58.[4]

The reason for the decline is fairly clear from a glance at Table 59. Close to 90 per cent of taxpayers in the lowest income group have been choosing the standard deduction since 1944. This ratio declines as we move to higher income groups; in the $5,000 to $10,000 group, two-thirds chose the standard deduction in 1949 and a little over one-half in 1956. As a result the amounts of itemized deductions have been rising, and the amounts of standard deduction falling, relative to total

[4] To isolate the effect of the movement of tax returns from the less-than-$10,000 group to the above-$10,000 group on the ratio of standard to total deductions, the $25,969 million deductions taken by the former group for 1956 (column 5, Table 58) was multiplied by 0.65; the result, when added to the amount in column 3, calls for: $18,118 ÷ 33,508 = 0.54.

Amount of Standard Deductions Compared with Total Personal Deductions on Taxable Returns, 1941-1956

(amounts in millions of dollars)

YEAR	Standard Deductions			All Personal Deductions			Standard Deductions as Per Cent of Total Deductionsᵃ		
	Total (1)	Below Upper Limitᵇ (2)	Subject to Upper Limitᵇ (3)	Total (4)	Corresponding to (2) (5)	Corresponding to (3) (6)	(1)÷(4) (7)	(2)÷(5) (8)	(3)÷(6) (9)
1941	401	401	—	4,033c	2,062	1,971	9.9	19.4	—
1942	1,112	1,112	—	7,000c	4,335	2,665	15.9	25.7	—
1943	1,814	1,814	—	8,610c	5,167	3,443	21.1	35.1	—
1944	7,883	7,226	657	12,477	10,005	2,472	63.2	72.2	26.6
1945	7,873	7,183	689	13,130	10,270	2,860	60.0	69.9	24.1
1946	7,455	6,594	862	13,168	9,672	3,496	56.6	68.2	24.7
1947	8,541	7,557	984	15,602	11,436	4,167	54.7	66.1	23.6
1948	9,545	8,938	608	16,472	13,742	2,730	57.9	65.0	22.3
1949	9,082	8,548	534	16,803	13,998	2,806	54.0	61.1	19.9
1950	10,135	9,472	662	19,043	15,713	3,330	53.2	60.3	19.9
1951	11,566	10,796	771	22,399	18,435	3,964	51.6	58.6	19.5
1952	12,069	11,231	838	24,622	20,225	4,397	49.0	55.5	19.1
1953	12,533	11,617	916	26,961	22,155	4,806	46.5	52.4	19.1
1954	11,600	10,687	914	27,476	22,188	5,288	42.2	48.2	17.3
1955	12,027	10,963	1,064	30,524	24,177	6,347	39.4	45.3	16.8
1956	12,471	11,232	1,238	33,508	25,969	7,539	37.2	43.3	16.4

ᵃ On individual returns only; does not include fiduciary returns.

ᵇ For the years 1941-1943, only taxpayers with less than $3,000 gross income, mainly derived from wages and salaries, could elect the standard deduction. From 1944 to 1947 taxpayers with more than $5,000 adjusted gross income were limited to a $500 standard deduction. From 1948 on this limit was raised to $1,000 for married persons filing joint returns and for single taxpayers.

c Total deductions for 1941-1943 in this table are not comparable to those shown in Tables 7, 8, and Appendix Table D-1 because no attempt was made to eliminate business-type deductions from the miscellaneous category, by income groups. Figures broken down by income groups had to be used to obtain the amount of deduction below and above the income level at which the limit on the standard deduction becomes effective.

adjusted gross income within each income group (Table 60). For 1956, the amount of itemized deductions rose from 3 to 9 per cent, and the amount of the standard deduction declined from 9 to 5 per cent of in-

CHART 15

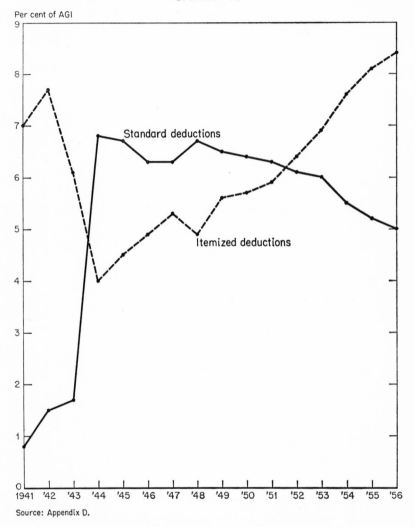

Standard and Itemized Deductions as Per Cent of Total Adjusted Gross Income, Taxable Returns, 1941-1956

come in the range to $10,000—the income range for which the minimum allowance was 10 per cent for all taxpayers. What explains such a sharp divergence? It is explained, to some extent, because the ratio of deducti-

TABLE 59

Number of Taxable Returns with Standard Deduction as
Per Cent of All Taxable Returns, by Size of Income
Reported, Selected Years, 1941-1956

INCOME GROUP[a] ($000's)	1941	1944	1947	1949	1952	1954	1956
Under 2	49.8	87.5	86.8	89.0	89.8	89.0	88.3
2-3	33.6	82.0	81.3	83.4	82.3	79.5	77.8
3-5	—	77.5	75.1	74.0	72.6	67.2	65.7
5-10	—	61.5	59.0	67.1	63.2	56.5	51.0
10-25[b]	—	34.2	34.5	53.5	53.9	49.4	43.0
25-50[b]	—	13.7	13.1	21.9	25.5	21.7	15.4
50-100	—	7.1	5.5	2.7	8.1	7.0	6.4
100-500	—	3.1	2.1	3.2	3.3	2.5	1.9
500 and over	—	1.8	1.2	0.4	0.5	0.3	1.1
Total	35.4	81.7	78.4	77.8	73.7	67.8	63.3

a For 1941, returns with standard deduction are classified by gross income; itemized returns classified by net income. For later years, classification by adjusted gross income.

b For 1952 and 1954, class limit is $20,000 instead of $25,000.

ble expenditures to income tends to rise somewhat over the income scale.[5] Hence as incomes rise, more taxpayers find that they lower their tax liability by itemizing deductions. But the modest rise in deductible expenses as per cent of income can hardly explain fully the pattern observed in Table 60.

The missing part of the explanation appears in the percentages shown in Table 61. Here we expressed the itemized deductions as per cent of the income of those itemizing (rather than of the income of all taxpayers as in Table 60). Now deductions fall as a per cent of income, even over that range for which the standard deduction is a flat 10 per cent for all taxpayers. In other words, among taxpayers who itemized deductions, those with the lowest incomes show the highest ratio of itemized deductions to income. This suggests strongly that, to undertake the labor of filing itemized returns, relatively larger amounts of deductible expenses were required for those in the lowest income groups than for those with somewhat higher incomes. It suggests that, on average, the further down taxpayers are in the income distri-

5 See Table 12 and the discussion of it in Chapter 3. But it should be borne in mind that the rise in the ratio of itemized deductions to income, as the income scale rises, was moderated by the introduction of the medical allowance in 1942. Thus for 1943 the increase in the deductions-income ratio was no longer as steep as in the earlier years (Table 12).

TABLE 60

Standard and Itemized Deductions as Per Cent of Total Adjusted Gross Income in Each Income Group, Taxable Returns, Selected Years, 1941-1956

INCOME GROUP[a] ($000's)	1941 Item-ized	Stand-ard	1944 Item-ized	Stand-ard	1947 Item-ized	Stand-ard	1949 Item-ized	Stand-ard	1954 Item-ized	Stand-ard	1956 Item-ized	Stand-ard
Under 2	5.5	1.6	2.5	8.7	2.8	8.6	2.6	8.8	2.9	8.7	3.2	8.7
2-3	6.3	1.3	3.1	8.2	3.3	8.1	3.4	8.3	4.5	7.9	5.0	7.7
3-5	8.6	—	3.6	7.7	5.0	7.5	5.1	7.4	6.7	6.6	7.1	6.5
5-10	10.0	—	5.8	4.8	7.1	4.5	6.3	6.7	7.9	5.7	8.9	5.1
10-25[b]	9.5	—	7.3	1.1	8.1	1.2	7.6	3.6	8.7	3.8	9.4	3.1
25-50[b]	9.2	—	7.7	0.2	8.7	0.2	9.3	0.6	10.5	0.8	10.8	0.5
50-100	9.7	—	8.7	0.1	9.9	c	10.3	0.1	11.9	0.1	12.2	0.1
100-500	10.8	—	10.9	c	12.0	c	12.8	c	15.9	c	17.1	c
500 and over	13.0	—	12.4	c	12.6	c	13.4	c	18.8	c	19.3	c
Average	7.4	0.8	4.0	6.8	5.2	6.3	5.6	6.5	7.6	5.5	8.4	5.0

a Net income groups for 1941; AGI groups for other years.
b For 1954, class limit is $20,000 instead of $25,000.
c Less than 0.1 per cent.

bution, the less inviting they find the possibility of reducing taxable income by, for example, 1 per cent, through itemizing their personal deductions rather than taking the standard allowance.[6] In more gen-

TABLE 61

Itemized Deductions as Per Cent of Income on Taxable Returns with Itemized Deductions, by Income Groups, Selected Years, 1941-1956

INCOME GROUP[a] ($000's)	1941	1944	1947	1949	1952	1954	1956
Under 2	10.0	18.3	20.1	21.4	24.2	23.7	24.2
2-3	7.5	17.0	19.3	20.1	21.7	21.8	22.2
3-5	8.4	15.9	18.9	19.3	19.8	20.0	20.2
5-10	9.5	14.4	16.7	19.1	18.2	18.3	18.1
10-25[b]	8.9	10.7	11.8	15.2	16.7	16.7	15.9
25-50[b]	8.6	8.9	10.0	11.7	12.7	13.1	12.7
50-100	9.8	9.4	10.4	11.2	12.2	12.8	13.0
100-500	9.9	11.2	12.2	13.1	15.2	16.2	17.4
500 and over	11.3	12.6	12.7	13.4	17.5	18.8	19.5
Average	9.1	14.0	15.7	17.1	17.5	17.8	17.6

a Net income groups for 1941; AGI groups for other years.
b For 1952 and 1954, group limit is $20,000 instead of $25,000.

6 An alternative, but somewhat far-fetched, explanation would be that although the ratio of personal deductions to income is a rising function of income over the range up to $10,000, the dispersion of the individual ratios about the mean is greater in the lowest income groups than further up. This would explain why the relatively few whose deductions exceed the 10 per cent minimum allowance in the lowest income group have higher deductions-to-income ratios than those with higher incomes who also itemize.

eral terms, it suggests that the lower their incomes, the more willing taxpayers are to forego in the interest of simplicity, some of the refinements of income and the subsidies implied by personal deductions.

Considerations in Determination of Size of Standard Deduction

The quantitative presentation so far shows that, if the primary aim was simplification, the extent to which taxpayers have used the standard deduction since 1944 indicates the success of the device. The Treasury saves a great amount of auditing and litigation as long as a large number of persons can be induced to use the minimum allowance.[7] Whether the taxpayers' "cost of compliance" has been comparably reduced depends on the extent to which they compute their tax liabilities both ways to find which is smaller. This in turn depends largely on the size of the minimum allowance.

Congress may attempt to set an allowance which permits the Treasury to collect approximately the same amount of gross revenue whichever tax form is selected. Taxpayers would still have to determine their monetary advantage by a trial of both methods. On the other hand, the government may aim at the same amount of net revenue obtainable if all taxpayers itemize, by passing on wholly or in part the savings in administrative expense to taxpayers who choose the simplified return. In that case only a minimum of taxpayers might find it necessary to compute their tax both ways.

It appears that, in effect, Congress has moved from the first approach to the second. In the 1942-1943 period, when the minimum allowance was 6 per cent, and close to the average ratio of itemized deductions to income of those eligible,[8] many taxpayers undoubtedly computed their taxes both ways. The 1944 move, to a more generous allowance (10 per cent of income) than the actual average, probably eliminated much of the taxpayer's paperwork, although the tendency to omit such comparisons appears greater the further down one goes in the income scale

[7] "The standard deduction has made a major contribution to the successful administration of the modern mass personal income tax by greatly reducing the importance of personal deduction errors." See Marius Farioletti, "Some Results from the First Year's Audit Control Program of the Bureau of Internal Revenue," *National Tax Journal*, March 1952, pp. 75-76. The Audit Control Program of 1948 uncovered major errors in personal deductions on one out of three returns with itemized deductions, but on only one out of 250 returns with standard deductions.

[8] In 1940, the last year prior to the first standard allowance, deductions in the group with incomes up to $3,000 were 7.5 per cent of income on average.

(Table 61). It may be that at the bottom of the income distribution, say up to $3,000, taxpayers are considerably more interested in convenience and simplicity than in small tax savings. That the rather sparse 1941 allowance of roughly 4 per cent enticed over 43 per cent of eligible taxpayers to adopt it, suggests that the government could get a considerable amount of tax simplification, even if those who obtained it had to pay for it. Such reasoning suggests a third possible guide to a standard deduction policy. The government, rather than passing the savings in administration cost on to the taxpayers who participate in the simplification program, might require these taxpayers to pay for the privilege of a simplified tax return in the form of a minimum allowance well below the previous average as it did, in effect if not intentionally, in 1941.

The question of the reason for the upper limit on the standard deduction—at first $500 and recently $1,000—remains. As we have seen, the average per cent of income deducted has been as large for those with high incomes as for those with low incomes (Table 12). Therefore, a changing functional relation between size of deductions and size of income could hardly have been the reason for the change from a flat percentage to a flat absolute amount at the $10,000 income level. It may be explained in part by a desire to protect deductible expenditures from the inroads of the tax rates that become operative above that level. But that explanation would be consistent only with the incentive aspects of the deductions, that is, with the view that gifts to philanthropy would be seriously reduced by a 10 per cent minimum allowance above $10,000 income, whereas the incentive effect does not operate below that level. It would not apply to the equity aspects of deductions, unless one wishes to argue that equity is more important for taxpayers subject to high tax rates than for the low-rate taxpayers. Or, the reason could rest mainly on grounds of differential audit expense, the argument being that above the $10,000 income level the cost of audit is warranted by the size of the deductions involved per return, whereas below that level it is not. The problem of tax return audit is considered in more detail in the next section dealing with the rationale of the standard deduction, as such.

Rationale of the Standard Deduction

In addition to the view that the standard deduction constitutes an audit-saving device to the Treasury and a convenience to the taxpayer, there is the view that it may bring about a net gain on equity grounds. It is argued that at least some, if not most, of the personal deductions are not justifiable in principle, and that a high standard deduction eliminates a large part of the differential advantage bestowed on those who itemize them.[9] But as a corollary to this, it has been said that to the extent that the deductions are now granted to everybody they are really granted to nobody, and the end result is a mere narrowing of the tax base, rather than the originally intended refinement of it. Indeed, the same result could be approximated without the attendant narrowing of the tax base and hence higher marginal tax rates, by restricting personal deductions to the amount of eligible expenses in excess of 10 per cent of income.[10] Though this would not lower anyone's tax bill,[11] it would permit the lowering of existing bracket rates. As to the alleged unequal treatment of taxpayers because of personal deductions, a preferable solution might be to go to the source of the difficulty rather than to rely on a method, such as the standard deduction, which tends to freeze inconsistencies into the tax system.

The proposition that the standard deduction would help solve the Treasury's audit problem is probably a major reason for its enactment. An audit program covering the deductions of some 40 million additional returns (Table 57) might constitute a difficult and unprofitable job. But such an enlarged audit program was not the only alternative, particularly in view of the actual result of the standard deduction— a minimum allowance of up to $1,000 for all taxpayers. An alternative solution might have been omission of auditing for returns with deductions below 10 per cent of income, or a token audit of such returns.[12] In favor of this alternative solution is the lower cost[13] and greater consistency with the purposes for which the various deductions had been enacted. Presumably there would have been no difference from

9 See Pechman, "Erosion of the Individual Income Tax," p. 11.

10 See also White, *op.cit.*, p. 365.

11 This is true in only an approximate sense. Some taxpayers might pay slightly more tax than previously and others slightly less, because the standard deduction is now computed, on incomes of $10,000 or less, as a per cent of adjusted gross income, rather than as a per cent of the tax base. Therefore, the precise tax equivalent of a taxpayer's standard deduction cannot be allowed for by a mere change in the rate schedule. However, this is at best a minor consideration.

12 Such a decision would not of course be announced. Taxpayers can be kept on their toes by the mere possibility of audit at any moment.

13 As we have shown on page 37, the 1944 change-over alone, from the initially small to the enlarged standard deduction, meant a loss in tax base of roughly $2.5 billion, or 40 per cent of the increase in the amount of standard deduction at that time.

present procedures in the audit program for returns claiming deductions in excess of 10 per cent of income, so that auditing costs would not have been greater than with the present standard deduction.

Thus there were three solutions to the Treasury's audit problem as it emerged in the early 1940's: (1) the current minimum allowance of 10 per cent of income up to $1,000 (or any other figure) for taxpayers who do not choose to itemize; (2) allowance of only deductions exceeding, in the aggregate, 10 per cent of income on the grounds, implicit in the current standard deduction, that deductions of most taxpayers need the restraint of audit; and (3) merely token audit for relatively small amounts of personal deductions, as those amounting to less than 10 per cent of income.

Finally, an important consideration is the taxpayer's convenience served by the simplicity of tax returns, which many undoubtedly prefer to whatever additional interpersonal equity and subsidy they might obtain under a system of itemized deductions. In this case analysis can provide little, if any, guide to policy. The two benefits are not only incommensurable, they are mutually exclusive. Only if a reader should decide that most, or all, of the personal deductions are uncalled for in principle would the two desires for a rational tax base and a simple tax return coincide.

CHAPTER 9

Summary of Findings

The Purpose of Personal Deductions

AT THE outset we find that the personal deductions, unlike the personal exemptions, were not established as a separate distinct category until World War II. This is largely because the personal deductions came into the tax law at widely separate points in time and under markedly different conditions. The interest paid, taxes paid, and casualty loss allowances are as old as the Civil War income tax, and may have been written into early tax laws with the businessman's circumstances in mind at a time when the income tax was not contemplated as a mass tax.[1] The allowance for philanthropic contributions, to protect philanthropy from the possible effects of high taxes, was enacted in 1917; the medical expense deduction was added to the list in 1942 in order to differentiate between taxpayers on the basis of their medical expenses of "extraordinary" size; and the child-care allowance, designed primarily for working mothers who are without husbands or who are supplementing family incomes below $5,100, was enacted in 1954 but has in its present form no quantitative significance. The long time intervals between enactment of the various personal deductions probably account for some of the features noted by critics as inconsistencies in the law. It is frequently pointed out, for instance, that the allowances both for medical expenses and casualty losses (fire, collision, storm, theft) attempt to deal with the subject of personal loss—one indirectly with loss of health (that is, only to the extent that there are actual expenditures), the other directly with loss of material belongings. Yet the casualty loss allowance has no lower or upper limits on the amount deductible (it even permits the carry forward and carry back of losses if they exceed current-year income), whereas the medical allowance has both quantitative restrictions.

At numerous points in our study, particularly in connection with the philanthropic contributions and medical expense allowances, a policy problem has persistently emerged—one that has become increasingly acute in recent times. How well is the income tax suited to serve as a vehicle for governmental action in the social welfare area? That is, how effectively can a tax rebate be substituted for an expenditure program? In a loose sense, a tax reduction conditional on a given

[1] For instance, note 18 of Chapter 6.

expenditure has some of the aspects of an expenditure program. In this context it becomes of immediate importance to identify the motivations and purposes underlying a deduction. A deduction may be intended to grant relief from a quasi-involuntary expenditure, and thereby differentiate between taxpayers whose incomes, though apparently equal, are of different sizes in some relevant sense; or a deduction may be geared as a stimulus to expenditures on which society is currently placing a high order of priority. The first is intended to further refine taxable income; the second has features of a government expenditure program.

Both these considerations are potentially present in the medical expenditures allowance. As constituted since 1942, the relief and interpersonal equity aspects, rather than the incentive aspects, have been the dominant consideration in the medical allowance. And, as we saw in Chapter 7, taxpayers who have been able to claim the deduction had medical expenses far above average for the population, both absolutely and relatively to income. Recent proposals, such as for no limit on deductibility of voluntary health insurance premiums[2] and addition to the list of personal deductions of an allowance for educational expenses beyond high-school level,[3] would tend to move the deductions further in the direction of indirect expenditure programs. Indeed Congress always has the option of making public expenditures in the form of tax concessions rather than budget appropriations.[4]

Quantitative Findings:
Deductions within the Tax Structure

Personal deductions reported on taxable returns have risen from an estimated 8 per cent of income reported in the years 1918-1921 to an average of over 13 per cent in 1953-1956 (Table 7). But the individual deductions have not uniformly behaved in this way. Particularly striking is the decline in the relative importance of interest paid, and the relative rise in taxes paid.

In 1929 over 40 per cent of the total consisted of personal interest

[2] See Chapter 7, p. 134.

[3] See, for instance, the President's Committee on Education Beyond the High School, *Second Report to the President*, Washington, D.C., July 1957, pp. 56, 90.

[4] The expenditure aspect of deductions and exemptions has been discussed by Clarence D. Long and Selma Mushkin in "Welfare Programs and Economic Growth and Stability," *Federal Expenditure Policy for Economic Growth and Stability*, Subcommittee on Fiscal Policy of the Joint Economic Committee, 85th Cong., 1st Sess., 1957, pp. 1028-31.

payments, one-fourth of nonbusiness taxes, and one-fifth of philanthropic gifts. For 1956, personal deductions amounted to $34 billion on taxable returns, of which 37 per cent was taken in the form of the standard deduction (first introduced in 1941). Of the $21 billion of itemized deductions, state and local nonbusiness taxes paid were over one-fourth, contributions and interest paid each over one-fifth, and medical expenses one-seventh.

Quantitatively, personal deductions have never been as significant as personal exemptions. For 1956, exemptions on taxable returns amounted to some $75 billion as against $34 billion for deductions. But the trend in the relative importance of deductions has been upward, while for exemptions it has been downward since prewar days (Table 3). Estimated effective exemptions (for all income recipients) declined from about seven-tenths of total adjusted gross income in prewar days to one-third in 1955. Effective personal deductions, on the other hand, rose from 7 per cent of total adjusted gross income in 1939 to 12 per cent in 1955. Thus personal allowances are less than formerly related to population and family size and more to selected types of expenditures and size of income (to income especially since the inauguration of the standard deduction).

The ratio of personal deductions to income varies only slightly between different income groups from the bottom to top of the income scale. In recent years a significant rise occurred only above the $100,000 income level (Table 12). This is a change from prewar years when total deductions exhibited a tendency to rise in relation to income reported over most of the income scale. The change may be ascribed primarily to the addition of the standard deduction and the medical expense allowance, which raised the ratio of deductions to income for low- and middle-income taxpayers. In contrast, the personal exemptions decline relative to income from the bottom of the income scale upward (Table 4). A striking contrast emerges in the differential effect of deductions and exemptions on the progression of effective tax rates. When we omit personal deductions (and retain exemptions) in order to isolate their effect on tax rates, the ratio of tax to income rises from 11 per cent in the lowest income group to 77 per cent at the top for the year 1953. When we omit personal exemptions (now retaining deductions), the ratio rises only from 20 to 61 per cent. Thus the personal deductions, as a group, have tended to dampen the progression of effective rates, and the exemptions have added considerably to effective rate progression (Table 5 and Chart 2).

How are personal deductions important to the total tax liability or tax rates? Again with 1953 incomes and 1953 tax rates, liabilities were reduced by the presence of personal deductions from an estimated $36 billion to $29 billion, or by $7 billion. In that year their revenue cost was somewhat less than one-fourth of the actual yield of the personal income tax. Alternatively, the over-all importance of the personal deductions might be expressed in terms of rates. If we hold tax liabilities approximately constant, the increase in tax base in a system without personal deductions permits a reduction of all nominal rates by close to 5 percentage points. The over-all average rate of tax (total tax liability divided by tax base) would then have been 20.7 instead of 25.4 per cent (Table 6).

Through their effect on the tax base, the personal deductions may also affect the built-in flexibility of the tax. We observed (Table 10) that the deductions have been slightly less sensitive than the current tax base to cyclical fluctuations in income. Hence, for a given level of tax liabilities, the deductions tend to reinforce built-in flexibility somewhat (Table 11). This means that at given levels of tax yield, changes in tax liabilities in response to changes in income tend to be a bit larger with than without the deductions. This is not necessarily so if fixed tax rates, with and without deductions, are assumed. Then the higher level of tax yield resulting without deductions might produce a change in tax liabilities with change in income greater than that in the presence of deductions.

Quantitative Findings:
Size and Significance of Major Deductions

Examination of the major individual deductions—philanthropic contributions, taxes paid, interest paid, and medical care expenses—reveals some striking differences in coverage of the underlying expenditure items for which these deductions were designed. This is illustrated in Table 62 for the years 1950, 1952, and 1954. Judging by the ratio of reported to estimated total expenditures, coverage appears to be greatest for contributions: eight-tenths according to one estimate, over nine-tenths according to another. Personal interest payments deducted came to one-half of the estimated total of such payments; nonbusiness tax payments to somewhat over four-tenths; and medical expenses to not

176

TABLE 62

Selected Deductions Compared with Estimated Total Expenditures,
by Category, 1950, 1952, and 1954

(dollar amounts in billions)

	1950	1952	1954
Philanthropic Contributions:			
Estimated total			
Andrews	3.7	4.5	4.8
Based on miscellaneous sources	2.7	3.4	4.1
Amount deducted	2.3	3.1	3.9
Deductions as per cent of total			
Andrews	61.3	68.6	81.3
Based on miscellaneous sources	82.8	93.0	94.0
Nonbusiness Tax Payments:			
Estimated total	6.6	8.5	9.8
Amount deducted	2.2	3.2	4.1
Deductions as per cent of total	33.8	37.6	41.5
Personal Interest:			
Estimated total	3.6	4.8	6.3
Amount deducted	1.5	2.2	3.2
Deductions as per cent of total	42.0	46.7	50.9
Medical Expenses:			
Estimated total	8.3	9.4	10.6
Amount deducted[a]	1.6	2.1	3.0
Estimated medical expenses of claimants[b]	2.5	3.4	4.5
Deductions as per cent of total	18.9	22.8	28.1
Claimant's expenses as per cent of total	30.6	36.0	42.2

[a] After exclusions.
[b] Estimated medical expenses of those claiming the deduction.
Source: Tables 16, 26, 34, 41, and 42, and *Statistics of Income.*

quite three-tenths. The ratio of medical deductions to estimated total medical expenses in the deductible category is particularly low, owing to the requirement that medical expenses below a stipulated percentage of the taxpayer's income be excluded from the deduction. When we include the amount falling below that floor for those who took the deduction, their medical expenses amount to approximately 40 per cent of the total of potentially deductible expense.

The tax equivalents of the amounts deducted in itemized form for the four major expenditure categories added to $3.5 billion in 1954 and $4.8 billion in 1956. The tax equivalents of each category are shown below.

	1954	1956
	(dollars in billions)	
Philanthropic contributions	1.1	1.5
Taxes paid	1.1	1.6
Interest paid	0.8	1.2
Medical expenses	0.6	0.7

These tax equivalents do not include the revenue foregone on account of the standard deduction. For instance, if we assign an appropriate fraction of the standard deduction to philanthropic contributions, the 1956 tax cost for the latter would be raised to $2 billion. (And if we wanted a still more inclusive figure to take account of all tax concessions in the area of philanthropy—as for corporation gifts, property transfers, and property income of philanthropic organizations—we would arrive at roughly $2.6 billion for 1956.)

Care must be taken not to designate the tax equivalents as simple tax losses. If intended to spur private expenditures, for instance, in the philanthropic domain, the figures represent more accurately the tax cost to the government of encouraging expenditures which might otherwise have to be undertaken by government. Two questions therefore need to be answered before the nature of this tax rebate can be appraised correctly: first, to what extent are philanthropic donations made for purposes in which the government's interest is considerable? Second, to what extent does the tax rebate affect the volume of giving? Only after these two questions are answered would we know enough to say whether, and to what extent, lower tax rates would be possible without the contributions deduction. If tax rates could not be reduced commensurately with the resulting broadening of the tax base, the deduction allowance may be said to constitute an indirect government expenditure which is not reflected in the government's budget.

The first question—the degree to which the typical philanthropic dollar and the typical tax dollar are complementary—may be referred to the estimated distribution of contributions by broad areas of activity. In 1954 an estimated two-thirds of the gifts of living donors went to religious organizations; over one-fifth for health, education, and welfare; and the remainder to private foreign aid, foundations, and a vast miscellany usually designated as philanthropy.

The second question—the effect of deductibility on the volume of giving—has two aspects: the effect of tax rates on the reported amounts of gifts and on the actual amount of gifts. The available evidence for both is highly tentative. The figures we were able to marshal suggest the possibility that deducted contributions are considerably over-reported; and they provide no evidence that philanthropic giving in the aggregate depends appreciably on tax incentives.

Without answering the questions raised, the considerations and data

178

mentioned give substance to two broad questions of tax policy: first, whether the government should have contributed $1.6 billion in the form of tax reduction to the living donors of the $4.2 to 4.8 billion gifts made in 1954; second, whether such a tax rebate might in future be most appropriately accomplished by a deduction from income, as at present, or through a tax credit.

A large part of the $2.8 billion tax equivalent of deductions for non-business taxes and interest paid in 1956 is probably for property taxes and mortgage interest of homeowners with mortgage debt. For that year, deducted nonbusiness taxes were 4.7 per cent of income reported on returns with itemized deductions; and estimated total deductible taxes were 4.0 per cent of total adjusted gross income. The discrepancy in the percentages is surprisingly small, for we naturally expect the amounts of taxes paid by those who itemize to show higher than average ratios to income. The small discrepancy may be explained by the somewhat regressive incidence of state and local tax systems, and by the compulsory nature of taxes, with the result that tax payments of those who itemize and those who choose the standard deduction are closer in amounts than some other expenditures are. By no means all homeowners itemize their deductions: in 1956 there were nearly 26 million nonfarm homeowners but only close to 18 million returns with an itemized tax deduction. Therefore, well over 8 out of 26 million nonfarm homeowners did not itemize, though they paid property taxes.

For homeowners with mortgage interest (as well as property taxes) the picture may be different. We estimate that there were close to 14 million nonfarm homeowners with mortgage debt in 1956. The number of tax returns reporting an itemized interest deduction was also just short of 14 million for that year (Table 36). It is thus likely that a much larger proportion of homeowners with mortgage debt than of homeowners in general itemize their deductions. Even for interest, however, the difference between the ratio of deducted interest to income reported on tax returns and the ratio of estimated total personal interest paid to total adjusted gross income has been narrowing recently. In 1944, deducted interest was 2.2 per cent of income on tax returns, and total deductible interest was 0.9 per cent of total income. In 1956, the respective percentages were 3.9 and 2.9 (Table 35), reflecting the sharp rise in installment interest payments for recent years.

The medical expense allowance, as we have seen, is quantitatively less significant than the three other major deductions. Owing to the 5 per cent floor and the standard deduction (which prevented many taxpayers from itemizing medical expenses, even if these exceeded 5 per cent of their income), the deductions claimed on tax returns were somewhat less than 20 per cent of total private medical outlays as estimated by the Department of Commerce in the period 1942-1950. By 1956 the deductions had risen to 29 per cent of total outlays, mainly because of the abolition of the percentage exclusion after age 65 and the lowering of the exclusion for all from 5 to 3 per cent. Total medical expenses incurred by those able to claim a deduction were about 30 per cent of estimated total medical expenses in 1942, and over 45 per cent in 1956 (Tables 41 and 42). The claimants of these relatively large amounts filed only 18 per cent of all returns (Table 43). In relation to income, we find that during the fifteen years under study medical deductions have been between 6 and 9 per cent of income reported by persons claiming the deductions, and total medical expenses of that group have been between 9 and 14 per cent of its income each year since 1942. Total personal medical expenditures for the United States have been about 4 per cent of total adjusted gross income over the same period (Table 45).

We conclude from the statistics presented that, in line with the law's intent, the medical deduction has benefited taxpayers whose average medical expenses are far above the average of the rest of the population in relation to income. In addition to being large relative to income, medical expenses of those taxpayers were also well above average in absolute size. The latter result is not a necessary consequence of the percentage floor under the deduction but may be caused largely by the standard deduction. If one wishes to view the medical deduction as an indirect government subsidy, its tax equivalent in 1956 was $700 million, about one-seventh of the nearly $5 billion medical expenses of taxable individuals who claimed the deduction. Of the $700 million, an estimated $133 million or one-fifth, was for taxpayers over 65 years old. One-fourth of their medical expenses, compared to 13 per cent for those under 65, was absorbed by the tax equivalent of the medical deduction.

Beginning with 1944, most taxpayers have chosen the standard deduction. In that year eight out of ten made use of it. Since then, there has been a decline to six out of ten in 1956 (Table 57). In dollar amounts, out of $12.5 billion total personal deductions on taxable returns in 1944, $8 billion or 63 per cent was accounted for by the standard deduction. In 1956, the total had risen to $33.5 billion, but only $12.5 billion or 37 per cent was in the form of the standard deduction (Table 58). In part, the decline has been caused by the rise in incomes during that thirteen-year period, since taxpayers in the low-income groups choose the minimum allowance with greater frequency than those in the middle- and high-income ranges (Table 59). The growth in deductible expenditures has also contributed to the decline, as, for example, expenditures resulting from the growth in homeownership. Certainly the liberalization of provisions for deductibility has had an effect in some cases, reinforced by the 1954 code, which lowered the floor for the medical allowance and added a new deduction, the child-care allowance for working mothers.

Quantitative Findings:
Size of Deductions by Income Groups

Although the ratio of total deductions (itemized and standard) to income has in recent years shown only small variations by size of income, ratios for the major allowances have exhibited substantially different patterns (Table 63). The philanthropic contributions deduction has tended to rise as a per cent of income, but perhaps not as steeply as is frequently suggested by those who consider philanthropy an activity of the very rich. There has been only a faint rise, if any, up to the $100,000 level of reported income for the years examined from 1922 to 1956 (Tables 19 and 20). Before 1943 the average ratio of contributions to income stayed as a rule under 3 per cent for incomes below the $100,000 level. After 1943 reported contributions have, on average, exceeded 3 per cent of income well before the $100,000 level was reached, but they still remained below 4 per cent in the $50,000 to $100,000 income group. For incomes above $100,000 the ratio turned up appreciably in all years. On returns with $500,000 and more it has been over 6 per cent in all years since 1943, and close to 12 per cent in 1956. Only in that income group has the average rate of giving moved halfway toward the limit on the amount deductible.

In view of two recent extensions of the limit above its original 15 per cent of income, its importance is of special interest. For 1949, 1954, and 1956, we estimate that in the under-$20,000 income range no more than 3 per cent of returns reported contributions in excess of the scriptural tenth (Table 22). There follows a mild rise up to $50,000, and only above that level does the ratio begin to rise significantly. Less than 0.5 per cent of all returns showed contributions in excess of 20 per cent of income in 1954 and 1956. The amount reported in excess of 20 per cent of income for 1954 was $68 million, or less than 2 per cent of total contributions for that year. The figures suggest that there were few persons with incomes below $50,000 whose contributions

TABLE 63

Major Itemized Deductions and Standard Deduction Reported on Taxable Returns: Per Cent of Income Reported and Percentage Frequency of Deductions on All Taxable Returns, by Income Groups, 1956

INCOME GROUPa ($000's)	Philanthropic Contributions (1)	Taxes Paid (2)	Interest Paid (3)	Medical Expenses (4)	Total Itemized (5)	Standard Deduction (6)
MAJOR DEDUCTIONS AS PER CENT OF INCOME ON RETURNS WITH ITEMIZED OR STANDARD DEDUCTIONS						
Under 2	6.1	5.1	2.3	7.0	24.2	10.0
2-3	5.2	4.9	2.7	6.1	22.2	10.0
3-5	4.2	4.7	4.1	4.2	20.2	10.0
5-10	3.5	4.7	4.7	2.5	18.1	10.0
10-25	3.5	4.7	3.3	1.7	15.9	7.7
25-50	3.3	4.3	2.0	0.9	12.7	3.1
50-100	4.1	4.1	1.8	0.6	13.0	1.6
100-500	6.9	4.3	2.6	0.3	17.4	0.7
500 and over	11.9	3.4	1.6	0.1	19.5	0.1
Total	3.9	4.6	3.8	2.5	17.6	9.6
NUMBER OF RETURNS WITH MAJOR DEDUCTIONS AS PER CENT OF ALL TAXABLE RETURNS						
Under 2	10.5	10.0	4.0	6.9	11.7	88.3
2-3	20.7	20.7	11.4	14.6	22.2	77.8
3-5	33.0	33.4	25.1	21.5	34.3	65.7
5-10	47.6	48.1	42.1	27.0	49.0	51.0
10-25	55.9	56.1	45.2	23.6	57.0	43.0
25-50	83.1	83.3	54.4	22.6	84.6	15.4
50-100	92.4	92.5	58.2	24.6	93.6	6.4
100-500	97.0	97.2	64.4	31.2	98.1	1.9
500 and over	97.3	96.6	71.0	36.8	98.8	1.2
Total	35.3	35.6	27.9	20.7	36.7	63.3

a Income is adjusted gross income.

might have been affected by the increase in the ceiling from 15 to 20 per cent in 1952, and to 30 per cent in 1954. In that income range originated well over nine-tenths of total contributions.

In contrast to the philanthropic contributions allowance, the relative size of medical deductions varies inversely with income. This is the pattern presumably desired for it. In 1942, the results of the consumer expenditure surveys of 1935-1936, and probably also of 1941, were already well known. They showed that medical expenditures rose as income rose, but not in proportion to it, and that medical expenses of all consumer units were about 4 per cent of money income (Table 39). The floor under the deduction was set at 5 per cent of income. It was clear from the start that medical hardship, as defined in the tax law, was most likely to occur among persons at the bottom of the income pyramid and to diminish with size of income, and that only a modest fraction of total medical expenditures would be deductible.

For 1956, medical deductions were 10 per cent of income on returns reporting medical deductions and less than $3,000 income, and 1 per cent on returns reporting $100,000 and over. For the same two groups, the proportion of total medical expense deductible was about four-fifths at the lower end and one-half near the upper (Tables 46 and 47). The frequency of medical deductions claimed among high-income taxpayers was very low until 1951. In that year, removal of the floor at 65 years was reflected in a sharp rise in the frequency of medical deductions on high-income tax returns—for instance, from 5 per cent in 1950 to 25 per cent in 1956 for the $50,000 to $100,000 income group (Table 51).

Of the 10.6 million returns with itemized medical deductions in 1956, 2.4 million showed medical expenses well in excess of 10 per cent of reported income (Table 52). They constituted 4 per cent of all tax returns filed. That figure is presumably a fair indication of the number of returns with relatively large medical expenses, since most taxpayers with medical outlays of 10 per cent of income would hardly choose the standard deduction.

That statement appears only approximately correct in relation to deductible expenses generally. Other evidence suggests that the preference for itemized deductions rises with income level, but not solely because of the slight increase in the ratio of deductible expenditures to income as its level rises. The ratio of itemized deductions to income on itemized returns falls markedly over the range up to $10,000. For 1956, the relatively few with incomes less than $2,000 who itemized claimed deductions equal to 24 per cent of reported incomes; those in the $5,000 to $10,000 group had deductions equal to 18 per cent (Table 63). This observation suggests that, on average, the further down taxpayers are in the income distribution, the less sensitive they tend to be to the possibility of reducing their taxable income by a given small percentage through itemizing their deductions rather than taking the standard deduction. In other words, taxpayers at the bottom of the income scale appear less inclined than those further up to compute their tax liability both ways in order to determine which would minimize their tax liability. The lower their income, the more willing taxpayers seem to be to forego, for the convenience of simplicity, some of the refinements of income and the subsidies implied by the personal deductions.

APPENDIXES

APPENDIX A

Estimates of Total Adjusted Gross Income, Total Deductions and Exemptions

NOTES TO TABLE 1

Line 1. The estimates of total adjusted gross income (AGI) from 1929 on were obtained by making appropriate adjustments in the Commerce Department's annual estimates of personal income. These adjustments follow for the most part the work of Selma F. Goldsmith ("Appraisal of Basic Data Available for Constructing Income Size Distributions," *Studies in Income and Wealth,* Vol. 13, National Bureau of Economic Research, 1951) and Joseph A. Pechman ("Yield of the Individual Income Tax During a Recession," *National Tax Journal,* March 1954, Appendix Table A). Pechman most graciously made all of his worksheets available to us, and our figures are, with some exceptions, the same as his. Although Pechman made no estimates for years before 1929, we followed his general outline in extending the figures back to 1918, using as a starting point Simon Kuznets' estimates of income payments as presented in two publications of the National Bureau of Economic Research: *National Product in Wartime,* 1945; and *National Income and Its Composition, 1919-1938,* 1941. The derivation of total AGI from personal income is shown for a recent year in Table A-1 (see end of Appendix A). While fairly representative, the adjustments shown for 1953 differ in some cases from those made for earlier years partly because of changes in the statutes defining taxable income, partly because figures were not available for all years from the same source.

Line 2. Taken as the difference between line 1 and line 8.

Line 3. For recent years, a rough clue as to size of AGI of nontaxable individuals is available in the form of AGI reported on nontaxable returns. The latter figure falls short of AGI of all nontaxable individuals for two main reasons. 1) It excludes the better part of the AGI of persons whose incomes fell below the filing requirement. The latter amounted to a gross income of $500 per taxpayer in the period 1944-1947, and a gross income of $600 from 1948 on. Because of withholding-at-the-source, a considerable number (possibly one-third) of those with incomes below the filing requirement level nevertheless filed returns in order to obtain refunds. Therefore not all the income at the bottom of the distribution is absent from tax returns. 2) AGI on non-taxable returns also misses the income of those who, though legally required to file, failed to do so because their deductions and exemptions exceeded their AGI and thus made them nontaxable. But this group is probably quite small since it consists entirely of persons who a) do not come under withholding and b) ignore the filing requirement.

We corrected roughly for the omission of those who did not file returns because their income was below the filing requirement. This necessitated first, an estimate of the income of persons who were not required by law to file tax returns. For the years 1945 to 1947 we used the estimates of income below $500 prepared by Ulric H. Weil ("A Note on the Derivation of Income Estimates by Source of Income of Persons Making Less Than $500 Per Annum, 1944-1948," *Journal American Statistical Association,* 1950, p. 440). For the years after 1947 we prepared rough estimates of AGI below the filing requirement. Weil's estimates of income below $500 (1) and ours of AGI below the filing level (2) are given below (in billions of dollars).

	Money Income Less Than $500[a]	AGI Less Than	
		$500	$600
	(1)	(2)	
1945	3.31	3.60	
1946	3.50	3.04	
1947	3.45	2.64	
1948	2.64	2.60	3.69
1949			3.49
1950			3.00
1951			3.69
1952			3.81
1953			3.90
1954			3.64
1955			3.41

[a] Excludes military pay and social security payments.

Since the per capita exemption, and hence the filing requirement, changed from $500 to $600 after 1947, Weil's estimates could be used only up to that year.

From 1948 on we estimated total AGI below the $600 level by blowing up the AGI reported in that income group by persons seeking refunds of tax withheld. The results shown in column 2 also include, for comparative purposes, estimates of total AGI below $500 for 1945-1948. The general order of magnitude—and that is all we are concerned with in the context of this study—is very close to Weil's. Thus for the period 1945-1955, AGI below the filing requirement level appears to have been between $3 billion and $4 billion in every year.

The blow-up factor to obtain our estimates is the ratio of the total number of persons with income of $1,000 and less to the number employed in occupations in which withholding of tax prevailed. The data used to obtain this ratio were the Census survey distributions of persons fourteen years and over by total money income and major occupation group. (For detail see Note c to Table A-2.) Since the Census money income concept includes certain transfer receipts (veterans' payments, social security benefits, and various relief payments), a considerable number of persons appear at higher income levels according to the census concept than they would according to the AGI concept. That is why we computed the ratio for money incomes up to $1,000. Census distributions exist for two types of reporting units: families and unrelated individuals; and persons fourteen years of age and over. The reporting unit on tax returns can of course be either of these. However, for the lowest income group a distribution of persons seems more appropriate. Our method makes various other rough assumptions. It is implicitly assumed that the average AGI of the group not subject to withholding tax is the same as the average AGI of those who were. It is also implicit in our method that all income recipients in this group who had tax withheld filed for a refund. Yet some persons might have considered their overpayments too small for the trouble of filing for a refund. The latter group, and the nontaxable income we miss as explained in 2) above, tend to make our estimates of the AGI of nontaxable individuals slightly low.

From the estimates of total AGI below the filing requirement we subtracted the amounts reported on tax returns (line 1c — line 1a of Table A-2) and thus obtained the estimated amount unreported by persons with income below the filing requirement. To this we added the amount reported on nontaxable returns, which gave us the figure in line 3 of Table A-2 (see end of Appendix A) for the years beginning after 1944. When we add the amount reported on taxable returns to that in line 3, Table A-2, and subtract the sum from the estimates of total AGI we obtain the figure for the amount unexplained. When expressed as a per cent of reported AGI (line 2 plus line 4), our estimate declined from 14.8 to 8.9 between 1945 and 1955 (line 7). The figures thus suggest a downward trend in this ratio. However, our estimates are too crude to furnish a basis for such a conclusion. As stated below (notes for line 7), the unexplained amount for the interwar period was obtained by extrapolating back the 1945 ratio of 0.15. The resulting figure was subtracted from line 2 in Table 1, and the figure for line 3 thus obtained for the selected years before 1945.

Lines 4, 5, and 6. The amount in line 3 of Table 1 was divided into personal deductions and exemptions in the same proportion that each of these constituted the combined total of deductions and exemptions reported on nontaxable returns in each of the eight selected years. Their combined total on nontaxable returns of course exceeded the income reported on these returns. We may nevertheless make the crude assumption that the relation of each to this combined total indicates their respective part in the total of AGI not reported on taxable returns. An earned-income credit against normal tax net income was in effect in 1939, and for that year we included the amount of the credit on nontaxable returns in the combined total in the same manner as deductions and exemptions in the other years.

Line 7. For the years later than 1944, shown in Table 1, the unexplained amount was estimated as the difference between line 2 and line 3 of that Table. For 1945 and 1946 it amounted to almost 15 per cent of reported AGI, as is shown in Table A-2. We carried this ratio back for years before 1945 to obtain a figure for the unexplained amount. Little positive basis exists for extrapolating this ratio back as far as 1918. Our main justification is that we had no evidence to the contrary to guide us, and furthermore that the magnitude we are interested in—estimates of the relative importance of deductions and exemptions—will be affected only slightly by errors in the ratio used for the interwar period. It might be argued that the ratio of amount unexplained to reported AGI was higher in the interwar period than in 1945 and 1946, because enforcement practices were less developed then and withholding of tax at the source nonexistent. On the other hand, tax rates were much lower, so that the urge to evade tax through underreporting of income may have been less strong than in the 1940's. Compared to the assumed understatement of income on tax returns for 1935-1936 (National Resources Committee, *Consumer Incomes in the United States*, Washington, 1938, p. 84), our assumptions for the interwar period are on the low side. In the NRC study, in addition to increasing the frequencies by from 25 to 5 per cent in the $5,000 to $20,000 income range to adjust for nonreporting, all incomes were raised by an average of 11 per cent to adjust for underreporting. Daniel M. Holland, on the other hand, found that the discrepancy between total estimated dividend payments and reported dividends has widened between 1939 and 1952, relatively as well as absolutely ("Dividend Underreporting on Tax Returns," *The Journal of Finance,* May 1958). Needless to say, the citation of these conflicting influences and views is no proof that the ratio in question has remained constant during the period 1918-1945. Contemplating them merely contributes to our doubts on the direction in which the ratio may have moved.

Lines 8 and 9. The figures for AGI on taxable returns for 1946, 1951, 1953, and 1955 are taken from *Statistics of Income,* Part I. For the years before 1944, when the AGI concept was not yet in use, the estimates are our own based on *Statistics of Income* data. The procedure consisted mainly of adding the deductions to the statutory net income figures given in *Statistics of Income* for those years, after substracting our estimates of some negative income items that were included in the deductions total before 1944. For more detail, see Appendix D.

Lines 10 and 11. *Statistics of Income.* The figure for the earned income credit for 1939 excludes the credit on returns with net incomes above $8,000. We assumed that all those with incomes above that level were subject to surtax, and the credit therefore did not diminish their tax base as defined below.

Line 12. The tax base figures are in a sense synthetic. We have ignored the fact that some income, either because of its source or because of the tax bracket in which it fell, was not taxable under one or the other of the components of the individual income tax. For instance, before 1941 a large part of income was subject to normal tax, but not to surtax which became due at a higher point on the income scale. On the other hand, some types of income, such as dividends, interest on federal government securities, and "earned" income have at various times been exempt from the normal tax but not from surtax; and some nonexempt net capital gains were taxed at an alternative rate. Thus the tax base as here defined includes all income to which an income tax rate was actually applied. The fact that the income tax has practically never had one unique base is disregarded.

TABLE A-1

Adjustments of Personal Income Estimate (Department of Commerce)
to Obtain Estimate of Total Adjusted Gross Income (AGI), 1953

(billions of dollars)

1.	Personal income	286,006
2.	Personal income not included in AGI—deduct	40,252
3.	Transfer payments	14,256
4.	Other labor income	5,532
5.	Income in kind	9,825
6.	Nonfarm inventory valuation adjustment (noncorporate)	—190
7.	Farm inventory change	—617
8.	Imputed interest	5,945
9.	Accrued interest (government bonds)	624
10.	Tax exempt interest	293
11.	Undistributed fiduciary income other than capital gains	1,123
12.	Property income of nonprofit organizations	520
13.	Nontaxable military pay	2,500
14.	Imputed rental value of tenant occupied houses	441
15.	AGI not included in personal income—add	8,696
16.	Personal contributions for social insurance	3,940
17.	Net gains from exchanges of property reported on tax returns	2,110
18.	Other income	1,049
19.	AGI of residents of Alaska and Hawaii	1,317
20.	Annuities and pensions	734
21.	Deductions for depletion	—252
22.	Net operating loss deduction reported on tax returns	—202
23.	Total AGI	254,450

Notes, by line

From Department of Commerce, *Survey of Current Business*, July 1957:
1. Table 3.
3. Table 36.
4. Table 34, line 12 minus lines (15 + 16).
5. Table 39, line 1 minus line 6 plus line 8.
6. Table 1.
7. Table 2.
8. Table 37, line 4 minus line 6.
9. *Treasury Bulletin*, June 1955, pp. 21-23. From the amount of "accrued discount" on outstanding debt during the calendar year, the total amount of accrued discount on redemptions during the year was subtracted. Accrued interest on series A-D bonds was obtained by subtracting the figures for series E-K from the figures for "all series combined." The amount of accrued interest received by individuals was obtained by assuming that 80 per cent of series A-D, 66⅔ per cent of series F, G, J, and K, and all of series E bonds were owned by individuals.
10. From Lawrence H. Seltzer, *Interest as a Source of Personal Income and Tax Revenue*, Occasional Paper 51, National Bureau of Economic Research, 1955, Table 15. For years after 1952 figures are from Seltzer's extended worksheets.
11. The 1953 figure is an interpolation between the 1952 and 1954 estimates, no 1953 figures for fiduciaries being published in alternate years. Following Pechman, we subtracted from the noncapital gains income reported by all fiduciaries an adjusted amount of fiduciary income reported on individual returns to obtain undistributed fiduciary income (other than capital gains) for 1952. The adjustment of fiduciary income reported by individuals was as follows: the reported amount was increased by 10 per cent to account for underreporting and income distributed to non-

taxable beneficiaries. This figure was then multiplied by the ratio of noncapital gain income to total income of fiduciaries.

12. Estimated by Pechman by extrapolating the average amount of interest, dividends, and rental income received by nonprofit institutions in 1944-1947. This amount was Selma F. Goldsmith's estimate by an index of personal interest, dividends, and rents as estimated by the Commerce Department, *op.cit.*, Tables 1 and 37.

13. Pechman subtracted from unpublished Commerce estimates of total military cash pay the estimated taxable military wages as obtained for 1953 from Selma Goldsmith. Taxable wages for earlier years were estimated by extrapolating the 1953 figure back on the basis of its relation to taxes withheld by the military, for which figures are available for earlier years.

14. Commerce Department, *op.cit.*, Table 30, line 4, 3 times 0.26 (ratio supplied by Selma Goldsmith).

16. Commerce Department, *op.cit.*, Table 35.

17. *Statistics of Income*, Part 1.

18, 19, 20. All three estimates are based on *Statistics of Income* reports. In these instances we considered appropriate an adjustment for unreported amounts, obtained by multiplying the reported amounts by the ratio of total estimated AGI to the reported AGI for all other items.

AGI of Alaska has not been tabulated separately since 1942, but is included in *Statistics of Income* in the AGI for the state of Washington. We estimated this item by extrapolating the 1939-1942 ratio of reported income for Alaska to that for Washington and Alaska combined by means of an index of the ratio of personal income tax collections in Alaska to collections in Alaska and Washington combined.

21. Estimated by extrapolating the 1945 depletion figure for proprietors and partners by an index of corporate depletion deductions in later years.

22. Net operating loss deductions are tabulated in *Statistics of Income* for 1945 and for 1951-1954. For other years our figures are estimates obtained with the aid of an index of corporate net operating loss deductions as reported in *Statistics of Income*, Part 2.

TABLE A-2

Gap between Total AGI and AGI Reported on Tax Returns, 1945-1955

(dollars in millions)

	1945	1946	1947	1948	1949	1950
1. Estimate of unreported AGI below filing requirement[b]						
a. Amount reported on tax returns	1,498	1,295	1,170	1,340	1,327	1,265
b. Amount reported by persons subject to withholding	1,312	1,111	965	1,097	1,016	1,006
c. Total estimated AGI below filing requirement[e]	3,310	3,500	3,450	3,690	3,490	3,000
d. Amount not reported (line c − line a)	1,812	2,205	2,280	2,350	2,163	1,735
2. Amount of AGI reported on nontaxable returns	2,447	16,033	14,435	21,459	22,008	20,603
3. AGI on nontaxable returns adjusted to include income of those below filing requirement (line d + line 2)	4,259	18,238	16,715	23,809	24,171	22,338
4. AGI on taxable returns	118,104	118,721	135,891	142,667	139,030	159,256
5. Estimated total AGI	140,185	156,065	171,563	184,795	184,292	201,446
6. Amount unexplained [line 5 − (3 + 4)]	17,822	19,106	18,957	18,319	21,091	19,852
7. Amount unexplained as a per cent of reported AGI [line 6 ÷ (2 + 4)]	14.78	14.18	12.61	11.16	13.10	11.04

(concluded on next page)

194

TABLE A-2, *concluded*

	1951	1952	1953a	1954a	1955a
1. Estimate of unreported AGI below filing requirement[b]					
a. Amount reported on tax returns	1,302	1,342	1,362	1,295	1,262
b. Amount reported by persons subject to withholding	1,006	1,116	1,125	1,060	1,013
c. Total estimated AGI below filing requirement[c]	3,690	3,810	3,900	3,640	3,410
d. Amount not reported (line c − line a)	2,388	2,468	2,538	2,345	2,148
2. Amount of AGI reported on nontaxable returns	19,093	18,699	18,225	19,553	18,935
3. AGI on nontaxable returns adjusted to include income of those below filing requirement (line d + line 2)	21,481	21,167	20,763	21,898	21,083
4. AGI on taxable returns	183,935	197,331	210,484	209,669	229,595
5. Estimated total AGI	226,603	240,645	254,450	252,987	272,723
6. Amount unexplained [line 5 − (3 + 4)]	21,187	22,147	23,203	21,420	22,045
7. Amount unexplained as a per cent of reported AGI [line 6 ÷ (2 + 4)]	10.44	10.25	10.15	9.34	8.87

AGI reported on tax returns includes deficit on returns with no AGI.

a Excludes fiduciary returns.

b The filing requirement was a gross income of $500 or more until 1947 and $600 or more thereafter.

c 1945-1947: Ulric H. Weil, op.cit. 1948-1955: line 16 times a blow-up factor obtained from annual Census survey figures.

The blow-up factor is the ratio of the number of income recipients to the estimated number of employees subject to withholding in the money income group 0 to $1,000. The figures used are from Current Population Reports, Series P-60, no. 5, Table 17; no. 6, Table 14; no. 7, Table 19; no. 9, Table 20; no. 11, Table 5; no. 14, Tables 4 and 5; no. 16, Tables 4 and 5; no. 19, Tables 4 and 5; no. 23, Tables 4 and 5.

APPENDIX B

Estimate of Personal Deductions on Taxable Returns for 1951-1953

The estimate of personal deductions for 1951-1953 from *Statistics of Income* was complicated by its inclusion in the taxable return category of returns with only self-employment tax liability. While *Statistics of Income* for those years includes a breakdown of adjusted gross income, by type of tax paid, it does not include such a breakdown of personal deductions. It was therefore necessary to correct the amount of personal deductions reported on taxable returns for a slight overstatement. This was done in the following manner:

1. The standard deductions were estimated by subtracting from total AGI reported on returns with income tax liability (that is, returns with normal, surtax, and alternative tax liability) our estimate of AGI on returns that have both itemized deductions and income tax liability; the resulting difference was then multipled by 0.10. AGI for returns with itemized deductions and income tax liability was obtained by multiplying, by income groups, the actually reported number of such returns by the average AGI on returns with income tax liability.

2. The amount of itemized deductions on returns with income tax liability was estimated by multiplying the average itemized deductions for each income group by the number of returns reporting income tax liability and itemized deductions.

APPENDIX C

Estimates of Tax Liabilities for Four Tax Base Variants for 1953

NOTES TO TABLE 5

Column 2. The tax liability figures presented in Table 5 differ somewhat from those published in *Statistics of Income* for 1953. To make the estimates presented in columns 3 and 4, an estimate of the tax base and its distribution was necessary. Since *Statistics of Income* for 1953 includes no data on the tax base itself, it was necessary to compute a tax base from the available data and recompute the 1953 tax liability to insure comparability between column 2 and columns 3 and 4. The published estimate of individual income tax liability, based on figures reported on tax returns, is $29,431 million. Our computed figure is $29,366 million, a difference of 0.22 per cent.

To obtain our estimate we constructed a frequency distribution of returns by AGI less deductions and number of exemptions. AGI less deductions was obtained by subtracting personal deductions (estimated as described in Appendix B) from the amount of AGI reported on taxable returns in each income group, and dividing by the number of returns in that group. The amount of error resulting from the use of averages was relatively small, since the available data permitted computations on the basis of twenty-five income groups, which made for small class intervals.

A somewhat arbitrary rearraying of the frequencies by exemption classes was necessary to include exemptions for age and blindness. *Statistics of Income* classifies the frequencies only by the number of ordinary exemptions. We therefore had to apportion the blind and aged exemptions among the regular exemption classes to obtain figures of total exemptions per return. In each adjusted gross income group, blind and aged exemptions were assumed to be claimed only on returns with one, two, or three regular exemptions. Blind and aged exemptions were distributed in the following manner: one-sixth into the class with one regular exemption; one-half into the class with two; and one-third into the class with three. The number of blind and aged exemptions claimed somewhat exceeded the number of returns with such exemptions. The excess was assigned to the two-regular-exemption class, but no return was assumed to have more than two blind and aged exemp-

197

tions. Once the blind and aged exemptions had thus been assigned to ordinary exemption classes, the number of returns affected were shifted into a correspondingly higher exemption class, and the result was a distribution of returns by total number of exemptions. The procedure just described was carried out separately for joint returns, since they cannot have less than two regular exemptions. It was assumed that 60 per cent of the returns with blind and aged exemptions fell into the class with two regular exemptions, and the rest into that with three regular exemptions.

The alternative tax returns were allocated, for each income group, among the exemption classes in the same proportion as the total number of returns in that income group were distributed among the exemption classes.

The next step was to obtain average taxable income for the frequencies in each cell by subtracting from its average AGI less deductions the value of the exemption. By multiplying the average taxable income by the corresponding frequencies, and summing the amounts thus obtained for each cell, we obtained an aggregate tax base from which tax liabilities could be computed.

Columns 3, 4, and 5. The estimates of total tax liability due on taxable returns when only exemptions are allowed were made by the same method as that for column 2, except that we subtracted the amount of exemptions from average AGI rather than average AGI less deductions for each income group of the distribution. For column 4, we simply computed the tax liability on the average AGI less deductions in each AGI group and multiplied this by the frequencies in the group.

For column 5, the adjusted gross income itself, as reported on taxable returns, constituted the tax base.

The four tax bases underlying the figures in Table 5 are presented in Tables C-1 to C-4, distributed by rate brackets and AGI groups. From the table the reader will be able to repeat our computations with such alternate sets of bracket rates as he might find of interest or consider more appropriate.

TABLE C-1, *concluded*

Taxable Net Income, by Rate Brackets and by Adjusted Gross Income Groups, 1953

(thousands of dollars)

AGI GROUP	Total Taxable Net Income[a]	RATE BRACKETS				
		0-2	2-4	4-6	6-8	8-10
Under 2	3,368,136	3,368,136				
2-3	7,561,161	7,561,161				
3-5	28,607,318	25,983,123	2,674,195			
5-10	46,161,260	39,028,785	6,436,512	621,884	74,079	
10-20	14,264,812	5,763,418	5,555,606	2,004,734	590,256	202,804
20-50	9,758,112	1,570,938	1,570,938	1,570,938	1,570,938	1,371,834
50-100	3,198,446	226,116	226,116	226,116	226,116	226,116
100-500	1,678,610	55,936	55,936	55,936	55,936	55,963
500 and over	291,438	1,728	1,728	1,728	1,728	1,728
Total	114,889,293	83,509,341	16,521,031	4,481,336	2,519,053	1,858,418

AGI GROUP	RATE BRACKETS					
	38-44	44-50	50-60	60-70	70-80	80-90
Under 2						
2-3						
3-5						
5-10						
10-20						
20-50						
50-100	44,772	43,308	31,234	67,080	49,847	35,100
100-500	158,595	96,468	114,625	8,640	8,640	8,640
500 and over	5,184	5,184	8,640			
Total	208,551	144,960	154,499	75,720	58,487	43,740

(concluded on next page)

TABLE C-1, *concluded*

AGI GROUP	RATE BRACKETS								
	10-12	12-14	14-16	16-18	18-20	20-22	22-26	26-32	32-38
Under 2									
2-3									
3-5									
5-10									
10-20	72,328	64,890	10,776	96,255	76,837	41,702	61,336	84,040	6,588
20-50	644,270	627,772	463,726	226,116	226,116	226,116	375,582	171,502	44,772
50-100	226,116	226,116	226,116	55,936	55,936	55,936	111,872	167,808	167,808
100-500	55,936	55,936	55,936	1,728	1,728	1,728	3,456	5,184	5,184
500 and over	1,728	1,728	1,728						
Total	1,000,378	976,442	758,282	380,035	360,617	325,482	552,246	428,534	224,352

AGI GROUP	RATE BRACKETS				Capital Gains Subject to Alternative Tax
	90-100	100-150	150-200	200 and over	
Under 2					
2-3					1,294
3-5					85,080
5-10					189,848
10-20					307,872
20-50					137,802
50-100	27,530	53,608	8,300		
100-500	8,640	43,103	23,838	4,673	
500 and over				138,097	
Total	36,170	96,711	32,138	142,770	721,896

a Excludes capital gains subject to alternative tax which appear in the last column.

TABLE C-2

Taxable Net Income if Deductions Had Not Been Allowed, by Rate Brackets and by Adjusted Gross Income Groups, 1953

(thousands of dollars)

AGI GROUP	Total Taxable Net Income	RATE BRACKETS 0-2	2-4	4-6	6-8	8-10
Under 2	4,469,087	4,469,087				
2-3	9,749,027	9,502,442	246,585			
3-5	36,756,189	30,746,947	5,947,589	61,653		
5-10	56,980,575	43,736,699	11,716,105	1,275,510	233,333	18,928
10-20	16,697,018	5,763,418	5,759,790	3,409,293	1,198,568	259,630
20-50	11,095,575	1,570,938	1,570,938	1,570,938	1,570,938	1,570,938
50-100	3,684,308	226,116	226,116	226,116	226,116	226,116
100-500	2,055,101	55,936	55,936	55,936	55,936	55,963
500 and over	388,991	1,728	1,728	1,728	1,728	1,728
Total	141,875,871	96,073,311	25,524,787	6,601,174	3,286,619	2,133,276

AGI GROUP	RATE BRACKETS 38-44	44-50	50-60	60-70	70-80	80-90
Under 2						
2-3						
3-5						
5-10						
10-20						
20-50						
50-100	44,772	44,772	67,196	22,729	67,080	67,080
100-500	167,808	167,808	194,996	111,373	8,640	8,640
500 and over	5,184	5,184	8,640	8,640		
Total	217,764	217,764	270,832	142,742	75,720	75,720

(concluded on next page)

TABLE C-2, concluded

AGI GROUP	RATE BRACKETS								
	10-12	12-14	14-16	16-18	18-20	20-22	22-26	26-32	32-38
Under 2									
2-3									
3-5									
5-10									
10-20	158,275	72,328	64,920	10,796	102,733	83,440	85,042	91,994	62,761
20-50	1,072,851	631,606	628,705	481,753	226,116	226,116	452,232	507,549	57,782
50-100	226,116	226,116	226,116	226,116	55,936	55,936	111,872	167,808	167,808
100-500	55,936	55,936	55,936	55,936	1,728	1,728	3,456	5,184	5,184
500 and over	1,728	1,728	1,728	1,728					
Total	1,514,906	987,714	977,405	776,329	386,513	367,220	652,602	772,535	298,535

AGI GROUP	RATE BRACKETS				Capital Gains Subject to Alternative Tax
	90-100	100-150	150-200	200 and over	
Under 2					
2-3					1,294
3-5					
5-10					85,080
10-20					189,848
20-50					
50-100					
100-500	65,229	112,658	25,200	13,085	307,872
500 and over	8,640	43,200	43,200	216,191	137,802
Total	73,869	155,858	68,400	229,276	721,896

a Excludes capital gains subject to alternative tax which appear in the last column.

203

TABLE C-3

Taxable Net Income if Exemptions Had Not Been Allowed, by Rate Brackets and by Adjusted Gross Income Groups, 1953

(thousands of dollars)

AGI GROUP	Total Taxable Net Income^a	RATE BRACKETS				
		0-2	2-4	4-6	6-8	8-10
Under 2	8,212,607	8,212,607				
2-3	15,462,179	14,570,168	892,011			
3-5	54,962,421	47,879,801	7,001,185	81,435		
5-10	70,925,941	47,701,116	21,520,440	1,481,160	215,379	7,846
10-20	17,269,327	5,763,418	5,763,418	4,008,607	1,250,702	264,342
20-50	10,615,345	1,570,938	1,570,938	1,570,938	1,250,702	1,570,938
50-100	3,318,682	226,116	226,116	226,116	226,116	226,116
100-500	1,707,131	55,936	55,936	55,936	55,936	55,936
500 and over	292,285	1,728	1,728	1,728	1,728	1,728
Total	182,765,918	125,981,828	37,081,772	7,425,920	3,320,799	2,126,906

AGI GROUP	RATE BRACKETS					
	38-44	44-50	50-60	60-70	70-80	80-90
Under 2						
2-3						
3-5						
5-10						
10-20						
20-50						
50-100	44,772	44,772	37,855			
100-500	167,808	99,322	124,134	67,080	52,801	36,205
500 and over	5,184	5,184	8,640	8,640	8,640	8,640
Total	217,764	149,278	170,629	75,720	61,441	44,845

(concluded on next page)

204

TABLE C-3, *concluded*

RATE BRACKETS

AGI GROUP	10-12	12-14	14-16	16-18	18-20	20-22	22-26	26-32	32-38
Under 2									
2-3									
3-5									
5-10									
10-20	105,904	72,412	40,524						
20-50	960,372	631,606	599,292	252,076	86,932	62,249	61,336	88,348	18,444
50-100	226,116	226,116	226,116	226,116	226,116	226,116	422,036	237,199	44,772
100-500	55,936	55,936	55,936	55,936	55,936	55,936	111,872	167,808	167,808
500 and over	1,728	1,728	1,728	1,728	1,728	1,728	3,456	5,184	5,184
Total	1,350,056	987,798	923,596	535,856	370,712	346,029	598,700	498,539	236,208

RATE BRACKETS

AGI GROUP	90-100	100-150	150-200	200 and over	Capital Gains Subject to Alternative Tax
Under 2					
2-3					
3-5					
5-10					
10-20					1,294
20-50					85,080
50-100					189,848
100-500	27,530	56,223	8,388	4,856	307,872
500 and over	8,640	43,200	24,112	138,573	137,802
Total	36,170	99,423	32,500	143,429	721,896

[a] Excludes capital gains subject to alternative tax which appear in the last column.

TABLE C-4

Taxable Net Income if neither Deductions nor Exemptions Had Been Allowed, by Rate Brackets and by Adjusted Gross Income Groups, 1953

(thousands of dollars)

AGI GROUP	Total Taxable Net Income	RATE BRACKETS				
		0-2	2-4	4-6	6-8	8-10
Under 2	9,313,411	9,313,411				
2-3	17,650,047	15,450,252	2,199,795			
3-5	63,113,542	50,942,235	11,408,919	762,388		
5-10	81,757,257	47,681,116	30,076,651	3,424,076	491,617	83,797
10-20	19,699,545	5,763,418	5,763,418	5,597,709	1,514,482	625,632
20-50	11,952,384	1,570,938	1,570,938	1,570,938	1,570,938	1,570,938
50-100	3,804,480	226,116	226,116	226,116	226,116	226,116
100-500	2,088,631	55,936	55,936	55,936	55,936	55,936
500 and over	389,840	1,728	1,728	1,728	1,728	1,728
Total	209,764,137	131,005,150	51,303,501	11,638,891	3,860,817	2,564,147

AGI GROUP	RATE BRACKETS					
	38-44	44-50	50-60	60-70	70-80	80-90
Under 2						
2-3						
3-5						
5-10						
10-20						
20-50						
50-100	44,772	44,772	70,548	27,465		
100-500	167,808	167,808	207,068	120,882	67,080	67,080
500 and over	5,184	5,184	8,640	8,640	8,640	8,640
Total	217,764	217,764	286,256	156,987	75,720	75,720

(concluded on next page)

TABLE C-4, *concluded*

				RATE BRACKETS					
AGI GROUP	10-12	12-14	14-16	16-18	18-20	20-22	22-26	26-32	32-38
Under 2									
2-3									
3-5									
5-10									
10-20	249,467	72,412	72,412	40,595	272,739	89,018	110,465	92,004	78,915
20-50	1,570,938	648,514	631,606	603,495	226,116	226,116	452,232	562,029	115,386
50-100	226,116	226,116	226,116	226,116	55,936	55,936	111,872	167,808	167,808
100-500	55,936	55,936	55,936	55,936	1,728	1,728	3,456	5,184	5,184
500 and over	1,728	1,728	1,728	1,728					
Total	2,104,185	1,004,706	987,798	927,870	556,519	372,798	678,025	827,025	367,293

	RATE BRACKETS				Capital Gains Subject to Alternative Tax
	90-100	100-150	150-200	200 and over	
Under 2					
2-3					
3-5					
5-10					1,294
10-20					85,080
20-50					189,848
50-100					307,872
100-500	67,080	117,196	25,350	13,495	137,802
500 and over	8,640	43,200	43,200	217,040	
Total	75,720	160,396	68,550	230,535	721,896

a Excludes capital gains subject to alternative tax which appear in the last column.

APPENDIX D

Supplementary Tables on Personal Deductions, Adjusted Gross Income, and Personal Exemptions, 1918-1956

TABLE D-2

Estimated Adjusted Gross Income on Tax Returns, 1918-1943, and Reported Adjusted Gross Income, 1944-1956

	Taxable Returns			All Returns		
Year	Net Income (1)	Personal Deductions (2)	AGI (3)	Net Income (4)	Personal Deductions (5)	(6)

PART A — RETURNS WITH ITEMIZED AND STANDARD DEDUCTIONS

Year	(1)	(2)	(3)	(4)	(5)	(6)
1918	13,893	1,041	14,934	15,925	1,156	17,—
1919	17,692	1,425	19,117	19,859	1,583	21,—
1920	20,229	1,651	20,880	23,736	1,835	25,—
1921	13,410	1,541	14,951	19,577	2,105	21,—
1922	15,044	1,634	16,678	21,336	2,241	23,—
1923	17,426	1,970	19,396	24,777	2,704	27,—
1924	19,469	2,072	21,541	25,656	2,812	28,—
1925	17,471	1,809	19,280	21,895	2,461	24,—
1926	17,423	1,932	19,355	21,959	2,647	24,—
1927	18,090	2,067	20,157	22,545	2,823	25,—
1928	21,032	2,275	23,307	25,226	3,247	28,4—
1929	20,493	2,232	22,725	24,801	3,424	28,2—
1930	13,693	1,736	15,429	18,119	2,997	21,11—
1931	9,297	1,108	10,405	13,605	2,462	16,0—
1932	7,920	1,086	9,006	11,656	2,174	13,8—
1933	7,373	917	8,290	11,109	1,855	12,964
1934	8,344	987	9,331	12,797	1,727	14,524
1935	10,034	1,106	11,140	14,910	1,773	16,683
1936	14,219	1,445	15,664	19,240	2,001	21,241
1937	15,264	1,633	16,897	21,239	2,239	23,478
1938	12,670	1,453	14,123	18,897	2,129	21,026
1939	15,804	1,663	17,467	23,192	2,326	25,518
1940	23,558	2,317	25,875	36,589	3,332	39,921
1941	45,481	3,838	49,319	58,226	4,806	63,032
1942	65,949	6,721	72,670	77,346	7,964	85,310
1943	96,336	8,218	104,554	97,721	8,428	106,149
1944			115,173			116,877
1945			118,104			120,552
1946			118,721			134,754
1947			135,891			150,326
1948			142,667			164,126
1949			139,030			161,116
1950			159,256			179,859
1951			183,935			203,028
1952			197,331			216,031
1953b			210,484			228,708
1954b			209,669			229,221
1955b			229,595			248,530
1956b			249,551			267,724

(concluded on next page)

TABLE D-1

Personal Expense Deductions by Major Types of Deductions, Taxable Individual and Fiduciary Returns, 1918-1956

(millions of dollars)

YEAR	Contributions (1)	Taxes Paid (2)	Interest Paid (3)	Property Losses* (4)	Medical Expenses (5)	Child Care (6)	Misc. Items (7)	Standard Deductions (8)	Total (9)
1918a	234	229	431	12			135		1,041
1919a	291	324	611	15			185		1,425
1920a	349	372	700	17			214		1,651
1921	319	339	674	9			200		1,541
1922	343	363	707	9			212		1,634
1923	422	394	886	13			255		1,970
1924	441	425	922	15			269		2,072
1925	371	456	734	13			235		1,809
1926	395	487	787	13			251		1,932
1927	423	537	827	11			268		2,067
1928	459	576	927	19			295		2,275
1929	441	560	922	19			289		2,232
1930	357	499	640	15			225		1,736
1931	242	340	371	12			144		1,108
1932	231	353	352	10			141		1,086
1933	185	308	296	9			119		917
1934	200	337	313	10			128		987
1935	227	386	327	12			143		1,106
1936	312	532	397	17			187		1,445
1937	352	649	405	15			212		1,633

* Personal Property.

(continued on next page)

TABLE D-1, continued

YEAR	Contributions (1)	Taxes Paid (2)	Interest Paid (3)	Property Losses* (4)	Medical Expenses (5)	Child Care (6)	Misc. Items (7)	Standard Deductions (8)	Total (9)
1938	310	602	340	12			188		1,453
1939	387	663	383	14			216		1,663
1940	570	901	467	22			356		2,317
1941	876	1,380	754	44			384	401	3,838
1942	1,320	1,893	1,010	91	534		762	1,112	6,721
1943	1,813	2,101	1,038	116	773		561	1,814	8,218
1944	1,235	1,152	696	149	722		695	7,883	12,582
1945	1,424	1,225	683	128	836		1,027	7,873	13,195
1946	1,559	1,269	694	137	906		1,225	7,455	13,245
1947	1,875	1,547	855	193	1,156		1,517	8,541	15,682
1948	1,756	1,500	903	179	1,040		1,648	9,545	16,571
1949	1,897	1,812	1,106	171	1,170		1,656	9,082	16,895
1950	2,129	2,068	1,372	248	1,260		1,940	10,135	19,152
1951	n.a.	n.a.	n.a.	n.a.	n.a.		n.a.	11,566	22,504
1952	2,968	3,034	2,095	293	1,843		2,440	12,069	24,742
1953	3,383	3,453	2,585	326	2,043		2,638	12,533	26,961
1954	3,671	3,826	2,985	359	2,482	73	2,479	11,600	27,476
1955	n.a.	n.a.	n.a.	n.a.	n.a.	n.a.	n.a.	12,027	30,524
1956	4,650	5,543	4,544	295	2,993	95	2,916	12,471	33,508

Deductions on fiduciary returns are included up to 1953.
They consist of interest, taxes, and miscellaneous items.
a Omits returns with net income below $1,000.

(concluded on next page)

TABLE D-1, *concluded*

Source, by column

(1) For 1917 and 1920 the contribution figure for all returns is given in *Statistics of Income* for 1949, Table 17. On the basis of their relation to net income, we estimated the contributions on taxable returns for 1918-1921. From 1922 on, the figures are from *Statistics of Income*.

(2) The *Statistics of Income* figures beginning with 1927 were extrapolated back to 1918 with the help of a series of state and local taxes given in *Historical Statistics on State and Local Government Finance, 1902-1953* (Bureau of the Census, 1955, p. 17).

(3) The relation between interest and interest deducted as personal expense on tax returns was found to be rather stable in the period 1928-1939. In most of the years of that period, personal interest deducted was somewhat over one-half of interest reported. We extrapolated the 1928-1939 relation into the 1918-1927 period. Beginning with 1928, actually reported figures are available.

(4) Casualty losses of personal property are separately tabulated only from 1939 on. The ratio of casualty losses to income in 1939-1940 was therefore used for all prior years.

(7) For 1940-1943, miscellaneous personal deductions were obtained as a residual after subtracting all other personal and business deductions (such as rents and royalties losses, bad debts, and net operating loss carryovers) from total deductions. The 1940-1943 figures are thus comparable to the miscellaneous deduction figures for the years after 1943. For the years prior to 1939, the 1940-1943 ratio of miscellaneous to all other personal deductions (contributions, taxes paid, interest paid, and personal property losses) was applied.

(5, 6, & 8) *Statistics of Income.*

(9) For the years 1944-1956, the total is more or less the sum of figures given separately in *Statistics of Income*, except that the standard deduction figure was computed by us on the basis of the amount of income reported on 1040A (short form) returns. For the years before 1944, the figures for total personal deductions are the sum of our estimates—in some instances very crude. They are at all times smaller than the figures for total deductions given in *Statistics of Income*, which for these years include various business deductions.

TABLE D-2, *concluded*

	Taxable Returns			All Returns		
YEAR	Net Income (1)	Personal Deductions (2)	AGI (3)	Net Income (4)	Personal Deductions (5)	AGI (6)
			PART B			
		RETURNS WITH ITEMIZED DEDUCTIONS ONLY				
1941	35,343	3,437	38,780	41,337	4,164	45,501
1942	48,525	5,609	54,134	53,173	6,421	59,594
1943	67,911	6,404	74,315	68,499	6,563	75,062
1944			32,880			33,106
1945			35,322			35,498
1946			38,844			40,240
1947			45,088			46,451
1948			43,522			45,500
1949			45,337			47,367
1950			53,820			55,827
1951			63,927			65,952
1952			72,422			74,383
1953b			80,817			82,871
1954b			89,381			92,334
1955b			104,641			108,528
1956b			119,731			123,719

a Omits returns with net income below $1,000. On the basis of 1921-1924 relationship, net income on all returns would be about 1 per cent higher, and deductions roughly 3 per cent, if the returns of persons reporting statutory net incomes of less than $1,000 had been tabulated. Almost all of the omitted incomes and deductions were reported on nontaxable returns.

b Excludes fiduciary returns.

Source: Net income figures from *Statistics of Income*. Personal deductions in column 2 from Table D-1. The personal deductions on all tax returns in column 5 were estimated by methods similar to those given for deductions on taxable returns. The AGI figures in columns 3 and 6 are the sum of net income and personal deductions in columns 1 and 2, and 4 and 5, respectively, for the 1918-1943 period. For the 1944-1956 period, the AGI figures are as reported in *Statistics of Income*.

TABLE D-3

Personal Exemptions as Per Cent of Adjusted Gross Income Reported on Taxable Returns, 1918-1956

(amounts in millions of dollars)

YEAR	Personal Exemptions[a] Amount (1)	Per Cent of AGI (2)	YEAR	Personal Exemptions[a] Amount (1)	Per Cent of AGI (2)
1918	5,772	38.6	1939	6,564	37.6
1919	6,957	36.4	1940	10,401	40.2
1920	8,813	40.3	1941	22,594	45.7
1921	5,766	38.6	1942	29,540	40.6
1922	6,054	36.3			
			1943	45,848	43.8
1923	7,521	38.8	1944	46,975	40.6
1924	8,170	37.9	1945	47,331	40.1
1925	6,298	32.7	1946	39,654	33.4
1926	6,244	32.3	1947	44,292	32.6
1927	6,152	30.5			
			1948	50,888	35.7
1928	6,385	27.4	1949	50,155	36.1
1929	6,270	27.6	1950	55,243	34.7
1930	5,164	33.5	1951	61,428	33.4
1931	3,842	36.9	1952	64,535	32.7
1932	3,431	38.1			
			1953	67,896	32.3
1933	3,094	37.3	1954	66,966	31.9
1934	3,175	34.0	1955	71,182	31.0
1935	3,748	33.6	1956	74,648	29.9
1936	5,001	31.9			
1937	5,794	34.3			
1938	5,240	37.1			

[a] Personal exemptions for the years 1918-1933 are normal tax exemptions; for 1934-1953 normal and surtax exemptions coincided except for the war years 1943-1945, for which surtax exemptions are shown.

Source: Column 1: *Statistics of Income*. Column 2: column 1 as per cent of column 3, Table D-2.

APPENDIX E

Items Included in Miscellaneous Deductions

The miscellaneous deductions category has always included business expense items. From 1944 on it has contained only those expenses of a business or professional nature which were incurred by persons not required to use the business schedules of the tax return, that is, mainly expenses incurred in the production of income of wage and salary earners and of investors and rentiers. But before 1944 some other business expenses were also included in the miscellaneous category, particularly whenever a schedule within a return reported a net loss.

Below are listed the main business expense and loss items, as well as some which have been included earlier in the miscellaneous category and later eliminated. The dates in parentheses are for the last year that each allowance was included in miscellaneous:

1. Capital net losses (1923)
2. Net losses from sales of real estate, stocks, bonds, etc., held less than two years (1925)
3. Net losses from business and partnerships (1929)
4. Gambling losses in excess of gambling gains (1933)
5. Amounts distributed to beneficiaries as reported on fiduciary returns (1936)
6. Bad debts (1938)
7. Net operating loss deductions resulting from unabsorbed net operating losses from business, partnerships, and common trust funds, for two preceding taxable years (1940-1943)
8. Current year net losses from rents and royalties (1943)

Business expense and loss items still included, as of the most recent year, are:

1. Gambling losses not exceeding gambling gains (since 1913)
2. Amortizable bond premiums (since 1943)
3. Expenses incurred in the production and collection of taxable income, or in the management of property held for the production of taxable income (since 1942)
4. Expenses in connection with taxpayer's job, such as union dues, tools and supplies, and employment agency fees (since 1945)

APPENDIX F

Notes on Estimates of Philanthropic Contributions

NOTES TO TABLE 16

Adjusted Commerce Department Estimates

From 1929 to 1942 the figures are those published in *Survey of Current Business*, June 1944, Table 3, except for gifts to political organizations, which we eliminated. For years later than 1942-1951, figures have been available to us only in unpublished form, covering only gifts to religion, local social and welfare agencies, national social and welfare agencies, and foreign relief agencies. For the major categories of health, hospitals, and education, no figures were available for that period. We therefore blew up the unpublished Commerce figures for the available categories, assuming that the 1943-1951 ratio of total contributions to them was the same, on average, as in the 1929-1942 period. This assumption, though crude, is not out of line with what we could gather from other sources on the relation of religious and welfare giving to total contributions. The estimates on which this judgment is based are presented in Table F-1. For the period 1929-1942, the average ratio of total contributions to contributions for religious, welfare, and foreign aid causes was 1.27. Our rough estimates in Table F-1 give a ratio of 1.24-1.26 in 1952, and 1.22-1.25 in 1954 for the same categories.

While we consider the general magnitude of the estimate presented for 1952 and 1954 probably correct, the roughness of several of the component estimates leaves considerable room for error. In the main, our estimate for contributions to foundations may be too low. The great increase in the number of family foundations in recent times may have led to a larger total of gifts to such foundations than the estimate includes. On the other hand, our method of determining contributions made by individuals as a residual may have led to overestimates for such fields as religion, health, and welfare. In these areas, unlike education, we had no direct evidence of individuals' gifts, but had to resort to subtracting major items on which there was some information from estimates of total philanthropic gifts. For health and welfare, our estimates of individuals' gifts are higher relative to the estimated total than for education (see notes to Table F-1). It is also possible that our subtractions for corporate contributions are too low since some corpora-

216

tion philanthropic gifts are apparently reported as business expense. This too would lead to an overestimate for individuals whenever we used the residual method.

Table F-2 shows a number of series which, though they cover only parts of philanthropy and are therefore fragmentary, nevertheless convey some idea of the trends that prevailed in the area of philanthropic giving for the period under study. For the series shown, the percentage rise for the ten-year period 1942-1952 is on the whole similar to that for the extrapolated Commerce Department estimates. While the series for fourteen Protestant denominations and higher education would suggest that the extrapolated Commerce series understates the rise in philanthropic giving, the other series presented all show a smaller relative increase. In addition to the Commerce figures, only the Community Chest series for 285 cities and the series for 14 churches cover primarily the gifts of living donors. The other series shown include substantial amounts from other sources, a particularly important point regarding the education series, in which the sharpest relative increases probably occurred in gifts from corporations and foundations.

Finally, data bearing on the reasonableness of the Commerce Department figures up to 1942, on our extension of the Commerce series beyond 1942, and on the estimates presented in Table F-1, are found in the three national surveys of family income and expenditures that included gifts to philanthropy explicitly. These are the 1935-1936, 1941, and 1950 (urban population only) survey data presented in Table 23, Chapter 4. The summary figures are restated below.

	1935-1936	1941	1950
	(per cent of income)		
Gifts to religious organizations	1.0	1.2	1.2
All others	0.2	0.5	0.6
Total	1.3	1.7	1.8
Total on tax returns[a]	1.9-2.0	2.1	2.4[b]

a See p. 81 of text.
b Estimated by assigning contribution rate of 1.66 per cent of income to returns with standard deduction.

As already noted, the survey figures show lower percentages of reported income for reported philanthropic contributions. This may, however, merely indicate that income is relatively less understated in the consumer surveys than on tax returns—a distinct possibility.[1] What appears of greater significance to us is the relationship between contributions to religious organizations and all others suggested by the survey figures. "All others" amount to about one-fourth of the total in the 1941 and 1950 surveys. In our estimates for 1952 and 1954 the ratios are slightly higher (31 to 35 per cent of the total). Some of the estimates, arriving at considerably higher figures for philanthropic contributions than those in this study, place contributions to other than religious groups at 50 per cent of the total.[2] If the survey figures are indicative of the actual relationship between gifts to religious and to other fields, and if the estimate that we used for gifts to religious groups is approximately correct, then it would appear that even our estimates are more likely to err on the high side than on the low.

TABLE F-1

Estimated Total Amount of Philanthropic Contributions by
Individuals, Classified by Area of Service, 1952 and 1954

(millions of dollars)

AREA OF SERVICE	*1952*	*1954*
1. Religion	2,281	2,776
2. Education	114	143
3. Health and hospitals	259-303	283-369
4. Social welfare	323	465
5. Private foreign aid	44-91	60-139
6. Foundations	153	160
7. Miscellaneous	122-138	156-187
Total	3,296-3,403	4,043-4,239

NOTES TO TABLE F-1

(Notes refer to 1952, but apply also to 1954)
Source, by line

1. *Religious organizations.* The only firmly based series on gifts for religious causes, covering a large segment of churches, is that published annually for about 50 Protestant and Eastern Orthodox churches in

[1] Most consumer expenditure surveys find that income is understated more than expenditures, so that even the survey data, as presented above, have an upward bias. See, for instance, Wharton School of Finance and Commerce, University of Pennsylvania, *Study of Consumer Expenditures*, Vol. xi: *Income, Savings, Insurance, and Gifts and Contributions*, p. xv.

[2] See, for instance, Andrews, *Philanthropic Giving*, p. 73 (see text Table 16, Chapter 4, above for Andrews' estimates); also Thomas Karter, *op.cit.*, and Research and Statistics Note No. 38, 1957, Division of Program Research, Social Security Administration.

the United States by the Joint Department of Stewardship and Benevolences, National Council of the Churches of Christ in the U.S.A., in *Statistics of Giving*. The figure for 1952, covering contributions to 48 religious bodies with a membership of 33.4 million, is $1.4 billion. It does not include contributions to Catholic and Jewish religious bodies and omits a significant number of Protestant churches. If we project the per member gifts of the 48 churches covered in *Statistics of Giving* to the denominations not covered (using for this membership figures published annually in the *Statistical Abstract of the United States*, and making rough adjustments for differences in concept of "membership"), we obtain a figure of $2.6 billion for total gifts in the field. Probably a more informed estimate is that prepared by Thomas Karter of the Division of Research and Statistics, Social Security Administration, Department of Health, Education and Welfare (hereafter referred to as HEW) in "Health and Welfare Expenditures of Private Philanthropic Agencies in 1954" (Research and Statistics Note No. 15, 1956).[1] We have adopted the HEW figure for our estimate:

Total contributions to religious organizations, 1952 $2,354 million

Minus: Contributions from:
    Foundations   8
    Corporations   16
    Bequests   49

Equals: Contributions from living donors $2,281 million

The small estimate of foundation grants is based on F. Emerson Andrews' discussion of this subject, which suggests that probably not more than 2 per cent of foundation grants go to organized religion (*Philanthropic Foundations*, pp. 17, 278, and 293-294). Andrews estimates total foundation grants to have been in the neighborhood of $400 million. The estimate for corporations is based on Andrews' survey of 326 corporations' contributions in 1950, 4 per cent of which went to religion (see *Corporation Giving*, New York, 1952, p. 221). Corporation tax returns show $399 million of deductible contributions for 1952 (*Statistics of Income*, Part II), which, with Andrews' ratio, produced our estimate above.

The figure for bequests is based on estate tax return tabulations. For

[1] See also Karter's estimates for more recent years in "Voluntary Agency Expenditures for Health and Welfare From Philanthropic Contributions, 1930-55," *Social Security Bulletin*, February 1958.

returns filed in 1954, bequests to religious bodies constituted 9.4 per cent of total bequests of $354.5 million out of gross estates of $7.4 billion. Estimates supplied by Robert J. Lampman show that these were the estates of the upper 2.4 per cent of decedents. He also estimates that the upper 2.4 per cent of living adults held in that year about 28 per cent of all gross estates. The distribution of wealth was somewhat more unequal among decedents than among adults. The estates for which tax returns were filed may thus have accounted for roughly 30 per cent of the wealth of all decedents. In other words about $17.3 billion of gross estates were not reported on tax returns. Examination of a distribution of taxable and nontaxable estate tax returns by size of gross estates suggests that about 1 per cent of gross estates under $60,000 may have been absorbed by philanthropic bequests.[2] This would add an additional $172.9 million of bequests to the reported $354.5 million. Since these are figures based on returns filed in 1954 and our estimates concern 1952, we lowered our total bequest estimate from $527.5 to $487.8 million, an interpolation between 1951 and 1954, the years for which estate tax return tabulations are available. We assumed one-tenth, or $49 million, of these bequests went to religious organizations.

2. *Education.* This estimate is based on Office of Education figures for total gifts and grants to institutions of higher education for 1951-1952. For the most part these figures are not broken down by source of gift, and we therefore made the necessary allocation on the basis of a very detailed survey of 701 institutions by the Council for Financial Aid to Education covering 1954-1955. Our computations are shown below (in millions of dollars):

	Office of Education Totals[a] (1)	% from Living Donors[b] (2)	Living Donors (1)×(2) (3)
Gifts and Grants for:			
Current purposes	149.8	27.5	41.2
Nonexpendable funds (endowment)	96.2	36.5	35.1
Student aid	10.5	29.1	3.1
Plant expansion (a) total	71.6		
(b) from individuals	38.5	90.2	34.7
Total	328.1	(34.8)	114.1

[2] *Statistics of Income,* 1953, Part I, pp. 72-75.

a *Statistics of Higher Education: Receipts, Expenditures, and Property*, 1951-1952, p. 46. Student aid figures were estimated by multiplying total student aid income for 1952 by the ratio of student aid funds from philanthropy to the total of student aid funds for 1954, when the distribution was made for the first time. Figures from individuals for plant expansion are an interpolation between 1950 and 1954, when both the total and the amount given by individuals were tabulated. For 1952 only the former is available.

b Council for Financial Aid to Education, *Voluntary Support of America's Colleges and Universities*, 1954-1955, 1956. The percentage for current purposes is based on Table 7A, lines d, e, and f; for endowment, on Table 7B, lines d, e, and f; for student aid, on Table 7A, column 4, lines d, e, and f; and for plant expansion, the ratio of lines d, e, and f to lines d, e, f, and g in column 3, Table 7A was used. To compute our percentages we, of course, omitted grants from governments from Tables 7A and 7B.

3. *Health and hospitals.* For 1951, the President's Commission on the Health Needs of the Nation estimated philanthropy's contribution to civilian expenditures for health and medical services and facilities at $400 million (see *Building America's Health*, Vol. 4, Washington, 1953, p. 151). Since the Commission's figure is for 1951, we estimated a comparable 1952 figure by assuming that the relation of philanthropic gifts to total medical expenditures was the same in 1952 as in 1951. We used the series in Table 36 for this purpose, which yielded an estimate of $428 million. The Commission considers its figure understated because of the inclusion of contributions for hospital construction elsewhere. We therefore added to the above estimate another $197 million, a figure cited by the American Association of Fund-Raising Counsel (hereafter AAFRC) in *The Bulletin*, Vol. 3, No. 12. These two figures suggest a total of $625 million for health and hospitals in 1952. We also have Thomas Karter's estimate of $675 million for the same year (HEW, *op.cit.*, Table 3) for total health expenditures from philanthropic contributions. Adjustments for these two estimates, in millions of dollars, are shown below:

Total contributions for health and hospitals	$625-675
Minus: Contributions from:	
Corporations	106
Religious organizations	70
Bequests	109
Foundations	81-87
Equals: Contributions from living donors	$259-303

The figure for corporation gifts was obtained by multiplying the $399 million of contributions reported on corporate tax returns for

1952 by 0.27, the proportion of contributions that the 326 corporations in Andrews' 1950 survey gave to health agencies (*Corporation Giving*, p. 70). The contributions from religious organizations are Karter's estimate (HEW, *op.cit.*, Table 3). Bequests to health organizations were estimated by multiplying our estimate of total bequests ($487.8, see note to line 1) by 0.224, a ratio arrived at by AAFRC on the basis of a study of published bequests of recent years (see AAFRC, *The Bulletin*, Vol. 3, No. 18). No direct information on foundation gifts to health and hospitals for any recent year has crossed our path. A recent analysis of charitable organizations registered in New York State by the Charities Registration Bureau of the Department of Social Welfare showed that of $463 million contributions reported $64 million came from foundations. For lack of other quantitative information we have utilized these figures in estimating the foundation component of contributions to both the health and welfare areas. Of the $463 million reported, about $50 million appears to have been destined for education,[3] an area in which foundation grants have constituted about one-fifth of the total (see the study by the Council for Financial Aid to Education cited in note to line 2 as well as a recent survey of 398 institutions by the American Alumni Council, which reported 21 per cent of contributions coming from foundations). This leaves about $54 million, or 13 per cent, of foundation grants out of total contributions of $413 million. Of the latter figure about $300 million was for health and welfare purposes, and 13 per cent may thus be a fair approximation of the foundation contribution to health and welfare combined. On this basis our estimate of foundation grants to health organizations comes to $81 to $88 million ($625 to $675 million × 0.13).[4]

4. *Social welfare.* For total contributions to welfare organizations in 1952 we adopted Karter's figure (*op.cit.*, Table 3). Karter estimated

[3] See Bernard Perlman, *Fund Raising in New York State*, Charities Registration, New York State Department of Social Welfare, June 1957.

[4] Assuming that 0.13 is an approximately correct over-all figure for health and welfare, the further division of the foundation component between these two areas does not affect the result we are ultimately seeking in this study, namely an estimate of the amount of philanthropic contributions of individuals. However, those interested in health and welfare as separate items should be warned that our division of foundation grants between health and welfare may be incorrect. For instance, F. Emerson Andrews observes that the "broad field of health" probably "receives larger foundation support than social welfare" (see *Philanthropic Foundations*, pp. 284-291). Thus our estimate of $81 to $87 million for health may be somewhat too low and that of $91 million for welfare (note to line 4) somewhat too high. In the absence of any more precise guide we preferred to leave these estimates unchanged.

total welfare expenditures financed by philanthropic contributions at $935 million, of which he assigns $235 million to church welfare, leaving us with $700 million of nonchurch contributions. The following subtractions were made for an estimate of contributions from individuals:

Total nonchurch contributions for welfare	$700 million
Minus: Contributions from:	
Corporations	177
Bequests	109
Foundations	91
Equals: Estimated from living donors	$323 million

Corporations undoubtedly made very substantial contributions for welfare purposes. For instance, 40 per cent of the amount raised by Community Chests has been obtained from corporations (see Community Chests and Councils of America, *Trends in Giving*, 1955, Bulletin 182, p. 4). Corporations contributed about $100 million to Community Chests in 1952. Andrews (*Corporation Giving*, p. 70) finds his sample of 326 corporations made 44 per cent of their gifts to welfare agencies. Using the reported contributions of $399 million and multiplying by 0.443 we obtain the above estimate for the corporations' share.

The estimate for bequests was arrived at by multiplying total bequests ($487.8 million, see note to line 1) by 0.223, a ratio cited by AAFRC (*The Bulletin*, Vol. 3, No. 18) on the basis of a study of publicly announced bequests. As already fully described in note to line 3, the foundations estimate is: $700 million $\times$ 0.13 = $91 million.

5. *Private foreign aid.* The Commerce Department's balance of payments statistics show that private institutional foreign aid was $175 million in 1952.[5] A large part of this, about three-fourths, is raised by, and channeled through, religious organizations; and a large part, except funds raised by Jewish groups, is included under religious organizations in Table F-1. Andrews has estimated gifts made directly to foreign relief organizations at $40 million for 1948 (*Philanthropic Giving*, p. 73), and an unpublished estimate supplied by Andrews places such gifts at $50 million for 1954. Apparently he considers all the contributions made to foreign aid agencies associated with particular religious

[5] See Jesse L. C. Adams, "Postwar Private Gifts to Foreign Countries Total $6 billion," *Foreign Commerce Weekly*, June 17, 1957.

denominations as already covered under religious organizations, and therefore to avoid duplication does not include them under foreign aid. On this basis only about one-fourth of the total reported by the Commerce Department as institutional remittances to foreign countries should be included in Table F-1 under foreign aid. However, it does not appear likely that gifts to the various Jewish foreign aid groups (such as the American Jewish Joint Distribution Committee) are duplicated by the estimates under religion. A 1954 tabulation of income and expenditures of some 60 voluntary relief agencies, which register with the Advisory Committee on Voluntary Foreign Aid (then under the Foreign Operations Administration), shows that about one-fourth of the total income (cash and in kind) of these agencies is accounted for by nonsectarian agencies and somewhat over one-fourth by Jewish groups. If we consider the latter as not duplicated in the religious sector, the estimate for giving to foreign aid groups in 1952 is $91 million, most of which probably came from individuals.

6. *Foundations.* In this we rely mainly on Andrews' estimates. He estimates foundation expenditures in 1953 at $371 million,[6] of which about $71 million constitutes the current gifts of individuals and corporations which are merely being channeled through the foundations to their ultimate recipients (*Philanthropic Foundations*, p. 17). An additional $150 million of current gifts "stays" with the foundations as additions to foundation capital according to an unpublished estimate of Andrews'.[7] Thus an estimated total of $221 million may have been given to foundations in 1952. Foundations receive their gifts from a number of sources. The $71 million of current gifts channeled through foundations comes mainly from individuals and corporations. Andrews estimates that about 20 per cent of foundation expenditures come from family foundations and 10 per cent from corporation foundations. We have used these proportions to allocate the $71 million of "through" gifts to individuals and corporations, that is, two-thirds for the former and one-third for the latter.

Of the estimated $150 million that goes into foundation endowment, the major part comes from individuals, much of it in the form of bequests from the estates of deceased persons rather than from living

[6] A much lower figure for foundation expenditures ("in excess of $140 million") is cited by John Price Jones (*The American Giver*, New York, 1954, p. 97) for 1952. Andrews' figure appears to be based on a more extended examination of available figures.

[7] Karter (*op.cit.*, p. 4) estimates this item at $100 million for 1954.

donors. We have no quantitative information on the importance of bequests as compared to gifts from living donors in the flow of funds to foundations. In their discussion of community trusts, Harrison and Andrews remark that "bequests are the chief source of capital funds."[8] Typically, most foundations are set up during the founder's lifetime and receive significant annual gifts out of his current income. At the founder's death (or after the death of members of his family) the foundation may receive further gifts from the estate of the deceased. For instance, of the over three million shares of nonvoting stock that the Ford Foundation has received at various times from the Ford family, almost one-half came from the estates of Henry and Edsel Ford.[9] Since community trusts hold only a small share of the total assets of all foundations, and since the case of the Ford Foundation, because of its size, may not be typical, a conservative estimate of the relative size of individuals' contributions to foundations in the form of bequests may be one-fourth of the total of such contributions by individuals. Some part of the funds that went into foundation endowment undoubtedly came from corporations. Andrews estimates the share of foundations assets held by corporation foundations at 6 per cent of the total. We have assumed this percentage to take account of corporation gifts to foundation capital. Thus we have estimated the gifts of individuals that merely flow through the foundations at $47 million and the gifts that are added to foundation capital at $106 million, resulting in a rough estimate of $153 million for gifts to foundations in 1952.

7. *Miscellaneous.* A large number of small and varied philanthropies have not yet been accounted for in the above categories, including organizations interested in humane care for animals, nature conservation, cultural activities, and museums. A clue to the size of gifts to these miscellaneous philanthropies is contained in the recent report of the Charities Registration Bureau of New York covering 1955. In the report,[10] the miscellaneous items constituted about 16 per cent of gifts classifiable under health, welfare, education, and foreign aid. Applying this ratio to our estimate of individuals' gifts to these four areas of philanthropy (those for New York are for total giving), we arrive at an estimate of $122 to $128 million.

[8] Shelby M. Harrison and F. Emerson Andrews, *American Foundations for Social Welfare*, New York, 1946, p. 33.
[9] See Andrews, *Philanthropic Foundations*, p. 59.
[10] *Op.cit.*, pp. 5-6.

TABLE F-2

Data on Philanthropic Contributions from Seven Selected Sources, 1929-1954

(millions of dollars)

Year	Community Chests 285 Cities (no corporations) (1)	8 Cities (2)	14 Protestant Bodies (3)	Jewish Community Campaigns (4)	Red Cross (5)	Extrapolated Commerce Series (6)	Higher Education[a] (current operating and endowment only) (7)
1929			445.5			1,449	
1930			420.7			1,378	89.7
1931			367.6			1,264	
1932			309.9			990	77.6
1933			260.6			806	
1934			260.5			832	
1935			267.5			902	
1936			279.7			952	
1937			296.0			1,099	
1938			307.2			990	
1939	45.0[b]		302.8			970	
1940	50.3		311.2			1,053	85.0
1941	54.0[b]		336.5			1,060	
1942	81.0[b]	33.2	358.2		71.0	1,259	84.4
1943	101.7		400.3		147.4	1,568	
1944	104.0[b]		460.8		216.4	1,824	120.1
1945	89.6		550.7	71.2	231.7	2,045	
1946	75.7		606.9	131.4	118.5	2,151	150.4[b]
1947	75.7		683.3	156.6	79.1	2,191	
1948	78.1		774.4	200.7	73.0	2,446	167.4
1949	77.5		874.2	170.3	67.5	2,549	
1950	86.1		934.1	142.2	64.2	2,729	185.4
1951	101.0		1,031.6	136.0	77.3	2,931	
1952	108.2	49.5	1,120.7	121.2	83.8	3,356	246.0
1953	118.8		1,232.0	115.3	85.5		
1954	119.6		1,350.0	107.5	81.5	4,153	297.8
1952 as per cent of 1942	134	149	313	151[c]	118	267	291

[a] Figures are for fiscal years ending June 30 of respective calendar years.
[b] Interpolated. For method see notes below.
[c] 1952 as per cent of 1945. The corresponding percentage for column 6 is 157.0.

Source by column

(1) Community Chests and Councils of America. Figures for the years 1940, 1943, and 1945 1954, excluding an estimated amount received from corporations, were supplied to us by Esther M. Moore, Director, Department of Research and Statistics. For 1939, 1941-1942, and 1944, the

APPENDIX F

NOTES TO TABLE 17

Column 1. *Statistics of Income.*

Column 2. This is the sum of reported contributions (shown in column 1) and an estimate of contributions by persons who did not file a tax return or who chose the standard deduction.

From 1924 to 1940, the estimates of unreported contributions are for those who did not file tax returns. They were computed by attributing a contribution rate to the income not covered on tax returns. We adhered throughout to the adjusted gross income concept. From total AGI (using the series described in Appendix A, notes to Table 1, line 1) we subtracted all AGI reported on tax returns as well as the amount of AGI unexplained. The difference is assumed to be the estimated AGI of nonfilers (the amount unexplained is discussed in Appendix A, notes to Table 1, line 7).

Since nonfilers are those not required to file tax returns, we imputed to them a contribution rate (ratio of contributions to AGI) equal to that reported for each given year on the tax returns of the income group into which most of the nonfilers might be expected to fall. To be on the conservative side in this hypothetical estimate, all the unexplained amount was allocated to tax return filers in proportion to their income, and the "reported" rate imputed to nonfilers was calculated

---

Notes to Table F-2, *concluded*

figures were interpolated by a charted index of total gifts in 285 cities (see Community Chests and Councils, *Trends in Giving*, 1955, Bulletin 182, p. 3).

(2) Community Chests and Councils, *Expenditures for Community Health and Welfare*, 1952, Bulletins 174 (p. 3) and 175 (p. 11).

(3) From a special compilation by the Department of Research and Survey, National Council of the Churches of Christ in the U.S.A.

(4) S. P. Goldberg, "Jewish Communal Services" in *American Jewish Yearbook*, 1957, p. 168.

(5) From Office of Research Information, American National Red Cross.

(6) *1929-1942*: Department of Commerce, *Survey of Current Business*, June 1944. *1943-1952*: Based on unpublished estimates by the Office of Business Economics, Department of Commerce, of contributions to religious organizations, social and welfare agencies, and foreign relief agencies for 1943-1951. The 1952 estimate for these items was obtained by extrapolating their 1951 relation to estimated religious and welfare consumption expenditures as given in *National Income*, 1954 Edition (Supplement to the *Survey of Current Business*), Table 30. These 1943-1952 estimates for religious, welfare, and foreign aid gifts were in turn blown up by multiplying by the average ratio of total contributions to these items for the period 1929-1942.

(7) See U.S. Office of Education, *Biennial Survey of Education in the United States*, beginning with issue of 1929-1930. The figures do not include gifts for plant expansion since for most years no estimates were given for this item. In 1951-1952 it amounted to $72 million and in 1953-1954 to $104 million. For 1945-1946, the figure for gifts to endowment was estimated by interpolating between the 1943-1944 and 1947-1948 figures.

with this broader income base, that is, it was lowered correspondingly. The income groups in which nonfilers were assumed to fall, in each period, and the contribution rates assigned to them, are shown below:

Year	Income Groups[a] ($000's)	Contribution Rates for Nonfilers (per cent)
1924	0-3	1.5
1925-1931	0-5	1.3-1.5
1932-1939	0-3	1.8-2.1
1940-1943	0-2	2.1
1944-1954	0-2	1.7-2.0

[a] Net income groups until 1943; AGI groups thereafter.

The contribution rates shown above were multiplied by the estimated AGI of nonfilers to obtain the estimates of unreported contributions for 1924-1940.

From 1941 on, estimated contributions not reported on tax returns also include estimates for persons filing returns with standard deductions. For the years 1941-1943, when the standard deduction could be taken only on returns with less than $3,000 gross income, the ratio of contributions to income on returns for 1940 in the 0 to $3,000 group was used to estimate contributions for that income group. This approach appears reasonable in the light of the ratios shown in Chart 3. In 1944 the standard deduction became available for all tax returns, and it was therefore necessary to impute contribution rates to returns in all income groups, although the relative frequency of returns with standard deduction was greatest for low income returns. An estimate of contributions for all tax returns in 1944 was obtained by applying to 1944 reported income the estimated 1943 ratio of contributions to reported income. From this figure the reported contributions on returns with itemized deductions were subtracted, and the residual taken as the contributions that would have been reported on short-form returns if none had used the standard deduction. A contribution rate of 1.5 per cent for returns with standard deductions was thus obtained for 1944.

We used this rate for all standard deduction returns from 1944 to 1947. Since we received this ratio by assuming no change in the overall reported contributions rate between 1943 and 1944, we may have established the level of contributions "reporting" for the years after

1944 somewhat too low. In 1948 the standard deduction was once more liberalized by a rise in its ceiling per return from $500 to $1,000 for almost all taxpayers. The resulting shift of some taxpayers from itemized deductions to the standard allowance, required an adjustment in the contributions rate on standard deduction returns, as estimated for 1944-1947. Accordingly, the amount of income shifted from the long-form to the short-form returns category was estimated, and to that amount of income we assigned the average contributions rate prevailing in 1947 on returns with itemized deductions. Thus the new estimated rate for contributions on standard deduction returns, 1948-1954, became 1.66 per cent.

To make the procedures outlined above somewhat more concrete, the figures below show for one year, 1952, how the estimate in column 2 of Table 17 was obtained (in millions):

Estimated contributions of nonfilers

1. Total AGI	240,645
2. Minus: AGI reported on all returns	216,030
3. Minus: Amount unexplained	22,147
4. Equals: AGI of nonfilers	2,468
5. Line 5 × 0.019 (adjusted contribution rate of 0 to $2,000 AGI group on taxable returns)	47

Estimated contributions of those filing returns with standard deduction

6. AGI on returns with standard deductions	141,647
7. Line 8 × 0.0166	2,358
Itemized contributions	3,116
Hypothetical estimate of total contributions, line 6 + line 9 + line 10	5,521

APPENDIX G

Note on Cost of Deductions to the Government

(TABLES 15, 25, 32, 33 AND 53)

The estimates of the tax cost of deductions are based on the average marginal rate of tax applicable to taxpayers in each income group. The income groups used are those given in *Statistics of Income* for each year for which estimates were made. Average marginal rates of tax were computed by dividing the change in average tax liability between two income groups by the change in average taxable income between the same two income groups. The amount of income subject to alternative long-term capital gains rate was subtracted before computing average taxable income. Similarly, the amount of long-term capital gains tax was subtracted before computing average tax liability.

Deductions in given income groups were then multipled by the marginal rate of tax as estimated by the above method, which gave us the tax cost to the government of philanthropic contributions, taxes paid, interest paid, and medical expenditures.

The estimates are obviously rough, since within each income group there are variations in the number of exemptions and the amount of income that taxpayers have.

APPENDIX H

Estimates of Nonbusiness Deductible Tax Payments

NOTES TO TABLE 26

A breakdown of our estimate of the amount of taxes that qualify as personal deductions is presented in Table H-1.

TABLE H-1
Estimated Nonbusiness Tax Payments in Deductible Category, 1922-1956

| | State and Local Taxes | | | | | Federal Excises (until 1943) | Total Deductible Taxes |
	Property (1)	Income (2)	Motor Vehicle Licenses (3)	Gasoline (4)	Sales and Poll (5)	(6)	(7)
1922	811	54	79	9	27	153	1133
1923	879	68	97	44	26	124	1238
1924	948	49	113	79	24	92	1305
1925	1017	60	128	114	25	50	1394
1926	1086	76	142	149	26	40	1519
1927	1155	90	149	185	26	33	1638
1928	1163	107	158	240	27	28	1723
1929	1172	133	187	296	24	22	1836
1930	1213	110	183	341	27	20	1894
1931	1196	74	171	373	34	17	1865
1932	1134	64	158	374	38	24	1792
1933	1005	67	152	387	36	34	1681
1934	1013	87	153	410	244	35	1942
1935	1033	121	163	448	334	37	2136
1936	1017	167	176	480	441	40	2321
1937	1032	204	183	524	478	43	2464
1938	1046	208	181	564	514	42	2555
1939	1019	201	190	595	515	44	2564
1940	1049	232	210	649	582	71	2793
1941	1068	258	219	690	650	192	3077
1942	1102	291	198	513	838	417	3359
1943	1164	330	183	279	869	665	3490
1944	1231	366	178	250	833		2858
1945	1307	402	182	341	889		3121
1946	1430	409	199	697	1084		3819
1947	1664	488	226	765	1388		4531
1948	1943	570	253	812	1649		5227
1949	2311	718	288	909	1731		5957
1950	2597	776	326	1005	1893		6597
1951	2995	910	373	1100	2191		7569
1952	3377	1007	397	1239	2456		8476
1953	3721	1047	421	1309	2661		9159
1954	4059	1143	456	1477	2698		9833
1955	4350	1356	496	1596	2977		10,775
1956	4672	1473	534	1901	3230		11,810

Source, by Column

Column 1. *1929-1956*: Commerce Department, *National Income*, 1954 ed., and *Survey of Current Business*, July 1957, Tables 8 and 39. *1922-1928*: Bureau of the Census, *Historical Statistics on State and Local Government Finances, 1902-1953*, Table 1. The figures in this source cover all state and local property taxes, whereas the Commerce Department figures for 1929-1952 are for taxes on personal property, owner-occupied farm and non-farm dwellings. We therefore multiplied the pre-1929 Census figures by the average 1932-1942 ratio of Commerce to Census figures to obtain an estimate of deductible property taxes for the 1922-1928 period. In each of the six years for which there are Commerce and Census figures in the 1932-1942 period, the former amounted to about one-fourth of the latter. The Census figures are given for only 1922 and 1927. The values for the other years 1922-1928 are our interpolations.

Column 2. *1930-1956*: Commerce Department, *op.cit.*, Table 8. *1925-1929*: Roy G. Blakey, *The State Income Tax*, p. 65. *1922-1924*: New York State individual income tax collections blown up by the 1925 ratio of total individual income tax (Blakey) to New York individual income tax collections. The New York figures are found in *Report of the New York State Commission for Revision of the Tax Laws*, 1932, Memorandum No. 11, p. 12.

Column 3. *1929-1956*: Commerce Department, *op.cit. 1922-1928*: The average cost of motor vehicle licenses in the 1929-1940 period was multiplied by a series on motor vehicle registrations for the 1922-1928 period. The annual number of registrations for the 1922-1940 period was taken from *Automotive Industries*, March 15, 1949, p. 91 (as cited in Wilfred Owen, *Automotive Transportation*, The Brookings Institution, 1949, p. 19).

Column 4. Gasoline taxes qualifying as personal deductions were estimated by multiplying total gasoline tax collections of state and local governments by the ratio of personal consumption of gasoline to total gasoline consumption. The latter ratio was obtained by dividing the Commerce Department personal consumption estimates (Commerce Department, *op.cit.*, Table 30) by the Commerce figures on total domestic consumption of gasoline. Total domestic consumption figures in current dollars were computed by multiplying domestic consumption in gallons by the annual price per gallon (Supplement to Survey of Current Business, 1940 and 1957). For years before 1929 the average of personal to total consumption for the 1929-1939 period was used. The gasoline tax figures are taken from Commerce Department, *op.cit.*, Table 8, for 1929-1952; and from Bureau of the Census, *op.cit.*, Table 2, for 1922 and 1927. The remaining years are interpolations.

Column 5. Sales taxes on personal consumption purchases rather than for final business use were estimated by applying to total sales tax collection figures the ratio of personal consumption expenditures to the total of personal consumption expenditures and gross private domestic investment (adjusted for change in inventories). For 1929-1956 we used Commerce Department, *op.cit.*, Table 2; for the earlier years, Simon Kuznets, *National Income and Its Composition, 1919-1938*, National Bureau of Economic Research, 1941, pp. 137, 269, 272. Sources of the sales tax figures used are: 1929-1952, Commerce Department, *op.cit.*, Table 8; 1922-1928, Bureau of the Census, *op.cit.*, Table 3.

The poll taxes included in column 5 are from the Census Bureau's annual publications dealing with state government finances, e.g. *Financial Statistics of States* for 1922-1928, and *Compendium of State Government Finances* for recent years. For 1933-1936, the poll tax figures are interpolations.

Column 6. This item comprises taxes on admissions, playing cards, passenger transport, dues, bowling alleys, slot machines, the use of boats and automobiles, and one-half of telegraph and telephone services. The figures as given in column 6 are placed on a calendar year basis by simple averaging. Source: *Annual Report of the Secretary of the Treasury*, Fiscal Year 1929, Table 10; and Annual Reports of the Commissioner of Internal Revenue (Treasury Department) for later years.

INDEX

Philanthropic contributions, *see* Deductions

Pigou, A. C., 2n.

Progression, *see* Tax rates, progression of

Property assessment, 108

Property tax, 4, 8n., 14n., 55, 92, 95, 100, 106, 108, 112; effect on itemizing, 148; estimates of, 231; revenue cost of, 179

Rate graduation, *see* Tax rate, progression of

Reciprocal deductibility, 102

Religious organizations, contributions to, 217-220

Revenue, collection cost of, 169

Revenue cost: as subsidy, 178, 180; of deductions, 30, 176-177, 230; of federal income tax, 7; *see also* Aged; Deductions; Subsidy

Rolph, E. R., 107n.

Royal Commission on the Taxation of Profits and Income, 2n., 87n.

Sales tax, *see* Taxes

Schanz, Georg, 3n., 121n.

Seltzer, Lawrence, 3n., 5n., 192

Shipman, George A., 135n.

Shultz, William J., 4n.

Simons, Henry C., 2n., 5, 58n., 88n., 121

Social health insurance, 136; *see also* Health insurance

State and local taxes: net cost to taxpayer, 103-106; *see also* Deductions, nonbusiness tax payments; State income tax

State income tax, 92; deductibility of, 100-101; effect on rate progression, 101-102, 106-107; net cost to taxpayer, 103-106; rate gradation of, 14n.; revenue cost of, 103-105, 154; *see also* Deductions, nonbusiness tax payments

Strayer, Paul J., 31n.

Subsidy, 11, 13-16, 59, 72, 88, 114-115, 124, 128, 134n., 136, 144, 158-159, 168, 170, 172, 174, 178

Tax base, 120, 128n., 191; definition of, 3-4, 17; effect of exemption and deductions on, 7, 17-25, 40-41, 171, 176; refining, 128n.; variants of, 197ff.

Tax benefit, 87

Tax cost, *see* Revenue cost

Tax credit, 15-16, 60, 67n., 87-90, 128n., 179; deduction from income as opposed to, 15-16, 88-90, 179

Tax equivalent of deduction, *see* Revenue cost

Tax liability, effect of deductions on, 28-30

Tax rates:

average: definition of, 30; effect of deductions on, 176

effective, xii, xiii, 84; definition of 26; effect of contributions on, 84; effect of exemptions and deductions on, 25-28, progression of, 28

marginal, 25, 84, 101, 154; effective, xii, 30

progression of: effect of contributions on, 83; effect of deductions and exemptions on, 25-28, 175-176; effect of state and local taxes on, 101, 106-107; effective tax rate, 28; state income taxes, 14n.

See also Deductions, total

Tax rebate, 62, 89, 91n., 173

Taxes: bequests and gifts, 56, 59n., 92; cigarette tax, 92; estate tax, 56, 220; gasoline tax, 92, 95, 231; motor vehicle tax, 108, 231; sales tax, 92, 95, 100, 107-108, 230; *see also* Civil War tax; Deductions; State income tax; Wisconsin tax

Ture, Norman, 39n.

Twentieth Century Fund, 4n., 5n.

Vickrey, William, 5n., 6n., 13n., 21n., 22n., 30n., 87, 89n., 101n., 107n., 108n., 120, 122, 123n., 158n.

Walker, Sydnor H., 47n., 48n., 72

Weil, Ulric H., 188-189, 195

Welfare, contributions to, 218, 223

White, Melvin I., 13n., 14n., 87n., 89n., 120-124, 136n., 171n.

Winston, Clement, 131n.

Wisconsin income tax, 119n.